CHINESE

AT A GLANCE

PHRASE BOOK & DICTIONARY FOR TRAVELERS

BY SCOTT D. SELIGMAN
Director, Public Relations
International Affairs and Government Relations
United Technologies Corporation
Washington, D.C.

and

I-CHUAN CHEN
Contract Conference Interpreter (Chinese and English)
Language Services
United States Department of State
Washington, D.C.

Second Edition

BARRON'S

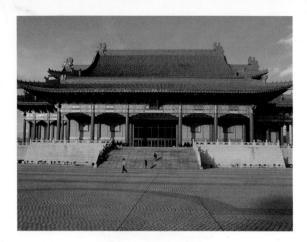

All inquiries should be addressed to:
Barron's Educational Series, Inc.
250 Wireless Boulevard
Hauppauge, New York 11788
http://www.barronseduc.com

Library of Congress Catalog Card No. 00-131723

International Standard Book No. 0-7641-1250-3

PRINTED IN Hong Kong
9 8 7 6 5 4 3 2

CONTENTS

PREFACE

So you're taking a trip to one of the many fascinating countries of the world. That's exciting! This new phrase book will prove an invaluable companion that will make your stay far more interesting.

This phrase book is part of a series in which we present the phrases and words that a traveler most often needs for a brief visit to a foreign country, where the customs and language are often different. Each of the phrase books highlights the terms particular to that country, in situations that the tourist is most likely to encounter. With a specially developed key to pronunciation, this book will enable you to communicate quickly and confidently in colloquial terms. It is intended not only for beginners with no knowledge of the language, but also for those who have already studied it and have some familiarity with it.

Some of the unique features and highlights of the Barron's series are:

- Easy-to-follow *pronunciation keys* and complete phonetic transcriptions for all words and phrases in the book.
- Compact *dictionary* of commonly used words and phrases—built right into this phrase book so there's no need to carry a separate dictionary.
- Useful phrases for the *tourist*, grouped together by subject matter in a logical way so that the appropriate phrase is easy to locate when you need it.
- Special phrases for the *business traveler*, including banking terms.
- Thorough section on *food and drink*, with comprehensive food terms you will find on menus; these terms are often difficult or impossible to locate in dictionaries, but our section gives you a description of the preparation as well as a definition of what it is.
- *Emergency phrases* and terms you hope you won't need: medical problems, theft or loss of valuables, replacement or repair of watches, cameras, and the like.

- *Sightseeing itineraries*, shopping tips, practical travel tips to help you get off the beaten path and into the countryside, to the small towns and cities, and to the neighboring areas.
- A *reference section* providing: important signs, conversion tables, holidays, telling time, days of the week, and months of the year.
- A brief *grammar section*, with the basic elements of the language quickly explained.

Enjoy your vacation and travel with confidence. You have a friend by your side.

INTRODUCTION

CHINESE DIALECTS

Spoken Chinese has many different dialects. Although the written language is essentially the same throughout China, the pronunciation of the characters varies tremendously in different regions. Speaking their native dialects, people from the north of China can communicate verbally with southerners about as easily as Frenchmen can speak with Italians.

It was in order to facilitate communication that the Chinese decided to establish a standard language for themselves. The dialect they chose as the standard is called Mandarin (*pǔtōnghùa* in Chinese), and it is native to the Beijing (Peking) area. Mandarin is taught throughout the People's Republic of China (PRC), as well as in Taiwan, where it is called *gúoyǔ*. It is also widely spoken in Singapore, Hong Kong, and other parts of Southeast Asia where there are large numbers of Chinese. Sometimes it is also referred to as *húayǔ* or *hànyǔ*.

Mandarin isn't the only dialect you'll come across on a tour of China. Among the dozens of other widely spoken dialects are Cantonese, which is heard in and around Guangzhou or Canton, the capital of Guangdong Province, as well as in Hong Kong and Macao; Shanghainese, which is spoken in the greater Shanghai area; Hunan dialect, spoken in the Hunan Province; and Sichuan (Szechuan) dialect, spoken in Sichuan Province. You'll also hear the Hokkien dialect in Fujian Province as well as in Taiwan and in many parts of Southeast Asia where Chinese people who trace their ancestry back to Fujian Province live. For the purposes of a tour of China, however, Mandarin is by far the best dialect to learn. You'll find plenty of Mandarin speakers no matter where you go in the PRC or Taiwan.

SPEAKING CHINESE

The Chinese are delighted when foreigners try to speak their language. They will forgive you a multitude of sins, try their best to understand you, even if your pronunciation is close to unintelligible, and probably even compliment you on your excellent command of Chinese. You needn't take such flattering compliments too seriously; they are simply the Chinese way of being polite and of expressing appreciation for your efforts.

In general, you'll have the best chance of being understood by Chinese who have had frequent contact with foreigners. They are more accustomed to, and better able to make sense of, the predictable mispronunciations. But don't let this stop you from speaking to anyone and everyone you meet. If all else fails, simply show the Chinese characters in this book for the phrase you wish to convey.

VISITING TAIWAN AND HONG KONG

Although this book has been written primarily for travelers to the PRC, the phrases included in it are also useful in Taiwan, where the Mandarin dialect is widely spoken. The native Taiwanese majority—those whose ancestors emigrated to Taiwan from southern Fujian Province during the nineteenth century, as opposed to the approximately 18 percent of "mainlanders" whose families arrived in the 1940s during the Communist takeover of the mainland—speak a dialect that is quite a bit different from Mandarin. But Mandarin has been taught widely in schools in Taiwan for many years, and one should have no trouble finding Mandarin speakers with whom to converse.

There are some linguistic differences to keep in mind, however. Though at least 98 percent of the vocabulary used in this book are understandable on both sides of the Taiwan Strait, some of the terms reflect PRC usage and are not widely used on Taiwan. A handful may not be understood at all. In general, basic conversational vocabulary varies very little, but words associated with the Communist system, such as *dānwèi*, or "work unit," and some technical terms referring to inventions of the last 30 years or so, may be troublesome in Taiwan.

There are also some pronunciation differences. Generally speaking, the further you are from Beijing, the less standard the Mandarin pronunciation of the local populace. Inhabitants of Taiwan have a distinct accent when they speak Mandarin, just as Australians and Americans do when they speak English. It's not impossible to understand, but it can take some getting used to.

The native dialect of most of the residents of Hong Kong and Macao is *Gǔangdōnghùa*, or Cantonese, unintelligible to native speakers of Mandarin and vice versa. Mandarin has become increasingly popular in Hong Kong since the colony returned to Chinese sovereignty in 1997. But because of Hong Kong's history as a British colony, the most widely spoken second language there is still English, and, in general, you should be able to get by in English with little difficulty. Mandarin is also spoken in Macao, which the Portuguese returned to China in 1999, but Cantonese is the native dialect and is heard far more frequently.

The written Chinese in this book is expressed in simplified characters. The Communists simplified many characters in the 1950s in order to make the language easier to learn and promote literacy among the masses. Most of these forms are not widely used in Hong Kong, however, and still less in Taiwan, so people in these places may not easily recognize some of the written characters in this book, though in many cases they'll be able to make good educated guesses.

QUICK PRONUNCIATION GUIDE

PINYIN SPELLING

The Chinese language in this book is rendered in characters as well as in a romanized system called *pīnyīn*, which translates quite simply as "spelling." The characters themselves give little or no phonetic information, and their pronunciation must normally be learned by rote. You won't be expected to learn characters to use this book effectively; we include them primarily to facilitate your communication with Chinese people when phonics fail you. Most Chinese can't read pinyin very well, even though many used it when learning Chinese in primary school. In Taiwan, it is hardly used at all.

Pinyin is the official romanization system of the People's Republic of China. It was adopted in the 1950s and has gained wide acceptance in China and abroad in recent years, essentially supplanting all previous romanization systems. Because pinyin is commonly used on street signs and storefronts in large cities, a knowledge of it can aid you as you make your way in China.

The traditional spellings of many names, such as *Peking, Tientsin, Canton,* and *Mao Tse-tung,* have been replaced with their less familiar but more phonetic pinyin forms: *Beijing, Tianjin, Guangzhou,* and *Mao Zedong.* The pinyin system is fairly accessible to native speakers of English. There are, however, a handful of notable exceptions. The table on page 3 explains pinyin pronunciation in detail.

Don't skip this section; you need to master pinyin for this book to be really useful to you. However, to help jog your memory, we include a summary of the hardest pinyin sounds to remember—both on page 10 and at the end of the book. And as an added convenience we have reprinted some of the most troublesome pinyin initials and their phonetic equivalents on the bottom of each left-hand page in the body of the book.

SYLLABLES

Syllables are the building blocks of Chinese words and phrases. In the written language, each syllable can be rendered as a distinct character. The syllable consists of three components: the *initial*, the *final*, and the *tone*. For example, in the word *táng*, which means "sugar," the initial is the *t* sound at the beginning of the syllable; the final is the *ang* sound at the end; and the tone, represented by the (´) mark, is the rising tone of voice in which the word is pronounced. All three components must generally be present for the word to be completely understandable in Chinese, though some syllables don't require initials.

INITIALS

Initials are always consonants, and in pinyin most of the pronunciations are fairly intuitive to native speakers of English. Following is a table of initials with an explanation of how to pronounce them.

PINYIN INITIAL	ENGLISH EQUIVALENT	EXAMPLES	APPROXIMATE PRONUNCIATION
b, p, m, f, d, t, n, l, g, k, j, s, w, y, ch, sh	approximately the same as in English	neng tou gan	*nung* *toe* *gone*
c	like the *ts* in *rats*	can cu	*tsahn* *tsoo*
h	more guttural than the English *h*. More like the German *ch* as in *ach*	hen hao	*hun* *how*
q	like the *ch* in *cheap*	qin qu	*cheen* *chü*
r	a cross between a *j* and an *r*. No English equivalent; something like the *z* in *azure*	ren ru	*wren* *roo*
x	like the *sh* in *sheen*	xiao xin	*shee-yow* *sheen*
z	like *dz* to sound like the *ds* in *kids*	zai zu	*dzye* *dzoo*
zh	like the hard *j* in *jack*	zhang zhou	*jahng* *joe*

FINALS

Finals always begin with vowels. They may end in vowels, consonants, or diphthongs. Study the list of finals below. In many cases they can be pronounced accurately by using your intuition as a native English speaker—but there are a few surprises.

PINYIN FINAL	ENGLISH EQUIVALENT	EXAMPLES	APPROXIMATE PRONUNCIATION
a	*ah* as in *rah*	ba	*bah*
		na	*nah*
ai	like the *y* in *rye* or *my*	tai	*tie*
		lai	*lye*
an	*ahn*, to rhyme with *John*	ban	*bahn*
		can	*tsahn*
ang	*ahng*, as in *angst*	tang	*tahng*
		chang	*chahng*
ao	like the *ow* in *cow*	chao	*chow*
ar	as in *are*	nar	*nar*
e	like the *u* sound in *bush*	de	*duh*
		le	*luh*
ei	like the *a* in *pay* or *play*	fei	*fay*
		shei	*shay*
en	like the *un* in *pun*	men	*mun*
eng	like the *ung* in *hung*	deng	*dung*
er	like the *ur* in *cur*	mer	*mur*
i	like the *ee* in *flee* when following *b, p, m, d, t, n, l, j, q,* and *x*	ji	*jee*
		xi	*shee*
	like a *zz* after *z, c,* and *s*	zi	*dz*
		si	*sz*
	like an *r* after *zh, ch, sh,* and *r*	zhi	*jr*
		shi	*shr*
ia	*ya*, like the *ia* in the name *Mia*, but said in one syllable	lia	*lya*
		xia	*shya*

PINYIN FINAL	ENGLISH EQUIVALENT	EXAMPLES	APPROXIMATE PRONUNCIATION
ian	*yen*	pian	*pyen*
iang	*yahng*, with the same vowel as in the word *angst*	liang jiang	*lyahng* *jyahng*
iao	*ee-yow*, to rhyme with the cat's *meow*, but said in one syllable	biao liao	*bee-yow* *lee-yow*
ie	*yeh*	bie	*byeh*
in	*een* as in *green*	qin xin	*cheen* *sheen*
ing	as in *sing*	bing	*bing*
iong	*yawng*, to rhyme with *strong*	qiong xiong	*chyuwng* *shyawng*
iu	like the *eo* in the name *Leo*, pronounced in one syllable	qiu liu	*cheo* *leo*
o	like the *aw* sound in *awe*, to rhyme with *saw*	mo po	*maw* *paw*
ong	like the *ong* in *wrong*, but with a rounder *o* sound	long zhong	*long* *jawng*
ou	like the *o* in *toe* or *ho*	mou zhou	*moe* *joe*
u	*oo* as in *boo* after most letters pronounced as *ü* (see below) after *j, q, x,* or *y*	mu du qu xu	*moo* *doo* *chü* *shü*
ü	no English equivalent; like the German *ü* or the French *eu*. Used only after *n* and *l*	nü lü	*nü* *lü*
ua	*wah*, like the *ua* in *guava*	zhua gua	*jwah* *gwah*

PINYIN FINAL	ENGLISH EQUIVALENT	EXAMPLES	APPROXIMATE PRONUNCIATION
uai	*wye*, to rhyme with *rye*	guai	*gwye*
uan	*wahn*, to rhyme with *swan* after most letters	tuan duan	*twahn* *dwahn*
	wen, to rhyme with *when* after *j, q, x,* or *y*	yuan juan	*ywen* *jwen*
uang	*wahng*, with the same vowel as the word *angst*	zhuang kuang	*jwahng* *kwahng*
ue or üe	*oo-eh*, to rhyme with *moo* and *yeh*, merged into one syllable. Written with (¨) symbol after *n* and *l*	xue lüe	*shooeh* *looeh*
ui	*way*	dui	*dway*
un	*one* is the closest sound in English, though the vowel is actually closer to the *oo* sound in *book*.	dun sun	*dwun* *swun*
	After *j, q,* and *x*, pronounced like the English *win*	jun xun	*jwin* *shwin*
uo	*waw*, to rhyme with *thaw*	duo cuo	*dwaw* *tswaw*

TONES

Each Chinese syllable also has a special intonation that must be used when it is pronounced. Spoken Mandarin has four distinct tones. They do not correspond to absolute musical pitches but rather, are spoken differently by different individuals, depending on the range of their voices. What is important is that the tones remain relatively distinct from one another.

For example, the first tone is pronounced at a high, level pitch at the top of one's vocal range. For a woman this will be a higher pitch than for a man, but this makes no difference as long as it's done at the top of one's register. The second tone rises from the middle of the voice to the top, as when asking a question in English, even though a rising tone implies no interrogative in Chinese. The third tone starts in the middle of the voice and dips to the bottom before rising at the end. The fourth tone starts high and ends low, as when scolding someone or emphasizing something in English. The figure below illustrates the four tones.

The tones are indicated by the use of diacritical marks above the syllables. The first tone, the even tone, is illustrated

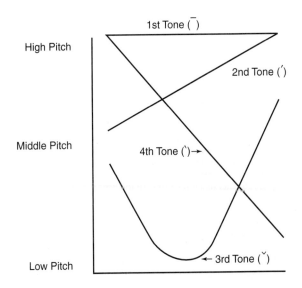

with a horizontal mark above the syllable (ˉ). The second tone, which rises, is shown with a line sloping up (ˊ). The third tone, which dips to the bottom of the voice, is indicated with a U-shaped mark (ˇ). The fourth, or falling, tone is illustrated with a line sloping down (ˋ).

The importance of the tones is clear from the example of the syllable *ma*. *Mā*, in the first tone, means "mother." In the second tone, *má* is understood to mean "hemp." The third tone form, *mǎ*, means "horse." And in the fourth tone, *mà* means "to scold." If you are careless with your tones, you are more than likely to make a serious mistake speaking Chinese, since the language is rich in homonyms. The tones help a Chinese listener to distinguish different words. Asking for *táng* at the table will get you sugar, but if you pronounce it *tāng*, you'll be given a bowl of soup.

Even a syllable with a given tone can have more than one meaning. *Shī*, for example, means both "lion" and "poem" in the first tone, as well as other things. A Chinese can generally figure out what you mean from the context of your remarks, but imagine how much harder you make his or her task if you mispronounce the word. In various other tones, *shi* can mean history, a teacher, an envoy, a market, to show, a lifetime, a test, a style, the number ten, a stone, or the verb "to be."

You'll notice that in this book we have frequently omitted the tone mark over a particular syllable. This simply means that the syllable should be unstressed and pronounced in a neutral tone of voice.

One more point: We've used standard punctuation marks in this text. These are as intelligible to the Chinese as to us. But when you're speaking Chinese, don't make the all-too-common mistake of raising your pitch at the end of a question or dropping it after an exclamation, as you might in English, for this will interfere with the proper pronunciation of tones. Just keep to the tones as marked and you will get the desired results.

SOME CONVENTIONS

We've adopted a few conventions in our use of pinyin that we hope will be helpful to you. First of all, we have omitted the space between two syllables when the syllables combine to form a common word. For example, to say "already" in Chinese requires two characters: *yǐ* and *jīng*. Neither can stand alone; the meaning comes from the combination. So for the sake of clarity we render it *yǐjīng*. This technique should help you to recognize words—as opposed to just syllables—a bit more quickly. We are also capitalizing the initial letter of words that begin sentences and that in English are considered proper nouns. Thus, *yīngwén* ("English language") is spelled throughout this book with a capital *Y*.

Finally, spoken Chinese occasionally involves a *change* in the tone of a syllable, depending on the context. When two third tones occur together, for example, the first one is generally pronounced as a second tone. We have built such changes in for you in this book, so you needn't concern yourself with these rules. It is for this reason, however, that the same word may occasionally appear in different tones in this book. An example is *wǒ* ("I" or "me"). This occasionally shows up as *wó*, depending on the tone of the word that follows it. Just say it the way it appears in the text and you won't go wrong. If you need to know the standard tone of the word out of context, check the dictionary at the end of the book.

THE COMMON PROBLEMS OF PINYIN

INITIALS*

c = *ts*, as in *rats*	**q** = *ch*	**z** = *dz*, like the *ds* sound in *kids*
x = *sh*	**zh** = *j*	

FINALS

ai rhymes with *rye*	**an** = *ahn*, rhymes with *John*	**ang** = *ahng* as in *angst*
ao rhymes with *cow*	**e** = *u* as in *bush*	**ei** rhymes with *pay*
en rhymes with *pun*	**eng** rhymes with *hung*	**ia** = *ya*
i sounds like *ee* after most letters, but like *zz* after *z*, *c*, and *s*, and like an *r* after *zh*, *ch*, *sh*, and *r*	**ian** = *yen*	**iang** = *yahng*
	iao = *ee-yow*	**ie** = *yeh*
	iong = *yawng*	**in** rhymes with *green*
iu rhymes with *Leo*	**o** = *aw*	**ou** rhymes with *toe*
u rhymes with *boo* in most cases, but becomes the German *ü* after *j*, *q*, *x*, and *y*	**ua** = *wah*	**uai** = *wye*
	uan = *wahn*; but *wen* after *j*, *q*, *x*, and *y*	**uang** = *wahng*; vowel as in *angst*
un = *one*, but the vowel is as in *book*	**ue** = *oo-eh*	**ui** rhymes with *way*
	ün rhymes with *win*	**uo** = *waw*

*The "Initials" of this table are hereafter repeated at the bottom of every left-hand page for the reader's convenience.

THE BASICS FOR GETTING BY

MOST FREQUENTLY USED EXPRESSIONS

The expressions in this section are ones you'll use again and again—they are the fundamental building blocks of conversation. They will help you to express your wants or needs, and they include some simple question forms. We suggest that you become very familiar with these phrases.

beautiful	*zhēn měi*	真美
Excuse me.		
(to apologize for something)	*Dùibuqǐ.*	对不起。
(to get attention)	*Láo jià!*	劳驾！
Forget it. Never mind.	*Sùan le.*	算了。
good	*hǎo*	好
Good-bye. (see you later)	*Zài jìan.*	再见。
Good morning.	*Zǎoshàng hǎo.*	早上好。
Good night.	*Wǎn ān.*	晚安。
Hello.	*Ní hǎo.*	你好。
I'm very sorry.	*Wó hěn bàoqìan.*	我很抱歉。
Is it convenient?	*Fāngbìan ma?*	方便吗？
It doesn't matter.	*Méi yǒu gūanxi.*	没有关系。
Just a second.	*Děng yīxìa.*	等一下。

May I trouble you?	*Máfan nǐ.*	麻烦你？
maybe	*kěnéng*	可能
No hurry.	*Bù jí.*	不急。
No problem.	*Méi wèntí.*	没问题。
not so	*bú shì*	不是
O.K.	*Kéyǐ.*	可以。
please	*qǐng*	请
right	*dùi*	对
See you tomorrow.	*Míngtīan jìan.*	明天见。
Thank you.	*Xìexie.*	谢谢。
That's all right.	*Xíng.*	行。
wonderful	*hǎo jí le*	好极了
wrong	*bú dùi*	不对
yes	*shì de*	是的
You're welcome.	*Bú kèqi.*	不客气。

FORMS OF ADDRESS

Traditional Chinese forms of address were used in prerevolutionary China but fell into disuse, especially during the Cultural Revolution of the 1960s and 1970s, when they were condemned as bourgeois. Since China's reopening to the West in the late 1970s, however, they have made a resounding comeback, to the extent that Communist-era terms like *tóngzhì* for "comrade" are now seldom heard. The traditional forms have been used continuously in Taiwan, Hong Kong, Macao, and Chinese communities elsewhere in the world.

c = ts; *q* = ch; *x* = sh; *z* = dz; *zh* = j

Sir	*Xiānsheng*	先生
Madame	*Fūrén*	夫人
	Tàitai	太太
Miss	*Xíaojǐe*	小姐
Ms.	*Nǚshì*	女士
Master (a respectful term used to address professional people, including chefs, waiters, and craftsmen)	*Shīfu*	师傅

COMMUNICATION

Do you speak English?	*Nǐ hùi shūo Yīngwén ma?*
	你会说英文吗？
I speak a little Chinese.	*Wǒ hùi shūo yīdǐan Zhōngwén.*
	我会说一点中文。
Do you understand?	*Ní dǒng ma?*
	你懂吗？
	Ní tīngde dǒng ma?
	你听得懂吗？
I understand.	*Wó dǒng.* 我懂。
	Wǒ bù dǒng.
	我不懂。
I don't understand.	*Wǒ tīng bù dǒng.*
	我听不懂。
Let me think.	*Ràng wó xǐang yī xǐang.*
	让我想一想。

What?	*Shénme?* 什么？
What did you say?	*Nǐ shūo shénme?* 你说什么？
How do you say ____ in Chinese?	____ *yòng Zhōngwén zěnme shūo?* ____用中文怎么说？
What does this (that) mean?	*Zhè shì shénme yìsi?* 这是什么意思？
Please speak more slowly.	*Qíng nǐ shūo màn yīdǐan.* 请你说慢一点。
Please repeat.	*Qíng nǐ zài shūo yíbìan.* 请你再说一遍。
That is not important.	*Nèige bú yàojǐn.* 那个不要紧。

INTRODUCTIONS

I'm American.	*Wǒ shì Měigúo rén.* 我是美国人。
My name is ____.	*Wǒ de míngzì jiào ____.* 我的名字叫____。
What's your name?	
■ (formal)	*Qǐng wèn gùi xìng dà míng?* 请问贵姓大名？
■ (colloquial)	*Nǐ jiào shénme míngzì?* 你叫什么名字？
How are you?	*Nǐ hǎo?* 你好？
Very well, thanks, and you?	*Hén hǎo, xìexie. Nǐ ne?* 很好，谢谢。你呢？

c = ts; *q* = ch; *x* = sh; *z* = dz; *zh* = j

GETTING AROUND

Where is ____?	____ zài nǎli?	____在哪里？
a bookstore	shūdìan	书店
the business center	shāngwù zhōngxīn	商务中心
a café	kāfēitīng	咖啡厅
a convenience store	xǐao mài bù	小卖部
the dining room	cāntīng	餐厅
the entrance	rùkǒu	入口
the exit	chūkǒu	出口
a gift store	lǐpǐn dìan	礼品店
the gym	jìanshēnfáng	健身房
the lobby	dàtīng	大厅
a newsstand	bàotān	报摊
a public telephone	gōngyòng dìanhùa	公用电话
a restaurant	fàngǔan	饭馆
the taxi	chūzū qìchē	出租汽车
a teahouse	chágǔan	茶馆
the telephone	dìanhùa	电话
the toilet	cèsǔo	厕所
the washroom	xíshǒu jīan	洗手间
May I ask you a question?	Qǐng wèn.	请问
Please help me.	Qǐng bāngmáng.	请帮忙。

I'm lost.	*Wǒ mí lù le.* 我迷路了。	
We're lost.	*Wǒmén mí lù le.* 我们迷路了。	
Where are my friends?	*Wǒ dē péngyou zài náli?* 我的朋友在哪里？	
Where is the tourist bus?	*Lǚyóu chē zài náli?* 旅游车在哪里？	
I am looking for ____.	*Wǒ zài zhǎo ____.* 我在找____。	
Which way did they go?	*Tāmén wǎng náli qù le?* 他们往哪里去了？	
■ to the left	*xiàng zuǒ*	向左
■ to the right	*xiàng yòu*	向右
■ straight ahead	*xiàng qián*	向前

c = ts; *q* = ch; *x* = sh; *z* = dz; *zh* = j

SHOPPING

How much does it cost?	*Dūoshǎo qían?*	多少钱？
I'd like ____.	*Wó xiǎngyào ____.*	我想要____。
Please give me ____.	*Qǐng géi wǒ ____.*	请给我____。
Please show me ____.	*Qǐng géi wǒ kàn ____.*	请给我看____。
just right	*gānggāng hǎo*	刚刚好
approximately; more or less	*chà bu dūo*	差不多
Too expensive!	*Tài gùi le!*	太贵了！
Can you come down in price?	*Píanyí dián, hǎo ma?*	便宜点好吗？
It's still too expensive.	*Háishi tài gùi.*	还是太贵。
I don't want it.	*Wǒ bù xiǎngyào.*	我不想要。
The quality is not so good.	*Zhìliàng bú tài hǎo.*	质量不太好。

MISCELLANEOUS

I'm hungry.	*Wǒ è le.*	我饿了。
I'm thirsty.	*Wó kǒ lo.*	我渴了。
I'm tired.	*Wǒ lèi le.*	我累了。
I don't feel well.	*Wǒ bù shūfu.*	我不舒服。
I'm sick.	*Wǒ bìng le.*	我病了。
What's that?	*Nà shì shénme?*	那是什么？

What's up? How's everything?	*Zěnme yàng?*	怎么样？
Do you know?	*Nǐ zhīdào ma?*	你知道吗？
I don't know.	*Wǒ bù zhīdào.*	我不知道。

QUESTIONS

How?	*Zěnme?*	怎么？
How much?	*Dūoshǎo?*	多少？
What?	*Shénme?*	什么？
When?	*Shénme shíhòu?*	什么时候？
Where is ____?	____ *zài nálǐ?*	____在哪里？
Which?	*Něige?*	哪个？
Who?	*Shéi?*	谁？
Why?	*Wèishénme?*	为什么？

PROBLEMS, PROBLEMS, PROBLEMS (EMERGENCIES)

Help! (for life-threatening emergencies only)	*Jìu mìng!*	救命！
Please help me quickly!	*Qǐng kùai lái bāng wǒ!*	请快来帮我！
Be careful! Watch out!	*Xǐao xīn!*	小心！
Look!	*Kànkan!*	看看！

c = ts; *q* = ch; *x* = sh; *z* = dz; *zh* = j

Listen!	*Tīng!*	听！
Wait!	*Děng yī děng!*	等一等！
Wait a moment!	*Děng yī xìa!*	等一下！
Fire!	*Qǐ huǒ le!*	起火了！
Stop him!	*Zhūazhù tā!*	抓住他！
I have lost ____.	*Wǒ dīu le ____.*	我丢了____。
▨ my suitcase	*wǒ de tíbāo*	我的提包
▨ my watch	*wǒ de shóubǐao*	我的手表

He has stolen ____.	*Tā tōu le* ____,	他偷了____。
▨ my passport	*wǒ de hùzhào*	我的护照
▨ my wallet; purse	*wǒ de qíanbāo*	我的钱包
Where is a policeman?	*Nálí yóu jǐngchá?*	哪里有警察

COMPLICATIONS

I haven't done anything wrong.	*Wǒ méi fàn cuò.*	我没犯错。
I want to go to ____.	*Wǒ yào qù ____.*	我要去___。
▥ the American consulate	*Měiguó Shíguǎn*	美国使馆
▥ the police station	*jǐngchá jú*	警察局
Can you help me, please?	*Nǐ kéyǐ bāng wǒ ma?* 你可以帮我吗？	
Who speaks English?	*Shéi néng shuō Yīngwén?* 谁能说英文？	
I need an interpreter.	*Wǒ xūyào fānyì.* 我需要翻译。	

NUMBERS

You will use numbers the moment you arrive in China, whether to exchange money at the airport, pay a taxi driver, or describe the length of your stay to an immigration official or hotel clerk. Here we list the cardinal numbers, give the rule for converting a cardinal to an ordinal number, and also specify fractions and other useful measures.

CARDINAL NUMBERS

0	*líng*	零
1	*yī*	一
2		

c = ts; *q* = ch; *x* = sh; *z* = dz; *zh* = j

▩	(the numeral)	*èr*	二
▩	(when used in collaboration with measure words)	*liǎng*	两
3		*sān*	三
4		*sì*	四
5		*wǔ*	五
6		*liù*	六
7		*qī*	七
8		*ba*	八
9		*jǐu*	九
10		*shí*	十
11		*shí yī*	十一
12		*shí èr*	十二
13		*shí sān*	十三
14		*shí sì*	十四
15		*shí wǔ*	十五
16		*shí lìu*	十六
17		*shí qī*	十七
18		*shí bā*	十八
19		*shí jǐu*	十九
20		*èr shí*	二十
21		*èr shí yī*	二十一
22		*èr shí èr*	二十二

30	*sān shí*	三十
31	*sān shí yī*	三十一
40	*sì shí*	四十
50	*wǔ shí*	五十
60	*liù shí*	六十
70	*qī shí*	七十
80	*bā shí*	八十
90	*jiǔ shí*	九十
100	*yī bǎi*	一百
101	*yī bǎi líng yī*	一百零一
102	*yī bǎi líng èr*	一百零二
103	*yī bǎi líng sān*	一百零三
110	*yī bǎi yī shí*	一百一十
120	*yī bǎi èr shí*	一百二十
130	*yī bǎi sān shí*	一百三十
200	*liáng bǎi*	两百
201	*liáng bǎi líng yī*	两百零一
300	*sān bǎi*	三百
400	*sì bǎi*	四百
500	*wú bǎi*	五百
600	*liù bǎi*	六百
1,000	*yī qiān*	一千

c = ts; *q* = ch; *x* = sh; *z* = dz; *zh* = j

1,001	*yī qiān líng yī*	一千零一
1,100	*yī qiān yī bǎi*	一千一百
1,200	*yī qiān èr bǎi*	一千二百
1,350	*yī qiān sān bái wǔ shí*	一千三百五十
2,000	*liǎng qiān*	两千
5,000	*wǔ qiān*	五千
10,000	*yī wàn*	一万
100,000	*shí wàn*	十万
1,000,000	*bǎi wàn*	百万
10,000,000	*qiān wàn*	千万
100,000,000	*yī yì*	一亿
1,000,000,000	*shí yì*	十亿
1,000,000,000,000	*wàn yì*	万亿
199____ (year)	*yī jiǔ jǔ ____ nían*	一九九____年
200____ (year)	*èr líng líng ____ nían*	二零零____年

ORDINAL NUMBERS

Making cardinal numbers into ordinal numbers is a simple task in Chinese. You simply add the prefix **dì** to the number. Note the following examples:

first	*dì yī*	第一
second	*dì èr*	第二
third	*dì sān*	第三

fourth	*dì sì*	第四
tenth	*dì shí*	第十
fiftieth	*dì wǔ shí*	第五十
one hundredth	*dì yī bǎi*	第一百
one thousandth	*dì yī qiān*	第一千

FRACTIONS AND QUANTITIES

a half	*yí bàn*	一半
half a	*bàn ge*	半个
a quarter	*sì fēn zhī yī*	四分之一
three-quarters	*sì fēn zhī sān*	四分之三
a third	*sān fēn zhī yī*	三分之一
two-thirds	*sān fēn zhī èr*	三分之二
a cup of	*yì bēi*	一杯
a dozen of	*yì dǎ*	一打
a gram of	*yí kè*	一克
a kilogram of	*yì gōng jīn*	一公斤
a catty of (Chinese measurement)	*yì jīn*	一斤
a liter of	*yì shēng*	一升
a little bit of	*yì diǎn*	一点
a lot of	*hěn dūo*	很多

c = ts; *q* = ch; *x* = sh; *z* = dz; *zh* = j

a pair of	*yí dùi*	一对
enough of	*gòu le*	够了
too much of	*tài dūo le*	太多了
ratio	*bǐ lì*	比例
____ percent	*bǎi fēn zhī* ____	百分之____
twenty	*èr shí*	二十
seventy-five	*qī shí wǔ*	七十五
____ times as much	____ *bèi*	____倍
six	*lìu*	六
one hundred	*yì bǎi*	一百

WHEN YOU ARRIVE

PASSPORT AND CUSTOMS

You need a visa to enter China. Normally this is a stamp on your passport issued before you arrive, though visas can sometimes be arranged at the port of entry. Group visas are also sometimes issued to tour groups that are traveling together. The visa specifies dates between which you are permitted to remain in China; if you wish to stay longer, it is necessary to extend your visa officially in order to avoid a fine.

Customs, once very stringent, have now become routine or even virtually nonexistent for most tourists and business travelers. Visitors may bring most items into China duty free, though large electronic appliances such as stereos, desktop computers, and television sets are dutiable. Smaller items such as cameras, watches, radios, jewelry, and calculators are technically supposed to be declared upon arrival and noted on the customs form; if they are carried out at the end of your stay in China, no duty is assessed. This rule is honored in the breach; however, in practice, such items are rarely declared and rarely taxed.

My name is ____.	*Wǒ de míngzì jiào ____.*	我的名字叫____。
I'm ____.	*Wǒ shì ____.*	我是____。
▓ American	*Měiguó rén*	美国人
▓ Canadian	*Jiānádà rén*	加拿大人
▓ British	*Yīngguó rén*	英国人
▓ Australian	*Aòzhōu rén*	澳洲人
▓ New Zealander	*Xīn Xīlán rén*	新西兰人
My address is ____.	*Wǒ de dìzhǐ shì ____.*	我的地址是____。

c = ts; *q* = ch; *x* = sh; *z* = dz; *zh* = j

I'll be staying at ____.	*Wǒ húi zhù zài ____.*	我会住在____。
Here is (are) my ____.	*Zhè shì wǒ de ____.*	这是我的____。
▦ arrival card	*rùjìng dēngjì kǎ*	入境登记卡
▦ customs certificate	*háiguǎn shēnbào dān*	海关申报单
▦ departure card	*chūjìng dēngjì kǎ*	出境登记卡
▦ documents	*wénjiàn*	文件
▦ health certificate	*jiànkāng shēnmíng kǎ*	健康申明卡
▦ passport	*hùzhào*	护照
▦ residence permit	*jūlíuzhèng*	居留证
▦ visa	*qīanzhèng*	签证
I've come ____.	*Wǒ lái ____.*	我来____。
▦ on a business trip	*zūo shēngyì*	做生意
▦ to participate in a conference	*cānjīa hùiyì*	参加会议
▦ to participate in an exhibition	*cānjīa zhánlǎn*	参加展览
▦ to participate in a delegation	*cānjīa dàibǐao túan*	参加代表团
▦ on a visit	*lǚxíng*	旅行
▦ on vacation	*dùjìa*	度假
▦ to visit relatives	*tànqīn*	探亲
I'm here with a group.	*Wǒ shì súi túantǐ lái de.*	我是随团体来的____。
I'll be staying ____.	*Wǒ yào zhù ____.*	我要住____。

▨ a few days	*jǐ tīan*	几天
▨ a few weeks	*jǐge xīngqī*	几个星期
▨ a week	*yíge xīngqī*	一个星期
▨ a month	*yíge yùe*	一个月
I'm traveling ____.	*Wǒ ____ lǚxíng.*	我____旅行。
▨ alone	*dāndú*	单独
▨ with my husband	*gēn wǒ zhàngfu*	跟我丈夫
▨ with my wife	*gēn wǒ tàitai*	跟我太太
▨ with my family	*gēn wǒ jīarén*	跟我家人
▨ with my friend	*gēn wǒ de péngyou*	跟我的朋友
▨ with my colleague	*gēn wǒ de tóngshì*	跟我的同事
▨ with a tour group	*gēn lǚyóu túan*	跟旅游团
These are my bags.	*Zhè shì wǒ de xíngli.* 这是我的行李。	
▨ checked luggage	*tūoyùn de xínglǐ*	托运的行李
▨ hand luggage	*shǒutí xínglǐ*	手提行李
Where shall I go to claim my luggage?	*Dào nálǐ qù qǔ xínglǐ?* 到哪里去取行李？	
Shall I open my bag?	*Xíngli yào dǎkāi ma?* 行李要打开吗？	
Must you x-ray my bag?	*Zhèijiàn xínglǐ yídìng yào jīnggùo X gūang jǎnchá ma?* 这件行李一定要经过X光检查吗？	

c = ts; *q* = ch; *x* = sh; *z* = dz; *zh* = j

Will the X ray damage my film?	*X guāng huì sǔnhuài wǒde jiāojuǎn ma?* X光会损坏我的胶卷吗？
I have very high-speed film.	*Gāo gǎn guāngdù jiāo juǎn.* 高感光度胶卷。
I have nothing to declare.	*Wǒ méi shénme yào bàoguān de.* 我没什么要报关的。
I have only a carton of cigarettes.	*Wǒ zhǐ yǒu yì tiáo xiāngyān.* 我只有一条香烟。
I have only a bottle of whiskey.	*Wǒ zhǐ yǒu yī píng wēishìjì.* 我只有一瓶威士忌。
They're gifts.	*Zhèixiē shì lǐpǐn.* 这些是礼品。
They're samples.	*Zhèixiē shì yàngpǐn.* 这些是样品。
This is for my personal use.	*Zhè shì zìjǐ yòng de.* 这是自己用的。
Do I have to pay duty?	*Wǒ yào fù shuì ma?* 我要付税吗？
I expect to take this out of China when I leave.	*Wǒ jiāng dài zhèige chūjìng.* 我将带这个出境。
Are you finished with your inspection?	*Jiǎnchá wánle ma?* 检查完了吗？
May I close my bag now?	*Xíngli kéyǐ shōu qǐlái ma?* 行李可以收起来吗？

LOST LUGGAGE

My luggage is lost.	*Wǒde xínglǐ bújiàn le.* 我的行李不见了。

Where do I report lost luggage?	*Dào nǎlǐ qù shēnbào yíshī de xínglǐ?* 到哪里去申报遗失的行李？
When will my luggage arrive?	*Wǒde xínglǐ shénme shíhòu dào?* 我的行李什么时候到？
Must I come back to the airport to claim it?	*Yídìng yào wǒ húi fēijīchǎng qǔ ma?* 一定要我回飞机场取吗？
Will you deliver it to my hotel?	*Nímén néng sòng dào lǚguǎn ma?* 你们能送到旅馆吗？

BAGGAGE AND PORTERS

Porters are hard to find at Chinese airports, but most major airports are equipped with baggage carts. You can usually wheel the carts through Customs right to the street.

baggage (luggage)	*xíngli* 行李
Where can I find a baggage cart?	*Nǎli yǒu xíngli chē?* 哪里有行李车？
Who can help me carry my bags?	*Shéi néng bāng wǒ bān xíngli?* 谁能帮我搬行李？
I need a porter.	*Wǒ xūyào fúwúyúan.* 我需要服务员。
These are my (our) bags.	*Zhè shì wǒ (wǒmén) de xíngli.* 这是我（我们）的行李。
■ that big one	*nèi jiàn dà de* 那件大的
■ these two little ones	*zhèi liǎng jiàn xiǎo de* 这两件小的

c = ts; *q* = ch; *x* = sh; *z* = dz; *zh* = j

| Please put them here. | *Qǐng fàng zhèli.*
请放这里。 |

| Please bring these to
the car. | *Qǐng bān dào chē shàng.*
请搬到车上。 |

| Please be careful. | *Qíng xiǎoxīn yīdiǎn.*
请小心一点。 |

| I'll carry this one myself | *Zhèi jiàn wǒ zìjǐ ná.*
这件我自己拿。 |

| This is for you. | *Zhè shì géi nǐde.*
这是给你的。 |

| Than you very much
for your help. | *Dūo xiè nǐ de bāngmáng.*
多谢你的帮忙。 |

AIRPORT TRANSPORTATION

Where is the information desk?	*Xúnwèn chù zài náli?*	
	询问处在哪里？	
Where is the hotel desk?	*Lǚguǎn fúwù chù zài nálǐ?*	
	旅馆服务处在哪里？	
Where is the representative from ____?	*____ dàibǐao zài náli?*	
	____代表在哪里？	
▩ the ____ Hotel	*____ Fàndiàn*	____饭店
▩ my host organization	*jiēdài dānwèi*	接待单位
▩ my travel service	*lǚxíng shè*	旅行社
▩ my school	*xúexìao*	学校
No one has come to meet me.	*Méi rén lái jīe wǒ.*	
	没人来接我。	
Where do I wait for a hotel shuttle bus?	*Zài náli děng lǚguǎn de bāshì?*	
	在哪里等旅馆的巴士？	
How do I pay?	*Zěnme fù qían?*	
	怎么付钱？	
I need a taxi.	*Wǒ xūyào chūzū qìchē.*	
	我需要出租汽车	
Where can I get a taxi?	*Náli yǒu chūzū qìchē?*	
	哪里有出租汽车？	
Is this the line for taxis?	*Zài zhèli páidùi děng chūzū chē ma?*	
	在这里排队等出租汽车吗？	

c = ts; *q* = ch; *x* = sh; *z* = dz; *zh* = j

BANKING AND MONEY MATTERS

EXCHANGING MONEY

Chinese currency is called **rénmínbì**, which means, literally, "the people's money." It is denominated in the **yúan**, which is also known colloquially as the **kùai**. The yúan breaks down into 10 **máo** (also called **jǐao**), or 100 **fēn**. Paper certificates come in 1, 5, 10, 20, 50, and 100 yúan denominations, and there are also 10- and 5-jǐao notes, as well as seldom-encountered 1-, 2-, and 5-fēn notes. One-yúan coins are in circulation, as are 1- and 5-jǐao coins and 1-, 2-, and 5-fēn coins, but the latter are of so little value that they are sometimes ignored when change is made. Taxi drivers, in particular, seldom give back such small change unless it is demanded of them.

Foreign currency, which can be imported in unlimited quantities, can be converted into rénmínbì throughout China at branch offices of the Bank of China (found at all airports), and also at stores with foreign clientele, nearly all hotels where foreigners stay, and a small number of other banks. Unlike the practice in other countries, the exchange rate is exactly the same whether you convert your money in a hotel, a shop, or a bank. By law, no commission other than the standard bank rate may be charged. Traveler's checks, however, have a slightly higher exchange rate than does cash. Be sure to bring your passport with you when you change money, and remember your hotel room number.

Rénmínbì is also available from ATM machines in large Chinese cities by using foreign ATM cards, but this can be spotty. Only certain ATMs permit rénmínbì withdrawal, and only certain cards are accepted. Your best bet is to bring enough traveler's checks for your trip, since you can't count on getting cash on a credit card guarantee outside of China's larger cities.

There is some black market money exchanging activity, but this is not recommended because it is illegal, because it's easy to be cheated with counterfeit bills, and because it can cause complications upon exiting China. Since the yúan is not yet freely convertible, reconverting unused Chinese money on departure requires that one produce the official exchange memos issued in the initial conversion of foreign currency together with a passport and an air ticket. Even so, one may reclaim only 50 percent of the funds initially converted, and the transaction must be done at the Bank of China.

Where can I exchange ____?	*Náli kéyǐ duìhuàn ____?*	哪里可以兑换?
▨ cash	*xìankǔan*	现款
▨ money	*qían*	钱
▨ rénmínbì (Chinese currency)	*rénmínbì*	人民币
▨ traveler's checks	*lǔxíng zhīpìao*	旅行支票
▨ U.S. dollars	*Měi yúan*	美元
▨ Hong Kong dollars	*Gǎng bì*	港币
▨ Japanese yen	*Rì yúan*	日元
▨ English pounds sterling	*Yīng bàng*	英镑
▨ Australian dollars	*Àodàlìyà yúan*	澳大利亚元
▨ a personal check	*gèrén zhīpìao*	个人支票
▨ a money order	*hùikǔan dān*	汇款单

c = ts; *q* = ch; *x* = sh; *z* = dz; *zh* = j

■ a cashier's check   *yínháng*   银行本票
                        běnpiào

Where is there a bank?	*Yínháng zài náli?*
	银行在哪里？

exchange rate	*dùihùan lù*
	兑换率

At what time do they ____?	*Jí diǎn ____?*
	几点 ？

■ open	*kāi mén*	开门
■ close	*gūan mén*	关门

office hours	*yíngyè shíjīan*	营业时间
Where is the cashier's counter?	*Náli yǒu chūnà guìtái?*	哪里有出纳柜台？
What is today's exchange rate for U.S. dollars?	*Jīntīan Měi yúan dùihùan lǜ dūoshǎo?*	今天美元兑换率多少？
I'd like to cash this check.	*Wǒ xǐang yòng zhèizhāng zhīpìao dùixìan.*	我想用这张支票兑现。
Where do I sign?	*Zài náli qīan zì?*	在哪里签字？
Where do I endorse it?	*Bèimìan qīan zì xǐe zài náli?*	背面签字写在哪里？
Please give me ____.	*Qǐng géi wǒ ____.*	请给我____。
▧ large bills	*dà é chāopìao*	大额钞票
▧ small bills	*xǐao é chāopìao*	小额钞票
▧ coins	*yìngbì*	硬币
Please give me two fifty-yúan bills.	*Qǐng géi wó lǐang zhāng wǔshi yúan de.*	请给我两张五十元的。
Please give me one hundred-yúan bill.	*Qǐng géi wǒ yì zhāng yìbǎi yúan de.*	请给我一张一百元的。
Do you accept credit cards?	*Nǐ shōu xìnyòng kǎ ma?*	你收信用卡吗？

c = ts; *q* = ch; *x* = sh; *z* = dz; *zh* = j

May I guarantee my check with a credit card?	*Wǒ kéyǐ yòng xìnyòng kǎ dānbǎo wǒ de zhīpiào ma?* 我可以用信用卡担保我的支票吗？
Where is there an automatic teller machine?	*Nálǐ yǒu tíkuǎn jī?* 哪里有提款机？
Does it accept foreign bank cards?	*Shōu wàiguó yínháng kǎ ma?* 收外国银行卡吗？

CREDIT CARDS

Can I use my credit card to get cash?	*Wǒ néng yòng xìnyòng kǎ dùihùan xiànkuǎn ma?* 我能用信用卡兑换现款吗？
Which credit cards do you accept?	*Nǐmén jiēshòu nǎxiē xìnyòng kǎ?* 你们接受哪些信用卡？
Do you need to ___ my credit card?	*Nǐ xūyào ___ wǒ de xìnyòng kǎ ma?* 你需要___我的信用卡吗？
▒ swipe	*shūa* 刷
▒ check	*chá* 查
Do you need another form of identification?	*Nǐ xūyào wǒ biéde zhèngjiàn ma?* 你需要我别的证件吗？
This is the only credit card I have.	*Zhè shì wǒ wéiyī de xìnyòng kǎ.* 这是我唯一的信用卡。
I don't have any other credit cards.	*Wǒ méiyǒu biéde xìnyòng kǎ.* 我没有别的信用卡。

BUSINESS BANKING TERMS

amount	*jīn é*	金额
bad check	*wúxìao zhīpìao*	无效支票
bank	*yínháng*	银行
Bank of China	*Zhōngguó Yínháng*	中国银行
bill (currency note)	*chāopìao*	钞票
bond	*Zhàiquàn*	债券
borrow	*jìe*	借
cash	*xìankuǎn*	现款
cash a check	*zhīpìao dùixìan*	支票兑现
cashier	*chūnàyúan*	出纳员
capital	*zīběn*	资本
check	*zhīpìao*	支票
close an account	*qùxīao zhànghù*	取消帐户
counter	*gùitái*	柜台
credit	*xìndài*	信贷
deposit	*cún kuǎn*	存款
dollar (U.S.)	*Měiyúan*	美元
endorse	*bèishū*	背书
equity	*gǔqúan*	股权
exchange rate	*dùihùan lù*	兑换率

c = ts; *q* = ch; *x* = sh; *z* = dz; *zh* = j

futures	*qīhùo*	期货
income	*shōurù*	收入
income tax	*sǔodé shùi*	所得税
insurance	*báoxǐan*	保险
interest	*lìxi*	利息
interest rate	*lìlǜ*	利率
investment; invest	*tóuzī*	投资
lend (to)	*jìe (gěi)*	借（给）
letter of credit	*xìnyòng zhèng*	信用证
loan	*dàikǔan*	贷款
loss	*sǔnshī*	损失
make change	*zhǎo língqían*	找零钱
money order	*hùikǔan dān*	汇款单
note	*pìaojù*	票据
open an account	*kāilì zhànghù*	开立帐户
▓ foreign exchange account	*wàihùi zhànghù*	外汇帐户
▓ local currency account	*rénmínbì zhànghù*	人民币帐户
personal check	*sīrén zhīpìao*	私人支票
principal	*běnjīn*	本金
processing fee	*shǒuxù fèi*	手续费
profit	*lìrùn*	利润
safe	*báoxǐan gùi*	保险柜
savings	*chǔxù*	储蓄

securities	*zhèngquàn*	证券
service charge	*fúwù fèi*	服务费
sign	*qīan zì*	签字
share	*gǔfèn*	股份
stock	*gǔpìao*	股票
stockbroker	*gǔpìao jīngjì rén*	股票经纪人
stock exchange	*zhèngquàn jīaoyì sǔo*	证券交易所
tax	*shùi*	税
tax rate	*shùi lǜ*	税率
traveler's check	*lǚxíng zhīpìao*	旅行支票
withdrawal	*tíkǔan*	提款
Have you received my wire transfer?	*Nǐ shōudào wǒ de dìanbào zhǔanzhàng ma?*	你收到我的电报转帐吗？

TIPPING AND GIFT GIVING

Although the Chinese government does not officially condone tipping, the practice has become commonplace on the mainland, and it has always been acceptable in Taiwan, Hong Kong, and Macao. While a gratuity is not always expected in China today, it is seldom refused.

Tips are both appropriate and welcome in hotels, for example, when a bellhop carries your luggage to your room or an enthusiastic travel guide or service person goes out of his or her way to help you. You may also tip a hairdresser, barber, or manicurist, or anyone else who performs a

c = ts; q = ch; x = sh; z = dz; zh = j

personal service. Chinese taxi drivers do not generally solicit tips directly, but sometimes they are slow to make change if they believe a foreign client is likely to let them keep it. Depending on the quality of service, you may request the change or not, as you wish.

Larger eating establishments that cater to foreigners, on the other hand, increasingly follow the practice of adding a service charge to their bills. In these situations you need not leave a tip. Nor are gratuities expected in smaller eating establishments that serve predominantly local clientele. Since local Chinese still do not tip as a regular practice, foreigners who patronize these establishments are not expected to do so either.

Cash is the currency of choice in most situations, but small items such as pens, cassettes, cigarette lighters, small calculators, sunglasses, or cosmetics may also be given.

Many formal occasions in China call for an exchange of gifts. A guest who visits a school or a factory, for example, may leave a souvenir of his or her visit. One generally accepts a gift graciously in China—refuse only if you suspect the gift would obligate you too much. Accept with both hands; this is the polite and customary way. As a rule, the Chinese do not open gifts in front of the gift giver, but it is not wrong to do so or to ask a Chinese recipient to open a gift immediately if you wish.

Don't be surprised if a Chinese refuses a gift from you the first time you offer it. This is a traditional polite gesture and may not mean that the gift is unwelcome. Try again; if you are repeatedly rebuffed, then by all means stop offering.

tip	*xiǎofèi* 小费
This is for you.	*Zhè shì gěi nǐ de.* 这是给你的。
Is tipping ____ here?	*Zhèlǐ ____ gěi xiǎofèi ma?* 这里____给小费吗？
▓ expected	*xūyào* 需要

■ permitted	*kéyǐ* 可以
How much should I tip?	*Yīnggāi gěi dūosháo xǐaofèi?* 应该给多少小费？
Is it all right to tip in foreign currency?	*Kéyǐ yòng wàibì gěi ma?* 可以用外币给吗？
I would like to give a tip.	*Wó xíang gěi yīdǐan xiǎofèi.* 我想给一点小费。
Is there a service charge on the bill?	*Zhàngdān bāokùo fúwùfèi ma?* 帐单包括服务费吗？

c = ts; *q* = ch; *x* = sh; *z* = dz; *zh* = j

AT THE HOTEL

GETTING TO YOUR HOTEL

There are a few ways of referring to hotels in Chinese, and they are mostly interchangeable. **Fàndiàn** (literally, "place for taking meals") and **lǚguǎn** ("place for travelers") are most commonly used in China, together with **bīnguǎn** ("place for guests"), which generally refers more to a guest house than a hotel. A guest house may also be called a **zhāodàisuǒ** ("place for reception or entertainment"). In Hong Kong and Taiwan you are more likely to hear the term **jǐudiàn** ("place for liquor").

Which hotel is our group staying at?	*Wǒmén de túantǐ zhù zài něige lǚguǎn?* 我们的团体住在哪个旅馆？
Will I stay in a guest house?	*Wǒ hùi zhù bīnguǎn ma?* 我会住宾馆吗？
I'm looking for the ____ Hotel.	*Wó zhǎo ____ Fàndiàn.* 我找____饭店。
Is it near?	*Hěn jìn ma?* 很近吗？
Where can I get a taxi?	*Náli yǒu chūzū qìchē?* 哪里有出租汽车？
How much is the fare?	*Dūoshǎo qían?* 多少钱？
How long is the trip?	*Yào dūoshǎo shíjīan?* 要多少时间？
Can I walk there?	*Zǒu de dào ma?* 走得到吗？

CHECKING IN

I have a room reservation.	*Wǒ yǐjīng yùdìng le fángjiān.* 我已经预定了房间。
Please check for my name.	*Qǐng chá wǒ de míngzì.* 请查我的名字。
My last name is ___.	*Wǒ xìng ___.* 我姓_____。
My first name is ___.	*Wǒ de míngzì jiào ___.* 我的名字叫_____。
My host organization is ___.	*Wǒ de jiēdài dānwèi shì ___.* 我的接待单位是_____。
I don't have a reservation.	*Wǒ méi yǒu yùdìng.* 我没有预定。
Please check for me which other hotels have vacancies.	*Qǐng bāng wó dǎtīng něi jiā fàndiàn yǒu kōng fángjiān.* 请帮我打听哪家饭店有空房间。

c = ts; *q* = ch; *x* = sh; *z* = dz; *zh* = j

I would like ____.	*Wó xiangyào*	我想要_____。
a single room	*dānjīan*	单间
a double room	*shūang rén fáng*	双人房
a suite	*tàojīan*	套间
I will be staying for ____.	*Wǒ yào zhù ____.*	我要住_____。
one night	*yī tīan*	一天
two nights	*liǎng tīan*	两天
a week	*yí xīngqī*	一个星期
I would like a room ____.	*Wǒ yào yǒu ____ de fángjīan.*	我要有_____的房间。
with a bath	*sīrén xízǎo jīan*	私人洗澡间
with a balcony	*yángtái*	阳台
with a double bed	*shūang rén chuáng*	双人床
with two single beds	*liǎngge dānrén chúang*	两个单人床。
with a nice view	*fēngjíng hǎo*	风景好
Does it have ____?	*Yǒu méi yǒu ____.*	有没有_____。
air conditioning	*kōngtíao*	空调
a coffeepot	*kāfēi hu*	咖啡壶
heat	*nǔanqì*	暖气
hot water	*rè shǔi*	热水
an in-room fax	*kèfáng nèi de chúanzhēnjī*	客房内的传真机
a refrigerator	*bīngxīang*	冰箱
a telephone	*dìanhùa*	电话
television	*dìanshì*	电视

I don't like this room.	*Wǒ bù xǐhuān zhèi jīan.* 我不喜欢这间。
May I change to another room?	*Kéyǐ hùan yī jīan ma?* 可以换一间吗？
This room is too noisy.	*Zhèige fángjīan tài chǎole.* 这个房间太吵了。
Do you have a nonsmoking room?	*Yǒu méiyǒu bù xīyān de fángjīan?* 有没有不吸烟的房间？
Do you have something ____?	*Yǒu méi yǒu ____ de?* 有没有_____的？

▨ better	*bǐjiào hǎo*	比较好
▨ brighter	*bǐjiào liàng*	比较亮
▨ cheaper	*bǐjiào píanyi*	比较便宜
▨ larger	*bǐjiào dà*	比较大
▨ quieter	*bǐjiào ānjìng*	比较安静
▨ smaller	*bǐjiào xǐao*	比较小

What floor is the room on?	*Fángjīan zài jǐ lóu?* 房间在几楼？
Where is the elevator?	*Dìantī zài náli?* 电梯在哪里？
Do you have a room that is equipped for handicapped people?	*Yǒu fāngbìan cánjī rén de fángjīan ma?* 有方便残疾人的房间吗？
Please carry my bags up to my room.	*Qíng bǎ xíngli sòng dào wǒ de fángjīan.* 请把行李送到我的房间。

HOTEL SERVICES

I would like to see ____.	*Wǒ xiǎng jiàn ____.*	
	我想见_____。	
▓ the assistant manager	*zhùlǐ jīnglǐ*	助理经理
▓ the bell captain	*fúwùyuán lǐngbān*	服务员领班
▓ the concierge	*fúwùtái jīnglǐ*	服务台经理
▓ the general manager	*zǒngjīnglǐ*	总经理
▓ the room attendant	*fúwùyuán*	服务员
front desk	*qiántái*	前台
service desk	*fúwùtái*	服务台
May I have my room key please?	*Qǐng géi wǒ fángjīan yàoshi.*	
	请给我房间钥匙。	
Shall I return the key to the service desk?	*Yàoshi yào huàn gěi fúwùtái ma?*	
	钥匙要还给服务台吗？	
I have lost my key.	*Wǒ diū le wǒ de yàoshi.*	
	我丢了我的钥匙。	
What is my room number?	*Wǒ de fángjīan hàoma dūoshǎo?*	
	我的房间号码多少？	
I am staying in room number ____.	*Wǒ zhù ____ hào fáng.*	
	我住_____号房。	
405	*sì líng wǔ*	
	四零五	

NOTE: Room and telephone numbers are read digit by digit in Chinese, so room 436 is not room *sìbǎi sānshílìu* (four hundred thirty-six) but rather room **sì sān liù** (four three six).

I have laundry to ____.	*Wó yǒu yīfu yào ____*	我有衣服要_____。
▧ dry clean	*gānxǐ*	干洗
▧ iron	*tàng*	烫
▧ wash	*xǐ*	洗

I need this done immediately.	*Wó mǎshàng jiù yào.* 我马上就要。	
My shirt is missing a button.	*Wǒde chènshān shǎole ge kòuzi.* 我的衬衫少了个扣子。	
When will you return this?	*Shénme shíhòu sònglái?* 什么时候送来？	
Where can I get my shoes shined?	*Zài nǎli kéyǐ cā xié?* 在哪里可以擦鞋？	

Where is ____?	____ *zài nǎli?*	____在哪里？
▧ the bathroom	*Cèsuǒ*	厕所
▧ the restaurant	*Cāntīng*	餐厅
▧ the telephone	*Diànhuà*	电话

I need ____.	*Wǒ xūyào ____.*	我需要_____。
▧ a towel	*máojīn*	毛巾
▧ a blanket	*yī chuáng tǎnzi*	一床毯子
▧ a light bulb	*dēngpào*	灯泡
▧ a pillow	*yígè zhěntóu*	一个枕头
▧ soap	*féizào*	肥皂
▧ some hangers	*yīxiē yījià*	一些衣架

Please send ____ to my room.	*Qǐng sòng ____ dào wǒde fángjiān.*	请送_____到我的房间。

c = ts; *q* = ch; *x* = sh; *z* = dz; *zh* = j

▥ an ashtray	*yānhuī gāng*	烟灰缸
▥ some cold (preboiled) drinking water	*lěng kāishuǐ*	冷开水
▥ some glasses	*jǐge bōlí bēi*	几个玻璃杯
▥ some hot water	*rè shuǐ*	热水
▥ some ice cubes	*yìxiē bīngkuài*	一些冰块
▥ some tea	*cháyè*	茶叶
▥ some toilet paper	*wèishēng zhǐ*	卫生纸

What's the voltage here?	*Zhèli diànyā duōshǎo?* 这里电压多少？
Please wake me tomorrow morning at ___ o'clock.	*Míngtiān zǎoshàng ___ dián qǐng jiào wǒ.* 明天早上＿＿＿＿点请叫我。
I don't wish to be disturbed.	*Qǐng bú yào dáráo wǒ.* 请不要打扰我。

AT THE DOOR

Who is it?	*Shéi?*	谁？
Just a minute.	*Děng yī xià.*	等一下。
Come in.	*Qǐng jìn.*	请进。
Please come back later.	*Qíng wǎn yīdian zài lái.*	请晚一点再来。

COMPLAINTS

My room ____.	Wǒ de fángjiān ____. 我的房间_____。	
has no air conditioning	méiyǒu lěngqì	没有冷气
has no electricity	méi yǒu diàn	没有电
has no heat	méiyǒu nuǎnqì	没有暖气
has no hot water	méi yǒu rè shuǐ	没有热水
has a strange odor	yǒu guài wèidào	有怪味道
is dirty	zāng le	脏了
is too cold	tài lěng	太冷
is too dark	tài àn	太暗
is too humid	tài cháoshī	太潮湿
is too noisy	tài chǎo	太吵

NOTE: China runs on a 220-volt, 50-cycle electrical system, so you can't just plug any appliance into the outlet in your hotel room and expect it to work efficiently. Furthermore, your room may contain electrical outlets in a number of different plug configurations. One of the most common outlets calls for a three-pronged "crow foot" plug that is rarely included in standard adaptor kits. A makeshift solution is to bend the two prongs in your adaptor out slightly to fit into two of the three crow feet, ignoring the third.

A good idea for those who expect to spend a fair amount of time in China is to buy appliances, such as electric razors, hair dryers, and portable tape recorders locally, or else those with conversion switches enabling them to be used at either 110 or 220 volts.

c = ts; q = ch; x = sh; z = dz; zh = j

At what time is there hot water?	*Shénme shíhòu cái yǒu rè shuǐ?*	什么时候才有热水？
When will the heat be turned on?	*Shénme shíhòu cái yǒu nuǎn qì?*	什么时候才有暖气？

The _____ is stuck.   _____ dǎ bu kāi.   _____ 打不开。

▓ curtain	*Chuānglián*	窗帘
▓ door	*Mén*	门
▓ window	*Chuāngzi*	窗子

The _____ is broken.   _____ huài le.   _____ 坏了。

▓ air conditioning	*Kōngtiáo*	空调
▓ doorbell	*Ménlíng*	门铃
▓ faucet	*Shuǐlóngtóu*	水龙头
▓ lamp	*Dēng*	灯
▓ plug	*Chātóu*	插头
▓ radio	*Shōuyīn jī*	收音机
▓ remote control	*Yáokòng qì*	遥控器
▓ shower	*Línyùqì*	淋浴器
▓ telephone	*Diànhuà*	电话
▓ television set	*Diànshì*	电视
▓ toilet	*Mátǒng*	马桶

This bulb is burned out.	*Dēngpào huài le.* 灯泡坏了
The drain is clogged.	*Páishuǐguǎn sāizhù le.* 排水管塞住了。

The _____ is leaking.   _____ lòu shuǐ.   _____ 漏水。

▓ bathroom	*Cèsuǒ*	厕所
▓ bathtub	*Zǎopén*	澡盆
▓ toilet	*Mátǒng*	马桶

Can you fix it?	*Nǐ néng xiū ma?* 你能修吗？
Can you make a phone call for me?	*Nǐ néng wèi wó dǎ ge diànhùa ma?* 你能为我打个电话吗？

ROOM SERVICE

What number do I dial for room service?	*Kèfáng yòngcān fúwùbù de diànhuà shì dūoshǎo?* 客房用餐服务部的电话是多少？
Where is the room service menu?	*Kèfáng yòngcān càidān zài nálǐ?* 客房用餐菜单在哪里？
Do you have any Western food?	*Yǒu Xīcān ma?* 有西餐吗？
Do you have any Japanese food?	*Yǒu Rìběn liàolǐ ma?* 有日本料理吗？
I would like to eat ____.	*Wó xiǎng chī ____.* 我想吃_____。
breakfast	*zǎocān*	早餐
lunch	*wǔcān*	午餐
dinner	*wǎncān*	晚餐
a late night snack	*yèxiāo*	夜宵
Do you have any ____?	*Yǒu méi yǒu ____?* 有没有_____？
bacon	*xūnròu*	熏肉
coffee	*kāfēi*	咖啡
donuts	*zhámìan bǐngqūan*	炸面饼圈

c = ts; *q* = ch; *x* = sh; *z* = dz; *zh* = j

▨ French toast	*Fǎshì tǔsī*	法式吐司
▨ fried eggs	*jīan dàn*	煎蛋
▨ fried potatoes	*zhá shūtíao*	炸薯条
▨ ham	*húotǔi*	火腿
▨ hot chocolate	*rè qǐaokèlì*	热巧克力
▨ milk	*níunǎi*	牛奶
▨ oatmeal	*mài pìan*	麦片
▨ orange juice	*júzi zhī*	橘子汁
▨ pancakes	*báojīan bǐng*	薄煎饼
▨ poached eggs	*zhǔ dàn*	煮蛋
▨ sausage	*xīangcháng*	香肠
▨ scrambled eggs	*chǎo jīdàn*	炒鸡蛋
▨ tea	*chá*	茶
▨ waffles	*húafū bǐng*	华夫饼
▨ yogurt	*sūan nǎi*	酸奶
I would like some more ____.	*Wǒ hái yào ____.* 我还要_____。	
▨ bread or rolls	*mìanbāo*	面包
▨ butter	*húangyóu*	黄油
▨ cream	*nǎiyóu*	奶油
▨ honey	*fēngmì*	蜂蜜
▨ jam	*gǔojìang*	果酱
▨ pepper	*húj̄iāo*	胡椒
▨ salt	*yán*	盐
▨ sugar	*táng*	糖
▨ syrup	*tángjīang*	糖浆
▨ toast	*kǎo mìanbāo*	烤面包

I think I'll have a Chinese breakfast.	*Wó xiǎng chī Zhōngshì zǎocān.* 我想吃中式早餐	
▨ crullers	*yóutíao*	油条
▨ dried minced fish	*yúsōng*	鱼松
▨ dried minced meat	*ròusōng*	肉松
▨ peanuts	*huāshēngmǐ*	花生米
▨ pickles; pickled vegetables	*pàocài*	泡菜
▨ rice gruel; congee	*xīfàn*	稀饭
▨ salty soybean milk	*xían dòujiāng*	咸豆浆
▨ sesame seed cake	*shāobǐng*	烧饼
▨ steamed bread	*mántóu*	馒头
▨ steamed stuffed buns	*bāozi*	包子
▨ sweet soybean milk	*tían dòujiāng*	甜豆浆
▨ thousand-year eggs	*pídàn*	皮蛋

DEPARTURE

We are leaving ___.	*Wǒmén ___ zǒu.* 我们___走。	
▨ tomorrow	*míngtīan*	明天
▨ today	*jīntīan*	今天

c = ts; *q* = ch; *x* = sh; *z* = dz; *zh* = j

Please send a porter to my room.	*Qing pài fúwùyúan lái qǔ xínglǐ.* 请派服务员来取行李。
I have two large bags.	*Wó yóu liǎng dà jiàn.* 我有两大件。
May I leave my bags in the room?	*Wǒ kéyí bǎ xínglǐ líu zài fángjīan lǐ ma?* 我可以把行李留在房间里吗？
Please send our baggage down to the lobby.	*Qíng bǎ xínglǐ sòng dào lóuxìa dàtīng.* 请把行李送到楼下大厅。
I would like to pay the bill.	*Wǒ yào fù zhàng.* 我要付帐。
Where shall I pay?	*Zài náli fù zhàng?* 在哪里付帐？
May I use my credit card?	*Wǒ kéyǐ yòng xìnyòng kǎ ma?* 我可以用信用卡吗？
What cards do you accept?	*Nǐmén jīeshòu shénme kǎ?* 你们接受什么卡？
May I check the bill a moment?	*Wǒ kéyi chákàn yíxìa zhàngdān ma?* 我可以察看一下帐单吗？
This is not my bill.	*Zhè búshì wǒde zhàngdān.* 这不是我的帐单。
There must be a mistake.	*Zhèlí yǒu cùo.* 这里有错。
What is this charge?	*Zhèi xìang shì shénme?* 这项是什么？
This charge is incorrect.	*Zhèi xìang bú dùi.* 这项不对。

I should not be charged for that.	*Wǒ bù yīnggāi fù zhèi xiàng.* 我不应该付这项。
I refuse to pay for that.	*Wǒ jùjúe fù zhèi xiàng.* 我拒绝付这项。
How much is the room tax?	*Fángjīan shùi dūoshǎo?* 房间税多少？
Please give me a separate bill for telephone calls.	*Qǐng lìngwài géi wǒ yīfèn dǎ diànhùa de zhàngdān.* 请另外给我一份打电话的帐单。
Where shall I sign?	*Wǒ zài nǎlǐ qīan zì?* 我在哪里签字？
I had a very comfortable stay.	*Wǒ zhù de hěn shūfu.* 我住得很舒服。
Your service was ____.	*Nǐ mén de fúwù ____.* 你们的服务_____。

▧ very good	*hén hǎo*	很好
▧ passable	*hái kéyǐ*	还可以
▧ not so good	*bú tài hǎo*	不太好
▧ very bad	*hěn chà*	很差

c = ts; *q* = ch; *x* = sh; *z* = dz; *zh* = j

Travel Tips It is possible, through diet and habit, to ease the transition to a new time zone, commonly referred to as "jet lag." Up to four days prior to your departure, begin accustoming your body to its future schedule by gradually changing the times you eat until they more closely match that of your destination. Eat lightly and avoid carbohydrates. If you are taking a night flight, eat very little the day of your departure and avoid alcohol and even dinner on the plane if it is offered. Instead, ask to have your breakfast earlier, then rest until it is served. When you arrive, you will have had your breakfast about the same time as people in that country, and be ready for your next meal at the appropriate time. When you do have your next meal, try to eat a lot of protein, followed in the next meal by a high-carbohydrate diet. Avoid taking a nap during your first day, and instead, go to bed a little earlier than usual.

GETTING AROUND TOWN

THE BUS

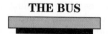

After bicycles, buses are the most common means of transportation in China. They run nearly everywhere in the major cities, and the fares are extremely low—just pennies. Foreigners seldom ride public buses in China, though a trip can be a real adventure. Because service personnel on public buses rarely speak English and stops are seldom marked in pinyin, be sure first to get someone to write down your destination in characters if you wish to take a bus.

At least two service personnel are assigned to each bus: a driver and one or two conductors, depending on the size of the bus (some buses have two coaches joined accordion-style). The conductor, usually a woman, accepts fares, gives out tickets, and yells out stops as they are passed. She is posted by the door of the bus to collect money. If you hand her a slip of paper with your destination in Chinese characters, she will let you know when it's time to get off.

One world of warning: Crowded buses are more the rule than the exception in urban China. Be prepared to be pushed and even squeezed if you board a bus in Beijing or Shanghai during rush hour.

Where is the bus terminal?	*Gōnggòng qìchē zhàn zài náli?* 公共汽车站在哪里？
Which bus do I take to get to ____?	*Dào ____ zuò jǐ lù chē?* 到___坐几路车？
How much is the fare?	*Pìaojìa dūoshǎo?* 票价多少？
In which direction should I go?	*Zóu něige fāngxiàng?* 走哪个方向？

c = ts; *q* = ch; *x* = sh; *z* = dz; *zh* = j

How often do the buses come?	*Qìchē duōjǐu yī bān?* 汽车多久一班？
Does the bus go to ____?	*Chēzi dào ____ qù ma?* 车子到____去吗？
Is it far from here?	*Lí zhèli yuǎn ma?* 离这里远吗？
How many stops are there?	*Yǒu duōshǎo zhàn?* 有多少站？
Must I change buses?	*Yào huàn chē ma?* 要换车吗？
Where do I have to get off?	*Zài nǎli xià chē?* 在哪里下车？
Please tell me where to get off.	*Qǐng gàosù wǒ zài nǎli xià chē.* 请告诉我在哪里下车。

TAXIS

If you are not part of a group traveling on a tourist bus, chances are you will find that taxis provide a reasonably priced and efficient means of getting around most of China's major cities.

Taxis can be hailed just about anywhere. Different car models fetch different rates, however, and in general, the better the car, the more expensive the ride. Most Chinese taxis have meters, and drivers will willingly issue receipts to those who request them.

It's an excellent idea to get someone to write down your destination in Chinese characters before you take a taxi; this can help a lot in preventing mishaps.

| Where can I find a taxi? | *Náli yǒu chūzū qìchē?* 哪里有出租汽车？ |

Please call me a taxi.	*Qǐng géi wǒ jiào chē.* 请给我叫车。	
Driver! Can you take me?	*Sījī, nǐ néng dài wǒ ma?* 司机，你能带我吗？	
I want to go to ____.	*Wǒ yào qù ____.* 我要去____。	
the airport	*fēijī chǎng*	飞机场
the hotel	*lǚguǎn*	旅馆
the railroad station	*huǒchē zhàn*	火车站
Please take me to____.	*Qǐng dài wǒ dào ____.*	请带我到____。
the bus station	*gōnggòng qì chēzhàn*	公共汽车站
this address	*zhèige dìzhǐ*	这个地址
Do you know where it is?	*Nǐ zhīdào zài nálǐ ma?* 你知道在哪里吗？	
How much is it?	*Yào duōshǎo qián?* 要多少钱？	
I will pay what is on the meter.	*Wǒ huì àn biǎo fù kuǎn.* 我会按表付款。	
Please turn on the meter.	*Qǐng dǎ biǎo.* 请打表。	
Please take the ____ route.	*Qǐng zǒu ____ de lù.* 请走____的路。	
fastest	*zuì kuài*	最快
most scenic	*fēngjǐng hǎo*	风景好
I'm in a hurry.	*Wǒ yào gǎn shíjiān.* 我要赶时间。	

c = ts; *q* = ch; *x* = sh; *z* = dz; *zh* = j

Please drive a little faster.	*Qǐng kāi kùai yìdǐan.* 请开快一点。	
I think you are going the wrong way.	*Wó xǐang ní zǒu cùo le.* 我想你走错了。	
Please drive a little more slowly.	*Qǐng kāi màn yìdǐan.* 请开慢一点。	
Please stop a moment ____.	*Qǐng tíng yíxìa.* 请停一下。	
▧ at the corner	*zài lùkǒu*	在路口
▨ at the next block	*zài xìa yī tíao jīe*	在下一条街
▧ in front of that building	*zài dà lóu qíanmìan*	在大楼前面。
Can you wait for me?	*Nǐ néng déng wǒ ma?*	你能等我吗？
I'll be right back.	*Wǒ mǎshàng jìu húilái.*	我马上就回来。
I expect to be back ____.	*Wǒ ____ jìu húilái.*	我____就回来。
▧ in a few minutes	*jǐ fēn zhōng*	几分钟
▧ in an hour or two	*yī líang xǐaoshí*	一两小时
▧ as soon as I'm through sightseeing	*kàn wán*	看完
How much do I owe you?	*Wǒ gāi fù nǐ dūoshǎo?*	我该付你多少？
Do not try to cheat me.	*Búyào qīpìan wǒ.* 不要欺骗我。	

I refuse to pay so much money.	*Wǒ jùjué fù zènme dūo.*	我拒绝付这么多。
You took a circuitous route.	*Nǐ ràole tài dūo wānlù.*	你绕了太多弯路。
I will report you to the authorities.	*Wǒ yào xiàng dāngjú tóusū nǐ.*	我要向当局投诉你。
Please give me a receipt.	*Qǐng géi wǒ kāi shōujù.*	请给我开收据。

SIGHTSEEING AND TOURS

Where is a travel agency?	*Náli yǒu lǚxíngshè?*	哪里有旅行社？
I need an English-speaking guide.	*Wǒ xūyào shūo Yīngwén de dǎoyóu.*	我需要说英文的导游。
How much will it cost ____?	____ *yào dūoshǎo?*	____要多少？
▦ per day	*Yī tīan*	一天
▦ per hour	*Yīge xǐaoshí*	一个小时
Where do they sell guidebooks?	*Náli yǒu mài lǚyóu shǒucè?*	哪里有卖旅游手册？
Where do they sell local maps?	*Náli yǒu mài běndì dìtú?*	哪里有卖本地地图？
What are the sights of interest here?	*Zhèli yǒu shénme míngshèng?*	这里有什么名胜？
Can you arrange a tour of the area?	*Nǐ néng ānpái běndì de lǚyóu ma?*	你能安排本地的旅游吗？

c = ts; *q* = ch; *x* = sh; *z* = dz; *zh* = j

How long is the tour?	*Lǚyóu yào duōjiǔ?* 旅游要多久？	
We would like to see_____.	*Wǒmén xiǎng qù kàn.*	我们想去看_____。
▦ an antique market	*gúdǒng shìchǎng*	古董市场
▦ an aquarium	*shuǐzúguǎn*	水族馆
▦ an art museum	*měishùguǎn*	美术馆
▦ a botanical garden	*zhíwùyúan*	植物园
▦ a Catholic church	*Tiānzhǔ jiàotáng*	天主教堂
▦ a department store	*bǎihùo shāngdìan*	百货商店
▦ the downtown area	*shí zhōngxīn*	市中心
▦ a flower garden	*hūayúan*	花园
▦ a foreign language bookstore	*wàiwén shūdìan*	外文书店
▦ a fruit and vegetable market	*cài shìchǎng*	菜市场
▦ a library	*túshūguǎn*	图书馆
▦ a museum	*bówùguǎn*	博物馆
▦ a park	*gōngyúan*	公园
▦ a Protestant church	*Jīdū jiàotáng*	基督教堂
▦ a scenic area	*fēngjǐng qū*	风景区
▦ a shopping center	*gòuwù zhōngxīn*	购物中心

■ a sporting arena	*tíyùguǎn*	体育馆
■ a stadium	*yùndòng chǎng*	运动场
■ a supermarket	*chāojí shìchǎng*	超级市场
■ a temple	*mìao*	庙
■ a university	*dàxúe*	大学
■ a zoo	*dòngwùyúan*	动物园

ADMISSIONS

Is it all right to go in now?	*Xìanzài kéyǐ jìnqù ma?* 现在可以进去吗？	
Is it open?	*Kāi le ma?* 开了吗？	
At what time does it ____?	*Jí diǎn zhōng ____?* 几点钟____？	
■ open	*kāi mén*	开门
■ close	*gūan mén*	关门
Where can I buy tickets?	*Dào nálí mǎi píao?* 到哪里买票？	
What is the admission?	*Pìaojìa dūoshǎo?* 票价多少？	
Are children's tickets ____?	*Xǐaohái ____ ma?* 小孩____吗？	
■ free	*mǐanfèi*	免费
■ half price	*bànpìao*	半票
Is it all right to take pictures?	*Kéyǐ zhàoxìang ma?* 可以照相吗？	
Do you have an English-language brochure?	*Yǒu Yīngwén zīlìao ma?* 有英文资料吗？	

c = ts; *q* = ch; *x* = sh; *z* = dz; *zh* = j

A SIGHTSEEING ITINERARY

China is just too vast and too varied for anyone to expect to see it all in one or two trips. Even a three-week tour of eight or nine cities is at best a whirlwind tour, what the Chinese would call *zou ma kan hua*, meaning "gazing at flowers from horseback." Here are some—but by no means all—of the important places and sights you should try not to miss.

BEIJING

Beijing is a "must see," since so many of China's cultural treasures and landmarks can be seen there, and since it figures so prominently in Chinese history, having served as the capital over many centuries. It's also one natural starting point for a journey into China, since it is the terminus of most of the international air routes into the PRC.

In the geometric center of the city is the *Gugong*, or **Forbidden City**, the Imperial Palace during the Ming and Qing Dynasties. A labyrinth of courtyards, formal halls, gardens, and ceremonial gates, it is now a museum that is open to the public and that can take a day or two to explore thoroughly. The southern gate of the Forbidden City is called **Tian'anmen**, or the "Gate of Heavenly Peace." It was from the top of this gate that Mao Zedong announced the founding of the People's Republic in 1949, and it bears his likeness today. It is the symbol of the new China, and the vantage point from which the leaders review parades on national holidays.

To the south of the gate is **Tian'anmen Square**, a vast plaza even larger than Moscow's Red Square, said to accommodate as many as half a million people. This was the site where student protesters were killed in 1989 after months of peaceful demonstrations urging democratic reform.

Tian'anmen Square is bounded on the west by the *Renmin Dahuitang*, the **Great Hall of the People**. The Great Hall, seat of the National People's Congress, is a mammoth structure built in the late 1950s that contains enormous reception rooms, auditoriums, and banquet halls. To the east are the **Museums of Chinese History and the Chinese Revolution**, best left for a rainy day. In the center of the square is the **Monument to the People's Heroes**, a memorial dedicated to those who died during the Chinese Revolution, and just to its south is the **Chairman Mao Memorial Hall**, which contains an exhibit devoted to a few prominent Communist revolutionaries and the remains of Mao Zedong himself, on view in a glass sarcophagus.

Completing the perimeter of the square at its south end is **Qianmen**, the "front gate," which originally was connected to an earth and stone wall that surrounded the entire city.

Southeast of the square is *Tiantan*, the **Temple of Heaven**, a complex of beautiful ceremonial buildings and an altar at which the Ming and Qing emperors made sacrifices to heaven to ensure a good harvest. The complex dates to the fifteenth century, and it is well worth visiting.

Northeast of the square is the **Lama Temple**, or *Yonghe Gong*, formerly the residence of an emperor's son, and later home to a Tibetan lamasery. Near it is the **Confucius Temple**, a thirteenth-century structure, and not too far away is **Ritan Park**, the gardens surrounding the Altar of the Sun.

Just across the street from the Forbidden City to the north is a park surrounding **Coal Hill** (Mei Shan or Jing Shan), an artificial hill created with earth excavated when the moat surrounding the Forbidden City was dug. The last emperor of the Ming Dynasty hanged himself on this hill. Nearby is **Zhongnanhai**, meaning "Central and South Sea," the compound in which the State Council's offices are located and that houses China's highest-ranking leaders. Chairman Mao lived there. It is closed to the public, but foreign dignitaries are occasionally received there. North of Zhongnanhai is **Beihai Park**, a public park with a lovely lake and a Tibetan-style Dagoba.

OUTSIDE BEIJING

The greater Beijing area also includes *Shisanling*, the **Ming Tombs**, the mausoleums of 13 Ming emperors set in a

c = ts; q = ch; x = sh; z = dz; zh = j

picturesque valley. The sacred way leading to the tombs begins with a marble gate of five archways and is guarded by a regimen of stone animals and statues of warriors and officials. One of the tombs has been excavated, and visitors may descend into it.

Yiheyuan, the **Summer Palace**, is also on most itineraries. It is a compound on the shores of Lake Kunming less than ten miles northwest of the city that was built in the late nineteenth century for the notorious Empress Dowager. Funds intended for China's imperial navy were appropriated for this purpose, and were used by the Empress in particular to construct a large marble pleasure boat on the edge of the lake that should not be missed. Not too far away you can still see some of the ruins of **Yuanmingyuan**, an earlier palace destroyed by foreign troops in 1860. Beyond the summer palace is Xiangshan, **Fragrant Hill**, a lovely park that contains the **Temple of the Sleeping Buddha** and the **Temple of the Azure Clouds**. The latter includes a memorial to Dr. Sun Yat-sen, the father of modern China.

About 40 miles north of Beijing is **Badaling**, the most popular site for viewing the Changcheng, or **Great Wall**. The wall is often seen together with the Ming Tombs on one trip outside of town. Its reputation precedes it and it is no disappointment—the Great Wall is well worth the trip. Other locations for visiting the wall are **Mutianyu**, a bit less crowded and built up than Badaling, and, somewhat further away, **Simatai**, where you can see unrestored sections of the wall in relative tranquility.

About nine miles southwest of Beijing you can visit the **Marco Polo Bridge** (Lugouqiao), an arched stone bridge said to have been admired by Marco Polo when he visited China in the thirteenth century. The bridge has two balustrades on which more than 400 white stone lions, no two of which are exactly alike, are perched. It is most famous as the site where, in 1937, Chinese forces shot at advancing Japanese troops and the Sino-Japanese war began. Further down the road is **Zhoukoudian**, the site at which the fossilized bones of Peking Man were unearthed in the 1920s.

Further outside of Beijing—a few hours in either direction by car—are Dongling, the **Eastern Qing Tombs**, and Xiling, the **Western Qing Tombs**, where the Qing emperors rest. They are in better condition than the Ming tombs, and there are a number of avenues of stone figures and animals to enjoy. The mausoleums of the Emperor Qianlong and of the Empress Dowager are located at the Eastern tombs; the latter was opened in the early twentieth century and one may descend into its inner chamber.

OVERNIGHT TRIPS FROM BEIJING

A number of places within striking distance of Beijing are good choices for overnight and weekend trips. Among these are **Chengde**, a mountain resort in northern Hebei Province that was used as a summer retreat for the Manchu court during the Qing (Manchu) Dynasty. To strengthen ties with Tibet, the Emperor Kangxi built a series of Tibetan-style temples in this city, including a replica of Lhasa's famous Potala Palace. A popular seaside resort located about four and one-half hours by train from Beijing is **Beidaihe**. It was a small fishing village until the early twentieth century, when it became a favorite retreat of foreigners who lived in Beijing during the hot summer months. They constructed many villas there, buildings now owned by the Chinese government and used by the senior party leaders every summer. Nearby is **Shanhaiguan**, the gateway to Manchuria and the eastern terminus of the Great Wall, the point at which the wall meets the sea.

Datong is another convenient destination, about ten hours by train from Beijing in northern Shanxi Province. The town is known for the magnificent Buddhist shrines that can be seen at the nearby Yungang grottoes, and for its many monasteries. Also accessible from Beijing is **Luoyang**, an ideal place to stop if you happen to be traveling by train between Beijing and Xi'an. Luoyang, known as the location where Buddhism was first introduced into China, boasts the White Horse Temple, reputed to be the first Buddhist Temple in China, as well as much Buddhist sculpture in the nearby Longmen caves.

c = ts; q = ch; x = sh; z = dz; zh = j

THE NORTHEAST

Northeast China, familiarly known as Manchuria, is heavily industrialized due to historical occupation by the Japanese and the Russians. The Japanese invaded officially in 1932 and stayed until 1945. The region is known for its bitter cold weather with winter temperatures falling as low as −22°F. Cities of interest in this region include **Harbin**, the capital of distant Heilongjiang Province, 700 miles northeast of Beijing, a 19-hour train ride. Russian influence is apparent from the architecture here, and the city is known for its annual ice festival in late January, when beautiful ice sculptures are displayed. **Shenyang**, formerly called Mukden, is the capital of Liaoning Province. The Manchus originated here before they conquered China in 1644, and Manchu tombs, plus an Imperial Palace used by them for the first eight years of their rule, are popular attractions. Also of interest in the Northeast is **Dalian** (formerly Dairen), a heavily industrialized manufacturing center an hour and a half by plane from Beijing.

EASTERN CHINA

Easily accessible from Beijing, **Shanghai** is China's most populous city, and it has a rich history. It was a nineteenth-century treaty port and a major foreign enclave until 1949, and its skyline bears this out. Tall European-style buildings line the Waitan, or **"Bund"** area between the Huangpu River and Zhongshan Road—a must for an evening stroll. Shanghai is a manufacturing and shipping center and is one of the leading commercial and cultural centers of China. Places to visit include the new **Shanghai Museum**, a world-class facility that is one of the most celebrated and successful examples of modern architecture in China today. It houses an internationally renowned collection of Chinese art and artifacts, including bronze, ceramics, painting, and calligraphy. Also of interest are Yu Yuan, the gardens of the Yu family, and **Chenghuang Miao**, a temple dedicated to the local gods, a short distance away. Other temples worth a visit include **Longhua Si**, which includes a wooden, seven-story pagoda, and **Yufo Si**, the Temple of the Jade Buddha. Don't forget a walk down crowded **Nanjing Dong Lu**, the major shopping area and an important Chinese fashion center.

Old Shanghai was built on the west bank of the Huangpu River; the east bank, called the **Pudong** area, was accessible from the city only by ferryboat and remained undeveloped until the 1990s. After the State Council approved a plan for its development, and two suspension bridges were built over the river, Pudong began to commercialize quite rapidly. It is one of China's principal foreign investment zones, and its symbol—indeed, the symbol of the new Shanghai—is the **Oriental Pearl Tower**, at just over 1,500 feet the highest television tower in Asia and the third-tallest in the world.

Suzhou, 50 miles west of Shanghai in Jiangsu Province, is aptly nicknamed "the Venice of the Orient" because of the many canals that crisscross the town. Suzhou is most famous for its landscape gardens, which number more than 150, some being more than 1,000 years old. Among the more famous: **Tiger Hill, the Pavilion of the Surging Waves, the Garden of the Humble Administrator**, and the **Lion Grove**. Since the 1980s Suzhou has also become one of China's most important manufacturing centers.

Hangzhou, a city in Zhejiang Province three and one-half hours by train from Shanghai, is renowned as one of the loveliest in all of China. An old Chinese saying goes, "There is paradise in heaven, and then there are Suzhou and Hangzhou on earth." Hangzhou is located near **West Lake**, which boasts lovely hills, stone bridges, pagodas, temples, pavilions, and many varieties of bamboo. Hangzhou is noted for its cuisine and for its silk and embroidery.

Also easily accessible from Shanghai are the cities of **Nanjing** and **Wuxi**, both in Jiangsu Province. Nanjing, 186 miles up the Changjiang (Yangtse River) from Shanghai, was China's capital during many dynasties. Don't miss the **Mausoleum of Dr. Sun Yat-sen** (1866–1925), the founder of modern China, in the **Purple Mountains** east of the city. Also nearby is the **Tomb of the Emperor Taizu** (Hong Wu), the founder of the Ming Dynasty. Wuxi, located on **Lake Tai**,

c = ts; q = ch; x = sh; z = dz; zh = j

is 87 miles west of Shanghai and is known as an industrial and resort center.

Also of interest is the city of **Qingdao** (Tsingtao), a seaport on the coast of Shandong Province occupied by Germany between the end of the nineteenth century and World War I, and later by Japan. Qingdao is a pleasant seaside resort with interesting European architecture. It is known worldwide for the excellent beer produced in a factory first set up by Germans.

THE SOUTHEAST

Guangzhou, formerly known as Canton, is one of China's gateway cities due to its proximity to Hong Kong, only three hours away by rail and even closer by hovercraft. The "City of Rams," as it is known, was where the Opium War began in 1839, and it was one of the treaty ports opened to the British at the end of that war in 1842. At the beginning of the twentieth century Guangzhou was also the site of early revolutionary activities that led ultimately to the overthrow of the Qing Dynasty (1644–1911). Guangzhou, heavily urbanized and relatively lacking in charm, is nonetheless home to monuments, museums, and temples, and of course to Cantonese cuisine, which is among China's finest.

Scenic spots near Guangzhou include the **Seven Star Rocks**, seven peaks standing in the formation of the Big Dipper, and **Conghua Hot Springs**, a health spa. Also not to be missed is the nearby town of **Foshan**, famous for the last 800 years as a center for pottery, porcelain, textiles, and other handicrafts. Of special interest are the tiny thumb-sized figurines crafted nearby.

Abutting Hong Kong is the city of **Shenzhen**, which was a quiet fishing village until the 1080s when it was designated by the central government as a "special economic zone" in order to absorb foreign investment. Shenzhen took maximum advantage of its proximity to Hong Kong and established itself as one of China's key manufacturing and financial centers. It has since become a metropolis where residents enjoy a much higher standard of living than do others in China.

Without a doubt, one of China's loveliest landscapes, **Guilin** (Kweilin) has been attracting tourists for hundreds of years. The town, located in Guangxi Zhuang Autonomous Region, is a short hop by plane from Guangzhou. A visit to Guilin is convincing evidence that traditional Chinese landscape paintings are not only symbolic but, in fact, can be completely realistic in their portrayal of exquisite scenery. Take a boat trip down the Li River to nearby Yangshuo and view the weathered limestone outcroppings for which the region is most famous.

Hainan, once part of Guangdong Province, was declared a province in its own right in 1988. It is China's second largest island and boasts a year-round tropical maritime climate. The authorities have successfully promoted Hainan, with its pleasant weather and pristine beaches, as a tourism destination. The island also boasts nature preserves where its lush tropical forests and rare animals and plants can be enjoyed.

CENTRAL CHINA

Xi'an, the capital of Shaanxi Province, is located more than 500 miles southwest of Beijing and about 1,000 miles inland from Shanghai. Xi'an shows China's ancient history more vividly than any other city. The first Emperor of China, **Qin Shihuang**, is buried nearby in a still-unexcavated tomb, guarded by an army of more than 6,000 terra-cotta warriors with horses and chariots that were discovered quite by accident in 1974 and subsequently unearthed. The **Terra-Cotta Warriors and Horses Museum** constructed on the site is a must-see in Xi'an.

Other sites of interest include the old city wall (one of the few in China still basically intact), the **Bell Tower**, and the two **Wild Geese Pagodas**, as well as the Shaanxi Provincial Musem, which houses a collection of important cultural relics, among them the "Forest of Tablet Stones" more than 1,000 steles that are calligraphic treasures dating back as far as the Han Dynasty.

c = ts; *q* = ch; *x* = sh; *z* = dz; *zh* = j

Outside of town, don't miss **Banpo Village**, an excavation of a 6,000-year-old neolithic village, the **Huaqing Pool**, a hot spring that dates back to the Tang Dynasty, and the **Qianling Tomb**, the joint mausoleum of Tang Emperor Gaozong and his consort, Empress Wu Zetian.

A favorite trek through central China begins in **Sichuan** Province and takes the traveler down the mighty Changjiang (Yangtse River) by boat. Sichuan, China's most populous province, is known for its lush vegetation, tremendous agricultural output, and of course its fiery cuisine. **Chengdu**, the provincial capital, is an industrial and agricultural center. Not too far away is **Emei Mountain**, known for spectacular scenery and for its famous Buddhist temple, traditionally a center for martial arts training in China. And don't miss **Chongqing** (Chunking), the other major city in Sichuan, which is also an industrial base. It was the provisional capital of the Chinese Nationalists during World War II.

THE FAR WEST AND SOUTHWEST

A number of destinations in China's Far West and Southwest are often omitted from tours but are worth visiting if time allows. Due west of Beijing is **Gansu** Province, which boasts the famous **Mogao Grottoes**, hundreds of caves containing Buddhist carvings dating from the Jin Dynasty (265–420). The grottoes are in the town of **Dunhuang**, which sits astride the ancient Silk Road near the border of **Xinjiang** Autonomous Region. Further down the **Silk Road** in Xinjiang is **Turpan** (Turfan), an oasis located in a geological depression about 500 feet below sea level. And half a day by car from Turpan is **Urumqi**, the capital of Xinjiang and home to 13 of China's many minority groups. The residents of Urumqi are principally Moslems.

Relatively few tourists are lucky enough to visit **Tibet** (Xizang). It is difficult to get there, but it is a fascinating journey nonetheless. **Lhasa**, the capital of the Autonomous Region, is 12,000 feet above sea level, and most visitors find that the altitude takes some getting used to. The most famous sight in Lhasa is the **Potala Palace**, a 13-story building on a cliff first built in the seventh century and since restored.

Visitors to **Kunming**, the capital of Yunnan Province, are generally impressed by the climate—perpetual springtime, according to the Chinese. Yunnan sits astride China's border with Burma, Laos, and Vietnam. Kunming was the terminus of the Burma Road, and American pilots flew there over the "Burma hump" to carry supplies to China during World War II. The Western Hills of Kunming boast temples and pavilions, and offer a magnificent view of the entire area.

One pleasant day trip from Kunming is to **Shilin**, the **Stone Forest**, a veritable thicket of slender limestone outcroppings that are compared to trees. A longer excursion will take the traveler to **Xishuang Banna**, a tropical paradise that is home to many minority peoples, the largest number of whom are of the Dai nationality.

HONG KONG

Hong Kong (pronounced *Xianggang* in Mandarin) has certainly earned the sobriquet "the pearl of the Orient." This gleaming metropolis adjacent to Guangdong Province was nothing more than a fishing port when, in the middle of the nineteenth century, the British acquired it in a series of treaties with China's Qing Dynasty government and turned it into a prosperous entrepôt.

After more than 150 years as a British crown colony, Hong Kong reverted to Chinese sovereignty in 1997 in a ceremony televised throughout the world. The reintegration was accomplished under a "one country, two systems" formula created by Deng Xiaoping whereby the Chinese government pledged to preserve Hong Kong's capitalist system for a period of 50 years and grant the region "a high degree of autonomy" in managing its internal affairs.

The "special administrative region" of Hong Kong consists of the island of Hong Kong, the adjacent **Kowloon** (*Jiulong* in Mandarin) peninsula, the "New Territories," which abut the city of Shenzhen, and more than 260 outlying islands.

Hong Kong is more of a shopper's paradise than a tourist

c = ts; q = ch; x = sh; z = dz; zh = j

destination, but there are some sights of interest worth visiting. Highest on the list is a trip to **Victoria Peak**, the summit of Hong Kong island from which the panoramic view of the colony is truly breathtaking. The Peak is reachable by taxi, but the better way to go is to take the Peak Tram, which climbs up the side of the mountain and offers some dramatic views of its own.

Other places of interest on the island include the **Aw Boon Haw (Tiger Balm) Gardens**, the **Flagstaff House Museum of Tea Ware**, and **Stanley Market**, where you can buy clothing and souvenirs.

You can get to **Kowloon** from Hong Kong island by subway, but many prefer to take the venerable Star Ferry instead. It's worth the ride for the harbor view alone. Kowloon is an excellent place to shop for electronics, jewelry, clothing, souvenirs, and just about everything else Hong Kong has to offer. Haggling is commonplace at the small stores, though not the custom at the larger department stores. If you have an evening free, visit the outdoor **Temple Street Market**, which features heavily discounted clothing and a wide variety of souvenirs and miscellaneous housewares. Or else, find your way to **Lei Yu Mun**, where you can pick out fresh seafood from any of several vendors and carry it down the road to a restaurant that will be only too happy to prepare it for you.

If you have a little more time to spend in Hong Kong, visit the New Territories, which have wonderful hiking trails, or take an inexpensive ferry ride from Hong Kong island to one of the outlying islands such as **Lantau**, **Cheung Chau**, or **Lamma Island**. There you can find Buddhist Temples, good hiking trails, and excellent seafood restaurants. On Lantau you can see the world's largest, outdoor, seated, bronze Buddha.

MACAO

When the Portuguese government lowered its flag over the enclave of Macao in December 1999 it returned to China the first—and last—European colony in Asia. The handover marked the end of nearly 450 years of Portuguese rule over this six-square-mile territory that was once part of Guangdong Province and is now a special administrative region of China.

Macao, far smaller in both size and population than Hong Kong, its neighbor to the east, consists of a peninsula that is connected to China and two islands, **Taipa** and **Coloane**, all linked by causeways. While it never enjoyed the larger colony's commercial success, its economy has relied primarily on tourism and, in particular, casino gambling, for many years. Known as "the Monte Carlo of the East," it is still the gambling capital of Asia.

Macao is also notable for its historic colonial-style European architecture, Chinese temples, and traces of Portuguese fortresses. Don't miss the plaza on which the **Church of St. Paul** (São Paulo) used to stand. Only the front of this richly decorated Baroque façade of this seventeenth-century building remains, but it is quite beautiful and has, in fact, become the symbol of Macao. For a bird's-eye view of the entire colony, visit its highest point, **Lighthouse Hill**.

You are likely to be well rewarded if you take the time to sample Macanese cuisine, an interesting blend of East and West. You can get pure Cantonese and classical Portuguese dishes there, of course, but make an effort to try some of the more exotic fare that features spices from Europe, Africa, Brazil, and Malaya.

TAIWAN

Known in the West for many years by the Portuguese name "Formosa," Taiwan has a varied colonial past. All or part of it has been held, at one point or another in its history, by the Dutch, the Spanish, the French, and the Japanese. Its history has thus often set it apart from the rest of the China mainland.

The island became a province in China in the late nineteenth century, and was ceded to Japan in 1895, together with the **Pescadore (Penghu) Islands**. Taiwan and the Pescadores were restored to Chinese rule in 1945 at the end

c = ts; q = ch; x = sh; z = dz; zh = j

of World War II. In 1949, after years of civil strife between the Nationalist government and the upstart Communist Party, the Nationalists were forced to retreat to Taiwan, thus paving the way for the founding of the People's Republic by the Communists on the mainland during that year.

For many years after that, the Nationalists and Communists put forth rival claims to sovereignty, each purporting to be the sole, legitimate government of all of China, even though the Communists held the mainland and the Nationalists controlled only Taiwan and several other islands. The PRC government views Taiwan as a renegade province of China whose reunification with the mainland is a high priority and is only a question of time. For their part, the authorities on Taiwan have renounced their claim to the mainland in recent years, but they have insisted on their legitimacy as the government of Taiwan.

Taiwan has much to offer the tourist. When the Nationalists beat their hasty retreat to Taiwan in 1949, they took with them the finest jade, porcelain, paintings, and bronzes from the Imperial Palace in Beijing. They deposited these in a museum they constructed in the capital city, **Taipei** (*Taibei*). As a result, Taipei is home to a treasure trove of some of the most breathtaking examples of Chinese art and artifacts that exist in the world today. A visit to the **National Palace Museum**, home to more than 620,000 of these objects from the imperial collection, is thus a "must-see" on a visit to Taipei. Because exhibit space is limited, however, only a small portion of the collection is on view at any given time.

Taipei's development has been quite rapid. What was rice paddies 30 short years ago is now boulevard after boulevard of gleaming office towers, apartment blocks, and department stores. But there are still hints of the past, as a visit to **Lungshan Temple**, the city's oldest and most famous, can testify. It is a fine example of traditional Chinese temple architecture. For a modern twist on these traditional Chinese forms, you can also visit the **Sun Yat-sen** and **Chiang Kai-shek Memorial Halls**.

Taipei's cultural life centers around the **National Theater** and **National Concert Hall**, which produce

Chinese and Western operas, dramas, symphonies, and ballets, and feature famous performers from around the world. And you'll find some of the world's finest Chinese cuisine—representative of all parts of China—in Taipei's restaurants.

If you have time for a trip around the island, there are many places worth a visit. A volcanically formed island, Taiwan has a spine of mountains at its center that gradually—and in some cases not so gradually—levels off into the sea. This makes it a fun place for mountain climbing. And don't miss sunrise over **Alishan**, Taiwan's most famous mountain.

A trip down the narrow **Suao-Hualian Highway** is a breathtaking experience. The winding highway is carved into the sides of steep mountains, and is perched as much as 2,600 feet above the Pacific Ocean. From **Hualian**, at the southern end of this road, you can travel inland to **Tienhsiang** via **Taroko Gorge**, a narrow ravine cut into solid granite mountains over the years by a river. Pagodas, temples, and waterfalls complete the exceptional experience. Tienhsiang itself is at the eastern end of the **Cross-Island Highway**, also carved into solid rock and well worth the journey.

It's not by chance that **Sun Moon Lake** in central Taiwan was Chiang Kai-shek's favorite retreat from the heat of Taipei. A beautiful lake in a natural setting with Chinese pavilions and temples perched on the slopes nearby, the lake today is one of Taiwan's most popular honeymoon destinations.

Historic **Tainan**, in the south of Taiwan, is Taiwan's oldest city. It features lots of reminders of the city's past, including dozens of temples, some of which date back to the seventeenth century, as well as the remains of Dutch forts that are equally old. Further south is **Kenting National Park**, where you can see interesting rock and coral formations. And at the very southern tip of the island you can visit **Oluanpi**, where you can see Taiwan's oldest lighthouse and visit a tropical recreation area.

c = ts; *q* = ch; *x* = sh; *z* = dz; *zh* = j

PLANNING A TRIP

LEAVING TOWN

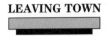

During your stay in China, you'll probably want to visit several cities. Air travel in particular is far more common and easier than ever, with travel agents and ticket offices in abundance and several airlines competing on specific air routes. But there are still formalities, such as producing your passport at the airport, even when traveling domestically, that you don't necessarily see in other countries.

I would like to visit ____.	*Wǒ xiǎng qù ____.*	我想去____。
How can I get to ____?	*Wǒ zěnméyàng qù ____?*	我怎么样去____?
You can go ____.	*Nǐ kéyǐ ____.*	你可以____。
by bicycle	*qí zìxíngchē*	骑自行车
by boat	*zuò chúan*	坐船
by bus	*zuò bāshì*	坐巴士
by car	*zuò qìchē*	坐汽车
by city bus	*zuò gōnggòng qìchē*	坐公共汽车
by plane	*zuò fēijī*	坐飞机
by taxi	*zuò chūzū qìchē*	坐出租汽车
by train	*zuò huǒchē*	坐火车
on foot	*zǒu lù*	走路

CHINESE PLACE NAMES

PINYIN SPELLING	CHINESE CHARACTER	TRADITIONAL SPELLING
Ānhūi	安徽	Anhwei
Aòmén	澳门	Macao; Macau
Běidàihé	北戴河	Peitaiho
Běijīng	北京	Peking; Peiping
Chángchūn	长春	Changchun
Chángjiāng	长江	Yangtse River
Chángshā	长沙	Changsha
Chéngdé	承德	Chengteh
Chéngdū	成都	Chengtu
Chóngqìng	重庆	Chungking
Dàlían	大连	Dairen
Dàtóng	大同	Tatung
Dūnhúang	敦煌	Tunhuang
Fújìan	福建	Fukien
Fúzhōu	福州	Foochow
Gānsù	甘肃	Kansu
Gāoxióng	高雄	Kaohsiung
Gǔangdōng	广东	Kwangtung
Gǔangxī	广西	Kwangsi
Gǔangzhōu	广州	Canton; Kwangchow
Gùilín	桂林	Kweilin
Gùiyáng	贵阳	Kweiyang
Gùizhōu	贵州	Kweichow
Hāěrbīn	哈尔滨	Harbin
Háikǒu	海口	Haikow
Hǎinán	海南	Hainan
Hángzhōu	杭州	Hangchow
Hànkǒu	汉口	Hankow
Héběi	河北	Hopeh
Héféi	合肥	Hofei
Hēilóngjiāng	黑龙江	Amur River
Hénán	河南	Honan
Hohhot	呼和浩特	Huhehot
Húang Hé	黄河	Hwang Ho; Yellow River
Húběi	湖北	Hupeh

c = ts; q = ch; x = sh; z = dz; zh = j

CHINESE PLACE NAMES

SPELLING COMPARISON CHART		
PINYIN SPELLING	CHINESE CHARACTER	TRADITIONAL SPELLING
Húnán	湖南	Hunan
Jiāngsū	江苏	Kiangsu
Jiāngxī	江西	Kiangsi
Jílín	吉林	Kirin
Jīlóng	基隆	Keelung
Jǐnán	济南	Tsinan
Jīnmén	金门	Quemoy; Kinmen
Kāifēng	开封	Kaifeng
Kāshí	喀什	Kashgar
Kūnmíng	昆明	Kunming
Lánzhōu	兰州	Lanchow
Lāsā	拉萨	Lhasa
Liáoníng	辽宁	Liaoning
Lùoyáng	洛阳	Loyang
Nánchāng	南昌	Nanchang
Nánjīng	南京	Nanking
Nánníng	南宁	Nanning
Níngbō	宁波	Ningpo
Níngxià	宁夏	Ningsia
Pǔdōng	浦东	Putung
Qīngdǎo	青岛	Tsingtao
Qīnghǎi	青海	Tsinghai
Qínhúangdǎo	秦皇岛	Chinhuangtao
Qǔfù	曲阜	Chufu
Shǎanxī	陕西	Shensi
Shāndōng	山东	Shantung
Shànghǎi	上海	Shanghai
Shàntóu	汕头	Swatow
Shānxī	山西	Shansi
Shěnyáng	沈阳	Mukden
Shēnzhèn	深圳	Shumchun
Shíjiāzhūang	石家庄	Shihchiachuang
Sìchūan	四川	Szechuan
Sūzhōu	苏州	Soochow
Táiběi	台北	Taipei
Tàiyúan	太原	Taiyuan
Táiwān	台湾	Taiwan; Formosa
Táizhōng	台中	Taichung

CHINESE PLACE NAMES		
SPELLING COMPARISON CHART		
PINYIN SPELLING	CHINESE CHARACTER	TRADITIONAL SPELLING
Táinán	台南	Tainan
Tīanjīn	天津	Tientsin
Túlǔfān	吐鲁番	Turfan; Turpan
Wūlǔmùqí	乌鲁木齐	Urumchi
Wǔhàn	武汉	Wuhan
Wúxī	无锡	Wuhsi; Wusih
Xī'ān	西安	Sian
Xìamén	厦门	Amoy
Xīanggǎng	香港	Hong Kong
Xīníng	西宁	Hsining
Xīnjīang	新疆	Sinkiang
Xīzàng	西藏	Tibet
Yán'ān	延安	Yenan
Yángzhōu	扬州	Yangchow
Yāntái	烟台	Cheefoo; Yentai
Yúnnán	云南	Yunnan
Zhèjīang	浙江	Chekiang
Zhèngzhōu	郑州	Chengchow
Zhūhǎi	珠海	Chuhai

BOOKING A FLIGHT

I would like to book a flight to ____.

Wó xiǎng zùo fēijī dào ____.

我想坐飞机到____。

When is there a flight to ____?

Shénme shíhòu yǒu fēijī dào ____?

什么时候有飞机到____?

c = ts; q = ch; x = sh; z = dz; zh = j

Which airlines fly to that city?	*Nǎjiā hángkōng gōngsī fēi nèige chéngshì?*	
	哪家航空公司飞那个城市？	
Do I have a choice?	*Yóu xuǎnzé ma?*	
	有选择吗？	
Can I fly directly from here?	*Néng zhí fēi ma?*	
	能直飞吗？	
Do I have to change planes?	*Yào zhuǎn jī ma?*	
	要转机吗？	
Where must I change planes?	*Zài nǎli zhuǎn jī?*	
	在哪里转机？	
Is it a nonstop flight?	*Shì zhídá de hángbān ma?*	
	是直达的航班吗？	
I would like a ____ ticket.	*Wǒ yào yìzhāng ____ piào.*	
	我要一张____票。	
▦ business class	*gōngwù cāng*	公务舱
▦ economy class	*pǔtōng cāng*	普通舱
▦ first class	*tóuděng cāng*	头等舱
▦ one-way	*dānchéng*	单程
▦ round-trip	*láihuí*	来回
I would like a ticket on ____ Airlines (Airways).	*Wó xiǎng mǎi ____ Hángkōng Gōngsī de piào.*	
	我想买____航空公司的票。	
▦ Aeroflot	*Égúo*	俄国
▦ Air China	*Zhōngguó Gúojì*	中国国际
▦ Air France	*Fǎguó*	法国
▦ All Nippon	*Quán Rì Kōng*	全日空
▦ British	*Yīngguó*	英国

■ Cathay Pacific	*Gúotài*	国泰
■ China Eastern	*Zhōngguó Dōngfāng*	中国东方
■ China Northern	*Zhōngguó Běifāng*	中国北方
■ China Southern	*Zhōngguó Nánfāng*	中国南方
■ Dragonair	*Gǎnglóng*	港龙
■ El Al	*Yǐsèliè*	以色列
■ Japan	*Rìběn*	日本
■ Korean	*Hánguó*	韩国
■ Lufthansa	*Déguó Hànshā*	德国汉莎
■ Malaysia	*Mǎláixīyǎ*	马来西亚
■ Northwest	*Měiguó Xīběi*	美国西北
■ Shanghai	*Shànghǎi*	上海
■ Singapore	*Xīnjīapō*	新加坡
■ United	*Měiguó Liánhé*	美国联合
I would like a seat ____.	*Wó xiǎngyào ____ de wèizi.*	我想要____的位子。
■ on the aisle	*kào gùodào*	靠过道
■ by the window	*kào chuāng*	靠窗
■ in the smoking section	*néng chōuyān*	能抽烟
■ in the nonsmoking section	*bù xǔ chōuyān*	不许抽烟

c = ts; *q* = ch; *x* = sh; *z* = dz; *zh* = j

What is the fare?	*Piàojià duōshǎo?* 票价多少？
Are meals served?	*Yǒu cāndiǎn ma?* 有餐点吗？
At what time does the plane take off?	*Fēijī jídiǎn qǐfēi?* 飞机几点起飞？
What time will we arrive?	*Wǒmén jídiǎn dào?* 我们几点到？
When will we land in ____?	*Jídiǎn dào ____?* 几点到____？
What is my flight number?	*Wǒ de hángbān hàomǎ duōshǎo?* 我的航班号码多少？
I want to ____ my reservation.	*Wǒ yào ____ wǒ yùdìng de wèizi.* 我要____我预定的位子。
■ confirm	*quèrèn* 确认
■ cancel	*qǔxiāo* 取消
What time shall I check in?	*Jídiǎn yào dēngjì?* 几点要登记？
Do I need to show my passport?	*Xūyào chūshì hùzhào ma?* 需要出示护照吗？
How long must we wait for departure?	*Yào tuīchí duōjiǔ cái qǐfēi?* 要推迟多久才起飞？
Will you provide a meal while I wait?	*Děng de shíhòu, gěi cāndiǎn chī ma?* 等的时候，给餐点吃吗？
Where shall I collect my meal?	*Dào nálǐ qù qǔ cāndiǎn?* 到哪里去取餐点？

AT THE AIRPORT

Which gate do we leave from?	*Zài jǐ hào mén hòujī?* 在几号门候机？
I'd like to check my bags.	*Wó xiǎng tūoyùn xíngli.* 我想托运行李。
I have only carry-on baggage.	*Wǒ zhí yóu shǒutíbāo.* 我只有手提包。

NOTE: Some high-speed film can be damaged by airport security X rays. It is best to pack your film in your suitcase, protected by a lead-insulated bag. If you have film in your camera or carry-on baggage, avoid problems by asking the guard to examine it by hand.

Please don't let the camera and film go through the machine.	*Qǐng búyào bǎ zhàoxiàng jī hé dǐpiàn tōngguò jīqì.* 请不要把照相机和底片通过机器。
Please examine my film (camera) by hand.	*Qǐng yòng shóu jiǎnchá dǐpiàn (zhàoxiàngjī).* 请用手检查底片（照相机）。
Where can I get a snack?	*Náli yóu xiǎochī diàn?* 哪里有小吃店？
Is there time for lunch?	*Yǒu shíjiān chī wǔfàn ma?* 有时间吃午饭吗？

c = ts; *q* = ch; *x* = sh; *z* = dz; *zh* = j

ON BOARD THE PLANE

flight attendant	*chéngwùyúan*	乘务员
pilot	*zhèng jiàshǐ*	正驾驶
copilot	*fù jiàshǐ*	副驾驶
Please fasten your seat belts.	*Xì hǎo ānqúandài.*	系好安全带。
My seat belt is already fastened.	*Wǒ de ānqúandài yǐjīng xìhǎole.*	我的安全带已经系好了。
My _____ is (are) broken.	*Wǒ de _____ yǒu máobìng.*	我的_____有毛病。

▨ earphones	*ěrjī*	耳机
▨ seat	*yǐzi*	椅子
▨ seat belt	*ānqúandài*	安全带
▨ television	*diànshì*	电视

May I use my _____ now?	*Xìanzài néng yòng wǒ de _____ ma?*	现在能用我的_____吗？

▨ CD player	*jīguāng chàng jī*	激光唱机
▨ cell phone	*shǒujī*	手机
▨ electronic game	*diànzǐ yóuxì*	电子游戏
▨ laptop computer	*bìanxíe shì diànnǎo*	便携式电脑
▨ tape recorder	*lùyīnjī*	录音机

I would like some _____.	*Wó xiǎngyào _____.*	我想要_____。

▨ beer	*píjǔ*	啤酒
▨ white wine	*bái pútáojiǔ*	白葡萄酒

■ red wine	*hóng pútáojiǔ*	红葡萄酒
■ cola	*kělè*	可乐
■ juice	*gǔozhī*	果汁
■ water	*kāishuǐ*	开水
■ tea	*chá*	茶
■ coffee	*kāfēi*	咖啡
■ milk	*níunǎi*	牛奶
■ peanuts	*huāshēngmǐ*	花生米
■ potato chips	*tǔdòupìan*	土豆片
Please bring me (a, an)____	*Qǐng géi wǒ ____.*	请给我___。
■ air sickness bag	*wèishēng dài*	卫生袋
■ blanket	*tǎnzi*	毯子
■ comb	*shūzi*	梳子
■ napkin	*cānjīn zhǐ*	餐巾纸
■ playing cards	*pǔkè pái*	扑克牌
■ postcards	*míngxìn pìan*	明信片
■ stationery	*xìn zhǐ*	信纸
■ toothbrush	*yáshūa*	牙刷
■ toothpaste	*yágāo*	牙膏
■ towel	*máojīn*	毛巾

Please ask that passenger not to smoke.	*Qǐng gàosu nèiwèi chéngkè búyào chōu yān.* 请告诉那位乘客不要抽烟。
Is the toilet occupied?	*Cèsǔo yǒu rén ma?* 厕所有人吗？

c = ts; *q* = ch; *x* = sh; *z* = dz; *zh* = j

| There is no toilet paper in the bathroom. | *Cèsuǒ méiyǒu wèishēng zhǐ.*
厕所没有卫生纸。 |

TRAIN SERVICE

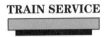

Train travel in China is a good way to see parts of the countryside you would never get to see otherwise, even if you can't stop to appreciate the local color. Long-distance trains are generally very comfortable, especially if, like most foreign guests, you travel "soft class." This generally means a cabin with four comfortable berths and a small table, no air conditioning, but reasonably good food service. "Hard class," a more spartan option, is also available, but it's a lot more crowded and much less comfortable. Don't be surprised if your Chinese hosts balk at your traveling that way; they are thinking only of your comfort.

The service person on the train will tell you when it is time to eat and will escort you to your assigned seat in the dining car.

Where is the train station?	*Huǒchē zhàn zài náli?* 火车站在哪里？
I want to travel to ____.	*Wǒ yào qù ____.* 我要去____。
I would like a ____ ticket.	*Wǒ yào yī zhāng ____ piào.* 我要一张____票。
▓ hard-class	*yìng wò pū*　　硬卧铺
▓ soft-class	*ruǎn wò pū*　　软卧铺
When does the train ____?	*Huǒchē jídiǎn ____?* 火车几点____？
▓ leave	*kāi*　　开
▓ arrive	*dào*　　到
Which platform?	*Něige yuètái?*　　哪个月台？

Does this train stop at ____?	*Zhèi bān chē zài* ____ *tíng ma?*	这班车在____停吗？
How long does it stop?	*Tíng dūojǐu?*	停多久？
Can I get off the train for a while?	*Kéyǐ xìa chē kànkan ma?*	可以下车看看吗？
All aboard!	*Shàng chē le!*	上车了！
Where is the dining car?	*Cānchē zài nálǐ?*	餐车在哪里？
Where shall I put my luggage?	*Xínglǐ yào fàng nálǐ?*	行李要放哪里？
Will you help me store my luggage?	*Nǐ néng bāng wǒ fàng xínglǐ ma?*	你能帮我放行李吗？
Will my luggage be safe there?	*Fàng zài nàlǐ fàngxīn ma?*	放在那里放心吗？
Where is the toilet?	*Cèsuo zài nálǐ?*	厕所在哪里？
Do you have a Western-style toilet?	*Yǒu Xīshìde cèsǔo ma?*	有西式的厕所吗？
Is it a(n) ____?	*Shì* ____ *ma?*	是____吗？
▪ local train	*pǔtōng chē*	普通车
▪ express	*kùai chē*	快车
Where are we now?	*Wǒmén xìanzài zài náli?*	我们现在在哪里？
Is it time to eat yet?	*Kéyǐ chīfàn le ma?*	可以吃饭了吗？

c = ts; *q* = ch; *x* = sh; *z* = dz; *zh* = j

Will we arrive on time?	*Wǒmén huì zhǔnshí dào ma?*
	我们会准时到吗？
Is this seat taken?	*Zhè wèizi yǒu rén zuò ma?*
	这位子有人坐吗？
Excuse me, this is my seat.	*Dùi bù qǐ, zhè shì wǒ de wèizi.*
	对不起，这是我的位子。

SHIPBOARD TRAVEL

Going by boat is a pleasant, relaxing way to see various parts of China. In many cities, such as Shanghai and Guilin, you can take a short pleasure tour on a boat and see a good deal of the local scenery. The half-day trip down the Lijiang (Li River) in Guilin offers one of the most spectacular views in all of China. One can also take longer boat tours—a favorite route is down the Changjiang (Yangtse River).

Chinese boats vary greatly as far as quality of accommodations. The best rooms are staterooms with two or four fairly comfortable beds. There are usually no private baths, but the common bathrooms do afford some privacy, and some boats have sinks in the higher-priced rooms. First-class passengers also generally have the use of a private lounge at the front of the boat. Other accommodations are more spartan; they are on the lower level of the boat and are noisier. There are eight bunk beds to a room and the toilets are common and often not well maintained.

Where is the dock?	*Mǎtóu zài nǎli?*
	码头在哪里？
When does the next boat leave for ____?	*Xià yī bān dào ____ de chúan jídiǎn kāi?*
	下一班到____的船几点开？
I'd like to go by ship.	*Wó xiǎng zuò chúan qù.*
	我想坐船去。

Does it take much longer by ship?	*Zùo chúan qù màn de dūo ma?* 坐船去慢得多吗？
How long does it take?	*Yào dūo jǐu?* 要多久？
Do we stop anywhere?	*Zhōngtú tíng ma?* 中途停吗？
How long will the ship remain?	*Chúan yào tíng dūojǐu?* 船要停多久？
When do we land?	*Shénme shíhòu xìa chúan?* 什么时候下船？

At what time do we have to be back on board?	*Shénme shíhòu zài shàng chúan?*	什么时候再上船？
I'd like a ____ ticket.	*Wó xǐangyào ____ pìao.*	我想要____票。
▦ first-class	*tóuděng cāng*	头等舱
▦ cabin-class	*èrděng cāng*	二等舱

c = ts; *q* = ch; *x* = sh; *z* = dz; *zh* = j

I don't fell well.	*Wǒ bú tài shūfu.*	我不太舒服。
I'm a little seasick.	*Wǒ yóu diǎn yūnchúan.*	我有一点晕船。
Is there any medicine to cure seasickness?	*Yǒu méi yǒu zhì yūnchúan de yào?*	有没有治晕船的药？

AVERAGE TEMPERATURES OF MAJOR CHINESE CITIES			
CITY	PROVINCE	SUMMER (° Fahrenheit)	WINTER (° Fahrenheit)
Beijing	—	80	23
Changsha	Hunan	85	42
Chengdu	Sichuan	85	45
Chongqing	Sichuan	82	47
Dalian	Liaoning	72	21
Fuzhou	Fujian	82	51
Guangzhou	Guangdong	84	57
Guilin	Guangxi	84	48
Hangzhou	Zhejiang	83	39
Haerbin	Heilongjiang	72	−3
Hohhot	Nei Menggu	70	20
Kunming	Yunnan	72	48
Lanzhou	Gansu	70	47
Lhasa	Xizang	63	32
Nanjing	Jiangsu	82	39
Qingdao	Shandong	77	28
Shanghai	—	80	38
Shenyang	Liaoning	75	10
Suzhou	Jiangsu	83	39
Taiyuan	Shanxi	77	17
Tianjin	—	79	24
Urumqi	Xinjiang	90	19
Wuhan	Hubei	85	40
Wuxi	Jiangsu	82	39
Xiamen	Fujian	86	55
Xi'an	Shaanxi	86	33

CAR RENTALS

Though some long-term foreign residents drive their own cars in China, it's not common for tourists to rent a car and drive it themselves, and given the casual approach to obeying traffic regulations on the part, not only of drivers but also of bicyclists and pedestrians, it's probably not advisable, either. What is possible, and recommended, is to rent a car with its driver for a day or two. This is a good way to see a lot of the sights at your own pace, without a large tour group to slow you down, and without auto repairs and similar headaches.

You can check with your local guide or your hotel to see about renting a private car for the day, but you can often rent a taxi for this purpose as well. Bear in mind that drivers expect to be able to rest for an hour or so at lunchtime, and that if you keep one occupied during meal hours, even if he or she is just waiting for you to eat, you are expected to provide money for the driver's meals.

Where can I rent ____?	*Náli kéyǐ zūdào*	哪里可以租到____？
a bicycle	*zìxíng chē*	自行车
a car	*chūzū qìchē*	出租汽车
a minibus	*miànbāo chē*	面包车
I want a(n) ____.	*Wó xiǎngyào yīliàng ____.* 我想要一辆____。	
American car	*Měigúo chē*	美国车
domestic car	*gúochǎn chē*	国产车
European car	*Oùzhōu chē*	欧洲车
imported car	*jìnkǒu chē*	进口车
Japanese car	*Rìběn chē*	日本车

c = ts; *q* = ch; *x* = sh; *z* = dz; *zh* = j

| van | *Miànbāo chē* | 面包车 |
| car with air conditioning | *yǒu kōngtiáo de chē* | 有空调的车 |

How much does it cost ____?	____ *yào dūoshǎo?*	____要多少？
per day	*Yì tīan*	一天
per week	*Yì xīngqī*	一星期
per kilometer	*Yì gōnglǐ*	一公里

How many kilometers per day do I get for the basic fee?	*Měitīan jīběn de gōnglǐshù shì dūoshǎo?* 每天基本的公里数是多少？
Does the price include gasoline?	*Jiàqián bāokùo qìyóu fèi ma?* 价钱包括汽油费吗？
Does the car come with a driver?	*Zūchē bāokùo sījī ma?* 租车包括司机吗？
Can the driver speak English?	*Sījī néng shūo Yīngwén ma?* 司机能说英文吗？
Will the driver stay with me all day?	*Sījī zhěngtīan dōu dài wǒ ma?* 司机整天都带我吗？
Shall I take care of the driver's meals?	*Wǒ yào fùzé sījī de fànqían ma?* 我要负责司机的饭钱吗？
I will settle up with the driver at the end of the day.	*Wǒ zùihòu zài gěi sījī fùzhàng.* 我最后再给司机付帐。
Does the price include insurance?	*Fèiyòng bāokùo báoxǐan ma?* 费用包括保险吗？
I'd like to buy insurance.	*Wó xíang mái báoxǐan.* 我想买保险

Please tell the driver ____.	*Qǐng gàosu sījī ____.* 请告诉司机____。	
▨ the car is to cold	*chēlǐ tài lěngle*	车里太冷了
▨ the car is too hot	*chēlǐ tài rèle*	车里太热了
▨ not to smoke	*búyào xīyān*	不要吸烟
▨ to turn on the heat	*dǎkāi nuǎnqì*	打开暖气
▨ to turn down the radio	*bǎ shōuyīnjī guan dī yìdiǎn*	把收音机关低一点
▨ to turn off the radio	*bǎ shōuyīnjī guāndiào*	把收音机关掉
▨ to close the window	*bǎ chuāng guānshàng*	把窗关上
▨ not to drive so fast	*búyào kāi de zhème kùai*	不要开得这么快
▨ not to drive so slowly	*búyào kāi de zhème màn*	不要开得这么慢
▨ I need to arrive by 3:00	*wó déi zài sāndiǎn zhīqián dào*	我得在三点之前到
▨ to wait for me here	*yào zài zhèlǐ déng wǒ*	要在这里等我
▨ to take me back to my hotel	*sòng wǒ húi fàndiàn*	送我回饭店

c = ts; *q* = ch; *x* = sh; *z* = dz; *zh* = j

Travel Tips When you are packing to leave home, leave a little space in your suitcase to hold the small purchases you will make while you are away. If you can't manage this, then pack a collapsible tote bag in you suitcase, to be filled up and carried separately on your return trip.

ENTERTAINMENT AND DIVERSIONS

NIGHTLIFE

In the past, China was not known for its nightlife, but in recent years a surprising variety of after-hours options have proliferated throughout the country. One can find bars, discos, karaoke parlors, bowling alleys, movie theaters, restaurants, and coffee shops. If you have energy left over after early-to-rise sightseeing trips to temples, pagodas, and other scenic and historic locations, there are plenty of late-night diversions.

There are also evening performances meant for tourists—and some aimed at locals as well—in major cities every night. It's not always easy to find out by yourself exactly what is being performed, and it's harder still to buy your own tickets, so let your guide or hotel help you. You might want to try to get in to see a martial arts or acrobatic performance, a sporting event, a concert, or a song-and-dance show. You don't need to speak Chinese to appreciate these activities, and they can be very entertaining. If you don't mind a little ambiguity, go to see a Chinese movie or a play. There will probably not be English subtitles or program notes provided, however, so you'll have to guess at the plot if you don't have an interpreter handy.

The Beijing Opera and regional operas of other provinces are also sights to behold. The Chinese love them for their portrayal of famous historic dramas and folk tales, for the symbolic and highly stylized makeup worn by the actors, and for the bright, colorful costumes. Westerners often find the singing rather shrill and unmelodious, however, and many report that without a clear idea of the plot, it is difficult to sit through an entire performance.

c = ts; q = ch; x = sh; z = dz; zh = j

MOVIES

Let's go see a movie.	*Wǒmén qù kàn diànyǐng hǎo bú hǎo?*	
	我们去看电影好不好？	
What are they showing today?	*Jīntiān yǎn shénme?*	
	今天演什么？	
It's a(n) ___ movie.	*Shì ge ___ piān.*	
	是个___片。	
■ American	*Měigúo*	美国
■ Chinese	*gúochǎn*	国产
■ Hong Kong/ Taiwan	*Gǎngtái*	港台
■ Japanese	*Rìběn*	日本
Is it in English?	*Shì shūo Yīngwén de ma?*	
	是说英文的吗？	
Are there English subtitles?	*Yǒu méi yǒu Yīngwén zìmù?*	
	有没有英文字幕？	
Where is the movie theater?	*Diànyǐng yùan zài náli?*	
	电影院在哪里？	
Where can I buy tickets?	*Zài nálǐ kéyǐ mǎi pìao?*	
	在哪里可以买票？	
How much for a ticket?	*Dūoshǎo qían yìzhāng?*	
	多少钱 张？	
action film	*dǎdòu piān*	打斗片
adventure film	*jīngxǐan piān*	惊险片
cartoon	*dònghùa piān*	动画片
documentary	*jìlù piān*	记录片

feature film	*gùshì pīan*	故事片
horror film	*kǒngbù pīan*	恐怖片
kung fu	*wǔxía pīan*	武侠片
mystery	*zhēntàn pīan*	侦探片
romance	*yángqíng pīan*	言情片
spy film	*jiāndíe pīan*	间谍片
war film	*zhànzhēng pīan*	战争片

Is there a refreshment stand?	*Yǒu xǐaomài bù ma?*
	有小卖部吗？
Where is the toilet?	*Cèsǒu zài nálǐ?*
	厕所在哪里？

THEATER

I'd like to see a play.	*Wó xǐang kàn hùajù.*
	我想看话剧。
Where can one buy tickets?	*Zài nálǐ kéyǐ mǎidào pìao?*
	在哪里可以买到票？
What time does the show begin?	*Shénme shíhòu kāiyǎn?*
	什么时候开演？
What time does the show end?	*Shénme shíhòu yǎn wán?*
	什么时候演完？
I would like to buy tickets for tonight.	*Wó xíang mǎi jīnwǎn de pìao.*
	我想买今晚的票。
I need two ____ tickets.	*Wǒ yào liang zhāng pìao.*
	我要两张票。

c = ts; *q* = ch; *x* = sh; *z* = dz; *zh* = j

■ orchestra seats	*lóuxià de wèizi*	楼下的位子
■ balcony seats	*lóushàng de wèizi*	楼上的位子

MUSICAL/CULTURAL PERFORMANCES

We would like to go to ____.	*Wǒmén xiǎng qù ____.*	我们想去____。
■ an acrobatic performance	*kàn zájì biǎoyǎn*	看杂技表演
■ a ballet	*kàn bāléi wǔ*	看芭蕾舞
■ a Cantonese Opera	*kàn Yùejù*	看粤剧
■ a classical Chinese music concert	*tīng gúoyùe yǎnzòu*	听国乐演奏
■ a comic dialogue performance	*tīng xiàngshēng*	听相声
■ a concert	*tīng yīnyùe hùi*	听音乐会
■ a local folk opera	*kàn dìfāng xì*	看地方戏
■ a magic show	*kàn móshù biǎoyǎn*	看魔术表演
■ a martial arts performance	*kàn wǔshù biǎoyǎn*	看武术表演
■ a Peking Opera	*kàn Jīngjù*	看京剧
■ a singing recital	*tīng gē chàng hùi*	听歌唱会

■ a song-and-dance show	*kàn gē wǔ bíaoyǎn*	看歌舞表演
Is there _____ here?	*Zhèlǐ yǒu méi yǒu _____?*	这里有没有____？
■ an auditorium	*lǐtáng*	礼堂
■ a concert hall	*yīnyuè tīng*	音乐厅
■ a movie theater	*dìanyǐng yùan*	电影院
What are they performing?	*Tāmén zài yǎn shénme?*	他们在演什么？
I enjoy _____.	*Wó xǐhūan _____.*	我喜欢____。
■ chamber music	*shìnèi yùe*	室内乐
■ classical music	*gùdǐan yīnyùe*	古典音乐
■ folk dances	*mínjīan wùdǎo*	民间舞蹈
■ folk songs	*míngē*	民歌
■ instrumental music	*qì yùe*	器乐
■ jazz	*jùeshì yīnyùe*	爵士音乐
■ modern music	*xìandài yīnyùe*	现代音乐
■ revolutionary model operas	*gémìng yàngbǎnxì*	革命样板戏
■ rock and roll	*yáogǔn yùe*	摇滚乐
■ symphonic music	*jiāoxiǎng yùe*	交响乐
■ vocal music	*shēng yùe*	声乐
■ Western opera	*Xīyáng gējù*	西洋歌剧

c = ts; *q* = ch; *x* = sh; *z* = dz; *zh* = j

Are there any tickets for tonight's performance?	*Yǒu méi yǒu jīnwǎn de piào?* 有没有今晚的票？
Must tickets be purchased in advance?	*Yídìng yào tíqián mǎi piào ma?* 一定要提前买票吗？
How much are front row seats?	*Qiánpái zuòwèi duōshǎo qián?* 前排座位多少钱？
How much are the least expensive seats?	*Zuì píanyi de zuòwèi duōshǎo qían?* 最便宜的座位多少钱？
May I have a program?	*Qíng géi wǒ yì zhāng jíemùdān.* 请给我一张节目单。
Is that performer famous in China?	*Nèi wèi yǎnyuàn zài Zhōnggùo yǒumíng ma?* 那位演员在中国有名吗？
What is the play being performed tonight?	*Jīnwǎn yǎn shénme hùajù?* 今晚演什么话剧？

BARS AND DISCOS

Where is the bar?	*Jǐubā zài nálǐ?* 酒吧在哪里？	
Please bring me a bottle of ___.	*Qǐng géi wǒ lái yìpíng ___.* 请给我来一瓶___。	
■ local beer	*běndì píjiǔ*	本地啤酒
■ imported beer	*jìnkǒu píjiǔ*	进口啤酒
I'd like a glass of whiskey.	*Wó xiǎngyào yī. bēi wēishìjì.*	我想要一杯威士忌。

■ straight	*bù jīa bīngkùai*	不加冰块
■ on the rocks	*jīa bīngkùai*	加冰块

Please bring me a glass of ____.	*Qǐng géi wǒ lái yìbēi ____.* 请给我来一杯____。	
■ cold beer	*lěngdòng de píjiú*	冷冻的啤酒
■ red wine	*hóng pùtáo jǐu*	红葡萄酒
■ white wine	*bái pùtáo jǐu*	白葡萄酒

Please bring me ____.	*Qǐng géi wǒ lái diǎn ____.*	请给我来点____。
■ cashew nuts	*yāoguǒ*	腰果
■ peanuts	*hūashēngmǐ*	花生米
■ potato chips	*tǔdòupìan*	土豆片

Let's go to a nightclub.	*Wǒmén qù yèzǒnghùi, hǎo ba.* 我们去夜总会，好吧。
Is there a disco here?	*Zhèlí yǒu dísīkē wǔtīng mā?* 这里有迪斯科舞厅吗？
Where can we go to dance?	*Dào nálǐ qù tiàowǔ?* 到哪里去跳舞？
Is there any cover charge?	*Yǒu rùchǎng fèiyòng ma?* 有入场费用吗？
How much is it to get in?	*Rùchǎng dūoshǎo qián?* 入场多少钱？
Where is the checkroom?	*Zài nálǐ cùn yīfu?* 在哪里存衣服？
At what time does the show begin?	*Shénme shíhòu kāishǐ bíaoyǎn?* 什么时候开始表演？

c = ts; *q* = ch; *x* = sh; *z* = dz; *zh* = j

May I buy you a drink?	*Wǒ kéyǐ qǐng nǐ hē jiǔ ma?* 我可以请你喝酒吗？
What would you like to drink?	*Nǐ xiǎng hē shénme?* 你想喝什么？
Would you like to dance?	*Nǐ xiǎng gēn wǒ tiàowǔ ma?* 你想跟我跳舞吗？
Would you like to take a walk outside?	*Wǒmén dào wàimiàn qù guàngguang hǎo ma?* 我们到外面去逛逛好吗？
Would you like to go back to my hotel?	*Nǐ gēn wǒ yīqǐ huì fàndiàn, hǎo ma?* 你跟我一起回饭店好吗？

KARAOKE

Karaoke, invented by the Japanese in the late 1980s, has taken China—and indeed, most of the rest of Asia—by storm. It provides the sound track and the lyrics that enable you to give your best imitation of Frank Sinatra or Barbra Streisand in front of an entire bar, or simply to entertain your fellow banquet guests in a private room. Karaoke machines seem to be omnipresent in restaurants, bars, banquet rooms, dining halls, dance halls, and nearly everywhere people in China relax.

Many karaoke establishments offer songs from various cultures. You can usually find Mandarin, Cantonese, Japanese, and English song titles. You may be called upon to perform with little notice and no opportunity for rehearsal. But the good news is that enthusiasm counts for more than perfect pitch when you're singing karaoke.

Does this place have a karaoke lounge?	*Zhèlǐ yǒu kǎlāōūkèi tīng ma?* 这里有卡拉OK厅吗？

Where can we go to sing karaoke?	*Dào nálǐ qù chàng kǎlāoūkèi?*	
	到哪里去唱卡拉OK？	
Do you have individual rooms?	*Yǒu dānjiān ma?*	
	有单间吗？	
How much is an individual room?	*Dānjiān dūoshǎo qián*	
	单间多少钱？	
Do you charge by the hour or by the song?	*Àn zhōngdiǎn háishi àn gēqǔ suàn?*	
	按钟点还是按歌曲算？	
How much per hour?	*Yì xiǎoshí dūoshǎo qián?*	
	一小时多少钱？	
How much per song?	*Yìshǒu gē dūoshǎo qián?*	
	一首歌多少钱？	
Do you have ____ songs?	*Nǐmén yǒu ____ gē ma?*	
	你们有____歌吗？	
■ Cantonese	*Yuèyǔ*	粤语
■ Chinese	*Zhōngguó*	中国
■ English	*Yīngwén*	英文
■ Hong Kong	*Xiānggǎng*	香港
■ Japanese	*Rìběn*	日本
■ Western	*Xīyáng*	西洋
■ Taiwanese	*Táiwān*	台湾
How do I ____?	*Zěnméyang ____?*	
	怎么样____？	
■ adjust the volume	*tíaojíe yīnliàng*	调节音量
■ adjust the pitch	*tíaojíe gāodī yīn*	调节高低音

c = ts; *q* = ch; *x* = sh; *z* = dz; *zh* = j

- adjust the speed — *tiáozhěng kuàimàn* 调整快慢

- change a song — *huàn lìngwài yìshǒu gē* 换另外一首歌

- cancel a song — *qǔxiāo yìshǒu gē* 取消一首歌

The room is too ____. — *Shìnèi guāngxiàn tài ____.* 室内光线太____。

- bright — *liàng* 亮

- dim — *àn* 暗

Is there a hostess? — *Yǒu xiǎojiě ma?* 有小姐吗？

Please sing a song for me. — *Qǐng wèi wǒ chàng yìshǒu gē.* 请为我唱一首歌。

You sing beautifully. — *Nǐ chàng de zhēn hǎo.* 你唱得真好。

Please sing another one. — *Qǐng zài chàng yìshǒu.* 请再唱一首。

How late are you open? — *Nǐmén kāi dào jǐdiǎn?* 你们开到几点？

We'd like to order ____. — *Wǒmén xiǎng diǎn ____.* 我们想点____。

- drinks — *yǐnliào* 饮料

- snacks — *xiǎochī* 小吃

Is the service charge included? — *Fùwùfèi zài nèi ma?* 服务费在内吗？

How much is the service charge? — *Fùwùfèi duōshǎo?* 服务费多少？

We would like a private room — *Wǒmén yào dānjiān.* 我们要单间。

We would like a private room with karaoke.	*Wǒmén yào yǒu kǎlāoōukèi de dānjiān.* 我们要有卡拉OK的单间。
We would like a room that can seat____ people.	*Wǒmén yào néng zuò ____ rén de dānjiān.* 我们要能坐____人的单间。

SPECTATOR SPORTS

I'd like to see a ballgame.	*Wó xiǎng qù kàn qíusài.* 我想去看球赛。
Where's the stadium?	*Tíyù chǎng zài náli?* 体育场在哪里？
When does the game begin?	*Bǐsài shénme shíhòu kāishǐ?* 比赛什么时候开始？
Which teams are going to play?	*Něixiē dùi cānjiā bǐsài?* 哪些队参加比赛？
What is the score?	*Bǐfēn dūoshǎo?* 比分多少？
Can we go to see a ____ game?	*Wǒmén kéyǐ qù kàn ____ bǐsài ma?* 我们可以去看____比赛吗？
▨ baseball	*bàngqíu* 棒球
▨ basketball	*lánqíu* 篮球
▨ hockey	*bingqíu* 冰球
▨ Ping-Pong	*pīngpōng qíu* 乒乓球
▨ soccer	*zùqíu* 足球
▨ softball	*lěiqíu* 垒球

c = ts; *q* = ch; *x* = sh; *z* = dz; *zh* = j

- swimming   *yóuyǒng*   游泳
- tennis   *wǎngqiú*   网球
- volleyball   *páiqiú*   排球

ACTIVE SPORTS

Do you play volleyball?	*Ní dǎ páiqiú ma?* 你打排球吗？	
I don't play very well.	*Wó dǎ de bù tài hǎo.* 我打得不太好。	
I need practice.	*Wǒ xūyào liànxí.* 我需要练习。	
I win.	*Wǒ yíng le.*	我赢了。
You lose.	*Ní shū le.*	你输了。
It's a tie.	*Dǎchéng píngshǒu.*	打成平手。
Where can I rent a bicycle?	*Náli kéyǐ zū zìxíngchē?* 哪里可以租自行车？	

BEACH OR POOL

Swimming is by no means the most popular leisure activity in China, probably due in part to Chinese modesty about the body, and in part to their preference for maintaining a light complexion. There are, however, many public swimming pools in the cities and some lovely bathing beaches along China's coast.

A favorite summer retreat for people who live in Beijing—and indeed, for China's senior leadership—is **Beidaihe**, a bathing beach on the coast of Hebei Province, four and one-half hours by train from the capital. Another popular spot is **Qingdao**, a city on the Shandong Province seacoast famous for its beer (Tsingtao beer). And in recent years, **Hainan** Province has become very popular with bathers from China, Hong Kong, and elsewhere in Asia.

Chinese beaches offer most of the amenities of beaches around the world. There are lifeguards on duty, and you can rent rafts, inner tubes, paddleboats, and umbrellas. Bring your own suntan lotion, however, because it won't necessarily be available for purchase.

Where is there a swimming pool?	*Náli yǒu yóuyǒng chí?*	哪里有游泳池？
Can we go swimming?	*Wǒmén kéyǐ qù yóuyǒng ma?*	我们可以去游泳吗？
Can we go to the beach?	*Wǒmén kéyǐ dào hǎitān qù ma?*	我们可以到海滩去吗？
Is it safe to swim here?	*Zài zhèli yóuyǒng ānquán ma?*	在这里游泳安全吗？

Are there ____?	*Yǒu ____ ma?*	有___吗？
■ sharks	*shāyù*	鲨鱼
■ jellyfish	*shùimǔ*	水母
Is there a lifeguard?	*Yǒu jìushēngyùan ma?*	有救生员吗？
Where can I get ____?	*Náli yǒu ____?*	哪里有___？
■ a bathing suit	*yóuyǒng yī*	游泳衣
■ a beach ball	*hǎitān wán de qíu*	海滩玩的球
■ a beach umbrella	*tàiyáng sǎn*	太阳伞

c = ts; *q* = ch; *x* = sh; *z* = dz; *zh* = j

| a chair | *yǐzi* | 椅子 |
| a towel | *máojīn* | 毛巾 |

| Where can I take a shower? | *Náli kéyǐ línyù?* |
| | 哪里可以淋浴？ |

IN THE COUNTRYSIDE

| I'd like to visit the countryside. | *Wó xǐang dào xiāngxìa qù kànkan.* |
| | 我想到乡下去看看。 |

| Where can I rent a car? | *Natl kéyǐ zū qìche?* |
| | 哪里可以租汽车？ |

| Can we go camping? | *Wǒmén kéyǐ qù lùyíng ma?* |
| | 我们可以去露营吗？ |

| Where can we go for a picnic? | *Wǒmén dào náli qù yěcān?* |
| | 我们到哪里去野餐？ |

| What a beautiful landscape! | *Fēngjǐng háo měi!* |
| | 风景好美！ |

| Look at ____. | *Kànkan ____ ba.* | 看看____吧。 |

the bridge	*qíao*	桥
the farmers	*nóngmín*	农民
the hill	*xǐao shān*	小山
the lake	*hù*	湖
the mountain	*shān*	山
the pagoda	*báotǎ*	宝塔
the rice paddies	*dàotían*	稻田
the temple	*mìao*	庙
the tractor	*tūolājī*	拖拉机

| ■ the water buffalo | *shuǐníu* | 水牛 |

| Isn't ____ beautiful? | ____ *dūo pìaoliang!* | ____多漂亮！|

■ the ocean	*Hǎi*	海
■ the pond	*Chítáng*	池溏
■ the river	*Hé*	河
■ the stream	*Xǐao xī*	小溪
■ the trees	*Shù*	树
■ the valley	*Shāngǔ*	山谷
■ the village	*Cūnzhūang*	村庄
■ the waterfall	*Pùbù*	瀑布

| Where does this road lead? | *Zhèi tíao lù tōng dào náli qù?* 这条路通到哪里去？|

| How far away is ____? | ____ *hái yǒu dūoyǔan?* ____还有多远？|

| ■ the city | *Shìqū* | 市区 |
| ■ the hotel | *Lǚgǔan* | 旅馆 |

| How long does it take to get to ____? | *Dào* ____ *qù yào dūojǐu?* 到____去要多久？|

| I'm lost. | *Wǒ mí lù le.* 我迷路了。|

| Please tell me how to get to ____. | *Qǐng gàosu wǒ dào* ____ *zěnme zǒu?* 请告诉我到____怎么走？|

c = ts; *q* = ch; *x* = sh; *z* = dz; *zh* = j

RELIGIOUS SERVICES

Where can I find a(an) ____?	*Nǎlí yǒu ____.* 哪里有___。	
■ Buddhist temple	*Fójìao mìao*	佛教庙
■ Catholic church	*Tīanzhǔ jìaotáng*	天主教堂
■ Confucian temple	*Kǒng mìao*	孔庙
■ Daoist temple	*Dào gùan*	道观
■ Lama temple	*Lǎmā mìuu*	喇嘛庙
■ Mormon church	*Mómén jìaotáng*	摩门教堂
■ Mosque	*Qīngzhēn sì*	清真寺
■ Orthodox church	*Dōng zhèng jìao jìaotáng*	东正教教堂
■ Protestant church	*Jīdū jìaotáng*	基督教堂
■ Synagogue	*Yóutàijìao hùitáng*	犹太教会堂

At what time do services begin?	*Shéngme shíhòu kāishǐ zùo lìbài?* 什么时候开始作礼拜？	

Do you celebrate ____ mass here?	*Zhèlǐ zùo ____ mísā ma?* 这里做 ___ 弥撒？	
■ Chinese	*Zhōngwén*	中文
■ English	*Yīngwén*	英文
■ Latin	*Lǎdīng*	拉丁

Is there an empty seat?	*Yǒu kōng wèi ma?* 有空位吗？	

May I make a contribution?	*Wǒ kéyǐ jūanxìan ma?*	
	我可以捐献吗？	
Where is your collection box?	*Fèngxìan xīang zài nálǐ?*	
	奉献箱在哪里？	
How old is this church?	*Zhèige jìaotáng dūo lǎo le?*	
	这个教堂多老了？	
I would like to meet a(n) ____.	*Wó xǐang jìan ____.*	
	我想见____。	
■ abbot (Buddhist)	*fāngzhàng*	方丈
■ abbot (Daoist)	*zhùchí*	住持
■ archbishop	*dà zhǔjìao*	大主教
■ bishop	*zhǔjìao*	主教
■ cantor	*lǐngchàngzhě*	领唱者
■ cardinal	*shūjī zhǔjìao*	枢机主教
■ clergy member	*shénzhi rényùan*	神职人员
■ elder	*zhánglǎo*	长老
■ imam	*āhōng*	阿訇
■ lama	*lǎmā*	喇嘛
■ metropolitan	*dū zhǔjìao*	都主教
■ minister; pastor	*mùshī*	牧师
■ monk (Buddhist)	*héshàng*	和尚
■ monk (Christian)	*xīushì*	修士
■ monk (Daoist)	*dàoshì*	道士
■ nun (Buddhist)	*nígū*	尼姑

c = ts; *q* = ch; *x* = sh; *z* = dz; *zh* = j

■ nun (Christian)	*xiūnǚ*	修女
■ priest	*jiàoshī; shénfù*	教士；神父
■ rabbi	*lābǐ*	拉比

EASTERN WORSHIP

Buddha	*Fó*	佛
burn incense	*shào xiāng*	烧香
chant	*niàn jīng*	念经
Goddess of Mercy	*Gūanyīn*	观音
hymn	*shèng gē*	圣歌
pray	*qídǎo*	祈祷
worship	*zùo lǐbài*	作礼拜

FOOD AND DRINK

MAKING DINING ARRANGEMENTS

It wasn't too many years ago that you could get any kind of food you wanted in China—as long as it was Chinese food! Today, however, a variety of cuisines are available, especially in China's larger cities. This includes food from other Asian countries such as Japan, Korea, and Thailand, as well as, increasingly, French, Italian, American, and other Western cuisines. In Hong Kong and Taiwan, food from all over the world has long been available.

If you are willing to experiment a little, and if you are amenable to exploring small establishments whose atmosphere and sanitary conditions don't necessarily measure up to international standards, you can taste some of the best Chinese food in the world. Lots of family-owned establishments are to be found in the alleyways of virtually all Chinese cities, and there is a variety of delicacies available from street vendors as well. Prices are generally extremely reasonable.

Most foreigners feel more comfortable in the higher-end restaurants where service is good, facilities are clean, and yes, the prices are higher. The good news is that with the exception of a relatively small number of very pricey and pretentious establishments, even in the better restaurants food is still a bargain in China.

If you have a large party, or if you are staging a formal banquet, it is usually necessary to make arrangements ahead of time. This involves calling ahead to the restaurant and telling the proprietor how many people will be in your party and what time you plan to arrive. If you intend to leave the menu selections to the discretion of the restaurant, you will also need to specify how much you wish to spend per person, exclusive of beverages. The restaurant may quote a minimum charge per head. The price is often negotiable, but generally

c = ts; q = ch; x = sh; z = dz; zh = j

only within 5 or 10 percent. There is seldom an upward limit, should you decide to go all out, but after a certain point the management doesn't add more courses to the meal, just more expensive ingredients.

If you've booked ahead of time, a table will be all set up for your group when you arrive, your entire menu will be planned, and one or two service people may be assigned exclusively to your table.

If you are taking a car to the restaurant and the driver has been with you for a good part of the day, it's a nice gesture to offer to pay for his or her meal. This is not necessary if you have engaged a cab simply to get to the restaurant; it is only for someone whose mealtime has been given up in your service. You can offer to have the restaurant add the cost of driver's meals to your tab, but most drivers prefer that you give them cash directly. In this way, they can eat where they like and spend as much or as little of the meal fee as they wish.

This section gives you the necessary vocabulary for making dining arrangements.

I would like to make a reservation for ____.	*Wǒ yào dìng ____.* 我要定____。	
■ dinner this evening	*jīntiān de wǎnfàn*	今天的晚饭
■ dinner tomorrow evening	*míngtiān de wǎnfàn*	明天的晚饭
■ lunch today	*jīntiān de wǔfàn*	今天的午饭
■ lunch tomorrow	*míngtiān de wǔfàn*	明天的午饭
■ lunch the day after tomorrow	*hòutiān de wǎnfàn*	后天的晚饭
There are ____ people in our party.	*Wǒmén yǒu ____ wèi.* 我们有____位。	
We would like to pay ____ per head.	*Wǒmén yào dìng ____ yīge rén.* 我们要定____一个人。	

■ fifty yuan	*wǔshí yuán*	五十元
■ two hundred yuan	*liángbǎi yuán*	两百元

Can you make it a little cheaper please?	*Nǐ kéyǐ sùan píanyi yīdǐan ma?* 你可以算便宜一点吗？
That doesn't include drinks, does it?	*Jíushǔi zài wài, shì ma?* 酒水在外，是吗？
We would like to arrive at ____.	*Wǒmén xiǎng ____ dào.* 我们想____到。

■ 6:00 P.M.	*xìawǔ lìu dǐan*	下午六点
■ 7:30 P.M.	*xìawǔ qī dǐan bàn*	下午七点半
■ exactly noon	*zhèngwǔ*	正午

We will order à la carte.	*Wǒmén yào língdǐan.* 我们要零点。

THE CHINESE BANQUET

The chances are excellent that some time during your stay in China you will find yourself the guest at a Chinese banquet. Whether your tour operator wants to give your tour group a taste of local cuisine, your business partner wants to celebrate a contract, or your government host simply wants to make you feel welcome, a banquet is usually in order when you visit the PRC.

The Chinese follow fairly predictable norms of behavior at banquets. They won't expect you to be completely schooled in banquet etiquette and will forgive you most of your errors. But they will be delighted at any attempt by you to follow their customs, so it's worth your while to learn a bit of the routine.

Your host will probably be there to greet you when you arrive at the restaurant. Generally, tea is served first, often before the guests actually sit down at the table. After small

c = ts; *q* = ch; *x* = sh; *z* = dz; *zh* = j

talk, the host will give the signal for all to take their seats. At formal banquets, seats are assigned according to a fairly orderly protocol pattern and placecards signal the arrangement; in less structured situations, the host may simply point you toward a particular seat. The guest of honor is usually seated to the right of the host.

The meal typically begins with a platter of cold appetizers. The Chinese hosts—or the restaurant staff—will serve these to you. It isn't polite to help yourself at first, and this is true of *each* dish as it is served. After the host has started a dish, however, you may begin to serve yourself. Bear in mind that the Chinese consider it their duty to see that your plate always has some food on it, so if you keep cleaning it, they will keep filling it up. Also be sure to pace yourself: if you eat the first two dishes to satiation, you won't have room for the eight to ten dishes that may follow. A meal will generally continue through sweet, sour, salty, and spicy dishes—four of the five basic Chinese tastes—and your signal that the end is drawing near is the fish dish and perhaps a bowl of rice. After these, there will likely be a soup and a dessert.

EATING OUT

Where is a good restaurant?	*Náli yóu hǎo de fàngǔan?*	哪里有好的饭馆？
Is it very expensive?	*Hěn gùi ma?*	很贵吗？
Which restaurant serves local dishes?	*Něige fàngǔan yóu běndì de míngcài?*	哪个饭馆有本地的名菜？
I would like to go to a ____ restaurant.	*Wó xǐang qù yīge ____ gǔan.*	我想去一个____馆。
■ Cantonese	*Gǔangdōng*	广东

■ French	*Fǎgúo cài*	法国菜
■ Fujian	*Fújiàn cài*	福建菜
■ German	*Dégúo cài*	德国菜
■ Hunan	*Húnán*	湖南
■ Indian	*Yìndù cài*	印度菜
■ Indonesian	*Yìnní cài*	印尼菜
■ Italian	*Yìdàlì cài*	意大利菜
■ Japanese	*Rìběn lìaolǐ*	日本料理
■ Korean	*Hángúo cài*	韩国菜
■ Mandarin	*Běifāng*	北方
■ Mexican	*Mòxīgē cài*	墨西哥菜
■ Middle Eastern	*Zhōngdōng cài*	中东菜
■ Mongolian	*Ménggǔ cài*	蒙古菜
■ Moslem	*Qīngzhēn cài*	清真菜
■ Peking duck	*Běijīng kǎoyā*	北京烤鸭
■ Russian	*Égúo cài*	俄国菜
■ seafood	*hǎixīan*	海鲜
■ Shandong	*Shāndōng*	山东
■ Shanghai	*Shànghǎi*	上海
■ Sichuan (Szechuan)	*Sìchūan*	四川
■ Southeast Asian	*Dōngnányà cài*	东南亚菜
■ Taiwan	*Táiwān cài*	台湾菜
■ Thai	*Tàigúo cài*	泰国菜
■ vegetarian	*sùcài*	素菜
■ Vietnamese	*Yùenán cài*	越南菜

c = ts; *q* = ch; *x* = sh; *z* = dz; *zh* = j

■ Western	*Xīcān*	西餐
■ Xinjiang	*Xīnjiāng cài*	新疆菜
Waiter! (younger man)	*Fúwùyúan!*	服务员！
Waiter! (older man)	*Shīfu!*	师傅！
Miss!	*Xíaojǐe!*	小姐！
A table for two, please.	*Lǐang wèi.*	两位。
We'd like to have lunch (dinner) now.	*Wǒmén xìanzài xǐang chī zhōng (wǎn) fàn.*	我们现在想吃 中（晚）饭。
The menu, please.	*Qǐng géi wǒ càidān.*	请给我菜单。
Where is the toilet?	*Cèsǔo zài nálǐ?*	厕所在哪里？
Where can I wash my hands?	*Nálǐ kéyǐ xǐ shǒu?*	哪里可以洗手？
Can you recommend some dishes?	*Nǐ géi wǒmén jièshào cài hǎo ma?*	你给我们介绍 菜好吗？
What is the chef's specialty?	*Dà shīfu náshǒu cài shì shénme?*	大师傅拿手菜 是什么？
Please bring us ———.	*Qǐng géi wǒmén ———.*	请给我们 ___。
■ an appetizer	*kāiwèi de xǐaocài*	开胃的小菜
■ a beer	*píjǐu*	啤酒
■ a bottle of mineral water	*yī píng kùangqúan shǔi*	一瓶矿泉水

■ some cold (preboiled) water	*lěng kāishǔi*	冷开水
■ some tea	*chá*	茶
May I order now?	*Xìanzài kéyǐ dǐan cài ma?* 现在可以点菜吗？	
I'd like ____.	*Wó xǐangyào ____.* 我想要____。	
Please also bring us ____.	*Qǐng lìngwài géi wǒmén ____.* 请另外给我们____。	
■ a bowl	*yíge wǎn*	一个碗
■ chopsticks	*kùaizi*	筷子
■ a fork	*yíge chāzi*	一个叉子
■ a glass	*yíge bēizi*	一个杯子
■ a hot towel	*rè máojīn*	热毛巾
■ a knife	*xīcān dāo*	西餐刀
■ a napkin	*yì zhāng cānjīn*	一张餐巾
■ noodles	*mìantiao*	面条
■ a plate	*yíge pánzi*	一个盘子
■ rice	*mǐfàn*	米饭
■ a spoon	*yíge tíaogēng*	一个调羹
■ steamed bread	*mántóu*	馒头
■ a toothpick	*yì gēn yáqīan*	一根牙签
■ a wet towel	*shī máojīn*	湿毛巾

NOTE: Chinese table manners dictate that one cover one's mouth with one's hand while using a toothpick. The teeth should be visible to others.

c = ts; *q* = ch; *x* = sh; *z* = dz; *zh* = j

SAUCES, SEASONINGS, AND CONDIMENTS

大蒜	*dàsuàn*	garlic
姜	*jiāng*	ginger
辣椒酱	*làjiāo jiàng*	hot pepper sauce
辣油	*làyóu*	hot sauce (oil)
芥末	*jièmò*	mustard
胡椒	*hújiāo*	pepper
盐	*yán*	salt
香油；蔴油	*xiāngyóu; máyóu*	sesame oil
酱油	*jiàngyóu*	soy sauce
蕃茄酱	*fānqié jiàng*	tomato sauce (also ketchup)
醋	*cù*	vinegar

CHINESE DISHES

APPETIZERS

叉烧肉	*chāshāo ròu*	barbecued pork
油焖笋	*yóumèn sǔn*	braised bamboo shoots
冷盘	*lěngpán*	cold platter
豆腐干	*dòufu gān*	dried bean curd
辣白菜	*là báicài*	hot pickled cabbage
海蜇皮	*hǎizhé pí*	jellyfish

酱牛肉	*jiàng niúròu*	marinated beef
锅贴	*guōtiē*	pan-fried pork dumplings
花生米	*huāshēng mǐ*	peanuts
腌黄瓜	*yān húanggūa*	pickled cucumber
泡菜	*pàocài*	pickled vegetables
芝蔴鸡	*zhīmá jī*	sesame chicken
熏鸡	*xūn jī*	smoked chicken
春卷	*chūnjǔan*	spring roll (egg roll)

c = ts; *q* = ch; *x* = sh; *z* = dz; *zh* = j

MEAT DISHES

肉	*ròu*	meat
■ 牛肉	*niúròu*	beef
■ 猪肉	*zhūròu*	pork
■ 羊肉	*yángròu*	lamb
扣肉	*kòuròu*	braised pork
宫保肉丁	*gōngbǎo ròu dīng*	diced pork with hot peppers
回锅肉	*huíguō ròu*	double-cooked pork
鱼香肉丝	*yúxīang ròu sī*	spicy shredded pork
木须肉	*mùxū ròu*	stir-fried pork with egg and black fungus (generally served with thin pancakes)
糖醋排骨	*tángcù páigǔ*	sweet-and-sour spareribs
糖醋里脊	*tángcù lǐjī*	sweet-and-sour boneless pork
牛肉丸	*niúròu wán*	beef meatballs
蚝油牛肉	*háoyóu niúròu*	beef with oyster sauce
红烧牛肉	*hóngshāo niúròu*	braised beef
蒙古烤肉	*Ménggú kǎo ròu*	Mongolian barbecue (beef and fresh vegetables grilled in a barbecue sauce)

干煸牛肉丝	*gānbiān niúròu sī*	sautéed shredded beef
青椒牛肉丝	*qīngjiāo niúròu sī*	shredded beef with peppers
芥兰牛肉	*gàilán niúròu*	sliced beef with Chinese broccoli
雪豆牛肉	*xuědòu niúròu*	stir-fried beef with snow peas
羊肉串	*yángròu chuàn*	lamb shish kabob
涮羊肉	*Shùan yángròu*	Mongolian hot pot (slices of lamb and assorted vegetables in a cauldron of boiling water, then dipped in sauce)
葱爆羊肉	*cōngbào yángròu*	quick-fried lamb with scallions

POULTRY

鸡	*jī*	chicken
鸭	*yā*	duck
鹅	*é*	goose
鸽子	*gēzi*	pigeon
醉鸡	*zùi jī*	chicken in wine
陈皮鸡	*chénpí jī*	chicken with orange peel

c = ts; *q* = ch; *x* = sh; *z* = dz; *zh* = j

棒棒鸡	*bàngbang jī*	cold chicken with spicy sesame sauce
脆皮鸡	*cùipí jī*	crispy-skin chicken
腰果鸡丁	*yāoguǒ jīdīng*	diced chicken with cashew nuts
宫保鸡丁	*gōngbǎo jīdīng*	diced chicken with hot peppers
柠檬鸡	*níngméng jī*	lemon chicken
纸包鸡	*zhǐbāo jī*	paper-wrapped chicken
怪味鸡	*gùaiwèi jī*	strange-tasting chicken (cooked chicken slices marinated in garlic and soy sauce)
樟茶鸭	*zhāngchá yā*	camphor and tea smoked duck
香酥鸭	*xiāngsū yā*	crispy duck
卤鸭	*lǔ yā*	duck braised in soy sauce
南京板鸭	*Nánjīng bǎn yā*	Nanjing steamed duck cutlets
北京烤鸭	*Běijīng kǎo yā*	Peking roast duck
咸水鸭	*xíanshǔi yā*	saltwater duck
红烧鸭	*hóngshāo yā*	stewed duck
炸鸽子	*zhá gēzi*	deep-fried pigeon

| 炒鸽松 | *chǎo gē sōng* | fried minced pigeon |

SEAFOOD

鲍鱼	*bàoyú*	abalone
红烧鱼	*hóngshāo yú*	braised fish
红烧鱼肚	*hóngshāo yúdǔ*	braised fish maw
红烧海参	*hóngshāo hǎishēn*	braised sea cucumber
蛤蜊	*géli*	clams
螃蟹	*pángxìe*	crab
脆皮鱼	*cùipí yú*	crispy-skin fish
墨鱼	*mòyú*	cuttlefish
炸虾球	*zhá xīa qíu*	deep-fried shrimp balls
鳗鱼	*mányú*	eel
鱼	*yú*	fish
豆瓣鱼	*dòubàn yú*	fish with hot bean sauce
炒螃蟹	*chǎo pángxìe*	fried crab
青豆虾仁	*qīngdòu xīarén*	fried shrimp with green peas
海蜇皮	*hǎizhé pí*	jellyfish
龙虾	*lóngxīa*	lobster
蚝	*háo*	oysters
明虾	*míngxīa*	prawns

c = ts; *q* = ch; *x* = sh; *z* = dz; *zh* = j

干炒明虾	gānchǎo míngxiā	sautéed prawns
干贝	gānbèi	scallops
海参	hǎishēn	sea cucumber (sea slug)
虾	xiā	shrimp
腰果虾仁	yāoguǒ xiārén	shrimp with cashew nuts
芙蓉虾仁	fúróng xiārén	shrimp with egg white
宫保虾仁	gōngbǎo xiārén	shrimp with hot peppers
熏鱼	xūn yú	smoked fish
鱿鱼	yóuyú	squid
清蒸鳗鱼	qīngzhēng mányú	steamed eel
清蒸全鱼	qīngzhēng quán yú	steamed whole fish
炒鱼片	chǎo yú piàn	stir-fried sliced fish
糖醋鱼	tángcù yú	sweet-and-sour fish
糖醋虾	tángcù xiā	sweet-and-sour shrimp
西湖脆鱼	Xīhú cùi yú	West Lake crispy fish
松子黄鱼	sōngzǐ húangyú	yellow croaker with pine nuts

VEGETABLES

竹笋	*zhúsǔn*	bamboo shoot
豆腐	*dòufu*	bean curd
豆芽	*dòuyá*	bean sprout
苦瓜	*kǔguā*	bitter melon
西兰花	*xīlánhuā*	broccoli
洋白菜	*yáng báicài*	cabbage
胡萝卜	*hú lúobo*	carrot
菜花	*càihuā*	cauliflower
腰果	*yāoguǒ*	cashew nut
芹菜	*qíncài*	celery
粟子	*lìzi*	chestnut
芥兰	*gàilán*	Chinese broccoli
韭菜	*jǐucài*	Chinese chives
玉米	*yùmǐ*	corn
黄瓜	*húanggūa*	cucumber
茄子	*qíezi*	eggplant
青椒	*qīngjīao*	green pepper
生菜	*shēngcài*	lettuce
莲藕	*líanǒu*	lotus root
蘑菇	*mógū*	mushroom
■ 草菇	*cǎogū*	straw mushroom
■ 香菇	*xīanggū*	black mushroom

c = ts; *q* = ch; *x* = sh; *z* = dz; *zh* = j

洋葱	*yángcōng*	onion
花生	*huāshēng*	peanut
土豆；洋芋；马铃薯	*tǔdòu; yángyù; mǎlíngshǔ*	potato
豌豆；雪豆	*wāndòu; xuědòu*	snow pea
黄豆；大豆	*huángdòu; dàdòu*	soybean
菠菜	*bōcài*	spinach
葱	*cōng*	spring onion (scallion)
扁豆；四季豆	*biǎndòu; sìjìdòu*	string bean
芋头	*yùtóu*	taro
西红柿；番茄	*xīhóngshì; fānqié*	tomato
萝卜	*lúobo*	turnip
核桃	*hétáo*	walnut
荸荠	*bíqí*	water chestnut
冬瓜	*dōngguā*	winter melon

VEGETABLE DISHES

沙锅豆腐	*shāguō dòufu*	bean curd in casserole
麻婆豆腐	*mápó dòufu*	bean curd with minced pork in hot sauce
红烧豆腐	*hóngshāo dòufu*	braised bean curd in soy sauce
家常豆腐	*jiācháng dòufu*	family-style bean curd

酿豆腐	*niàng dòufu*	stuffed bean curd
蚝油芥兰	*háoyóu gàilán*	broccoli in oyster sauce
奶油白菜	*nǎiyóu báicài*	Chinese cabbage in cream sauce
炒双冬	*chǎo shuāngdōng*	sautéed black mushrooms and bamboo shoots
素什锦	*sù shíjǐn*	sautéed mixed vegetables
干煸四季豆	*gānbiān sìjìdòu*	sautéed string beans
鱼香茄子	*yúxiāng qiezi*	spicy eggplant with garlic

SOUPS

青菜豆腐汤	*qīngcài dòufu tāng*	bean curd and vegetable soup
牛肉汤	*niúròu tāng*	beef broth
玉米汤	*yùmǐ tāng*	corn chowder
蛋花汤	*dànhuā tāng*	egg-drop soup
火腿冬瓜汤	*húotǔi dōngguā tāng*	ham and winter melon soup
醋辣汤	*sūan là tāng*	hot-and-sour soup
海鲜汤	*hǎixiān tāng*	seafood soup
鱼翅汤	*yúchì tāng*	shark's fin soup

c = ts; *q* = ch; *x* = sh; *z* = dz; *zh* = j

榨菜肉丝汤	*zhàcài ròusī tāng*	shredded pork and preserved vegetable soup
汤	*tāng*	soup
馄饨汤	*húndùn tāng*	wonton soup

STARCHES

米饭	*mǐfàn*	rice
■ 蒸饭	*zhēng fàn*	steamed rice
■ 炒饭	*chǎo fàn*	fried rice
面包	*miànbāo*	bread
馒头	*mántóu*	steamed bread
牛肉饺	*níuròu jiǎo*	beef dumplings
猪肉饺	*zhūròu jiǎo*	pork dumplings
■ 水饺	*shúijiǎo*	boiled pork dumplings
■ 锅贴	*gūotīe*	fried pork dumplings
■ 蒸饺	*zhēngjiǎo*	steamed pork dumplings
三鲜饺	*sānxīan jiǎo*	"three delights" dumplings (usually shrimp, chicken, and pork or beef)
素菜饺	*sùcài jiǎo*	vegetarian dumplings
面条	*miàntiáo*	noodles

____炒面	____ *chǎo mìan*	fried noodles
■ 牛肉	*níuròu*	with beef
■ 猪肉	*zhūròu*	with pork
■ 鸡肉	*jīròu*	with chicken
■ 虾仁	*xīarén*	with shrimp
■ 素菜	*sùcài*	with vegetables
汤面	*tāng mìan*	noodles in broth
担担面	*dàndan mìan*	spicy sesame noodles
薄饼	*báobǐng*	Mandarin pancakes
花卷	*hūajǔan*	steamed rolls (flower-shaped)
包子	*bāozi*	steamed stuffed pork buns
番薯	*fānshǔ*	sweet potato
馄饨	*húndùn*	wontons

ORDERING

I (don't) like to eat fish.	*Wǒ (bù) xǐhūan chī yú.* 我（不）喜欢吃鱼。
I love to eat shrimp.	*Wǒ ài chī xīa.* 我爱吃虾。
Is the fish fresh?	*Yú xīnxīan ma?* 鱼新鲜吗？
I'd like to eat meat.	*Wǒ hén xǐang chī ròu.* 我很想吃肉。

c = ts; *q* = ch; *x* = sh; *z* = dz; *zh* = j

I don't eat meat.	*Wǒ bù chī ròu.* 我不吃肉。	
I don't like pork.	*Wǒ bù xǐhuan chī zhūròu.* 我不喜欢吃猪肉。	
I like to eat chicken.	*Wó xǐhuan chī jīròu.* 我喜欢吃鸡肉。	
I don't want to try pigeon.	*Wǒ bú yuànyì chī gēzi.* 我不愿意吃鸽子。	
I'd like to eat a lot of vegetables.	*Wó xiǎng dūo chī sùcài.* 我想多吃素菜。	
I hate vegetables.	*Wó tǎoyàn chī sùcài* 我讨厌吃素菜。	
What kind of soup do you have?	*Nǐmén yǒu shénme tāng?* 你们有什么汤？	
I want a bowl of ____.	*Wǒ yào yī wǎn ____.* 我要一碗____。	

FRUITS AND DESSERTS

Dessert doesn't play the central role in Chinese cuisine that it does in the West. It often doesn't figure at all in the daily fare of the Chinese, who generally enjoy tea after a meal, occasionally complemented by fresh fruit. In a banquet situation, something sweet is usually served at the end of the meal, either fruit or some sort of steamed pastry.

杏仁豆腐	*xìngrén dòufu*	almond gelatin
苹果	*píngguǒ*	apple
拔丝苹果	*básī píngguǒ*	hot candied apples
香蕉	*xiāngjiāo*	banana

拔丝香蕉	*básī xiāngjīao*	hot candied bananas
豆沙包	*dòushā bāo*	sweet bean buns
豆腐花	*dòufuhūa*	sweet bean curd pudding
蛋糕	*dàngāo*	cake
樱桃	*yīngtáo*	cherry
椰子	*yézi*	coconut
新鲜水果	*xīnxīan shúiguǒ*	fresh fruit
葡萄	*pútáo*	grape
绿豆汤	*lǜdòu tāng*	green bean soup
冰淇淋	*bīngqílín*	ice cream
柠檬	*níngméng*	lemon
荔枝	*lìzhī*	lichee
芒果	*mángguǒ*	mango
哈密瓜	*hāmìgūa*	muskmelon
橘子	*júzi*	orange
木瓜	*mùgūa*	papaya
桃子	*táozi*	peach
梨子	*lízi*	pear
柿子	*shìzi*	persimmon
菠萝;凤梨	*bōlúo; fènglí*	pineapple
李子	*lǐzi*	plum
红豆汤	*hóngdòu tāng*	red bean soup

c = ts; *q* = ch; *x* = sh; *z* = dz; *zh* = j

八宝饭	*bābǎo fàn*	eight-treasures glutinous rice pudding
西米露	*xīmǐlù*	tapioca cream
西瓜	*xīgūa*	watermelon
千层糕	*qiāncéng gāo*	steamed layer cake

BEVERAGES

Do you have any ___ ?	*Nǐmén yǒu ___ ma?* 你们有___吗？	
I want a glass (cup) of ___.	*Wǒ yào yì bēi ___.* 我要一杯___。	
■ milk	*niúnǎi*	牛奶
■ juice	*gǔozhī*	果汁
■ tea	*chá*	茶
■ coffee	*kāfēi*	咖啡
■ hot chocolate	*rè kěkě*	热可可
Please give me a bottle of ___.	*Qǐng géi wǒ yī píng ___.* 请给我一瓶___。	
■ beer	*píjǐu*	啤酒
■ brandy	*báilándì*	白兰地
■ Champagne	*xīangbīnjǐu*	香槟酒
■ cognac	*shàngděng báilándì*	上等白兰地
■ mineral water	*kùangqúan shǔi*	矿泉水
■ wine	*pútáo jǐu*	葡萄酒
■ rice wine	*mǐjǐu*	米酒

■ yellow rice wine	*húangjiǔ*	黄酒
■ soda (pop)	*qìshuǐ*	汽水
■ soda water	*sūdá shuǐ*	苏打水
■ whiskey	*wēishìjì*	威士忌
白酒	*báijiǔ*	spirits (general term for liquor distilled from wheat, sorghum, or corn)
高粱酒	*gāoliángjiǔ*	kaoliang (also a sorghum-based spirit)
茅台酒	*Máotái jiǔ*	Maotai (distilled sorghum liquor made in Guizhou Province)
绍兴酒	*Shàoxīng jiǔ*	Shaoxing rice wine (fermented wine made in Zhejiang Province)
五粮液	*Wǔlíangyè*	Five-grains liquor (made in Sichuan Province)
汾酒	*Fénjiǔ*	Fenjiu (a sorghum spirit made in Shanxi Province)

c = ts; *q* = ch; *x* = sh; *z* = dz; *zh* = j

WESTERN FOOD

Where is the closest Western restaurant?	*Zùijìn de Xīcānguǎn zài nálǐ?* 最近的西餐馆在哪里？	
Where is a fast-food restaurant?	*Nálǐ yǒu kuàicān diàn?* 哪里有快餐店？	
I would like to order ____.	*Wó xiǎng diǎn ____.* 我想点____。	
■ a cheeseburger	*nǎilào hànbǎo bāo*	奶酪汉堡包
■ french fried potatoes	*zhá shǔtiáo*	炸薯条
■ fried chicken	*zhá jī*	炸鸡
■ a hamburger	*hànbǎo bāo*	汉堡包
■ a hot dog	*rè gǒu*	热狗
■ onion rings	*zhá yángcōng qūan*	炸洋葱圈
■ a pizza	*bǐsā bǐng*	比萨饼
Do you have any ____?	*Nǐmén yǒu méiyǒu ____?* 你们有没有____？	
■ baked potato	*káo tǔdòu*	烤土豆
■ mashed potatoes	*tǔdòuní*	土豆泥
■ spaghetti	*Yìdàlì shì miàntiáo*	意大利式面条
■ steak	*niúpái*	牛排
I would like my meat cooked ____.	*Wǒde kǎoròu yào ____.* 我的烤肉要____。	
■ rare	*nèn yīdiǎn*	嫩一点
■ medium	*bú nèn bù lǎo*	不嫩不老
■ well-done	*lǎo yìdiǎn*	老一点

I would like ____ chops.	*Wó xiǎngyào ____ pái.*	我想要____排。
■ lamb	*yáng*	羊
■ pork	*zhū*	猪

Please bring me a (an) ____ sandwich.	*Qǐng géi wǒ ____ sānmíngzhì.* 请给我____三明治。	
■ bacon	*xūnròu*	熏肉
■ bacon, lettuce, and tomato	*xūnròu shēngcài xīhóngshì*	熏肉、生菜、西红柿
■ cheese	*nǎilào*	奶酪
■ chicken	*jīròu*	鸡肉
■ club	*zǒnghùi*	总会
■ egg	*jīdàn*	鸡蛋
■ fish	*yúròu*	鱼肉

Do you have a salad bar?	*Nǐmén yǒu méiyǒu shālā zìzhùgùi?* 你们有没有沙拉自助柜？	

What kind of salad do you have?	*Nǐmén yǒu shénme yàng de shālā?* 你们有什么样的沙拉？	
■ Caesar salad	*Kǎisā shālā*	凯萨沙拉
■ chicken salad	*jīròu shālā*	鸡肉沙拉
■ egg salad	*jīdàn shālā*	鸡蛋沙拉
■ green salad	*shūcài shālā*	蔬菜沙拉
■ spinach salad	*bōcài shālā*	菠菜沙拉
■ tuna salad	*jīnqiāng yú shālā*	金枪鱼沙拉

I would like ____ dressing on my salad.	*Wó xiǎngyào ____ shālā jiàng.* 我想要____沙拉酱。	

c = ts; *q* = ch; *x* = sh; *z* = dz; *zh* = j

■ bleu cheese | *lán nǎilào* | 蓝奶酪

■ French | *Fǎguó* | 法国

■ Italian | *Yìdàlì* | 意大利

■ oil and vinegar | *yóu cù* | 油醋

■ Russian | *Éluósì* | 俄罗斯

■ thousand island | *qiān dǎo* | 千岛

Do you have any ____? | *Nǐmén yǒu méiyǒu ____?*
你们有没有____？

■ cheese | *nǎilào* | 奶酪

■ chili sauce | *làjīao jiàng* | 辣椒酱

■ horseradish | *làgeň ʃluny* | 辣根酱

■ ketchup | *fānqíe jiàng* | 番茄酱

■ mayonnaise | *dànhuáng jiàng* | 蛋黄酱

■ mustard | *jièmò* | 芥末

■ pepper | *hújiāo* | 胡椒

■ salt | *yán* | 盐

■ sour cream | *sūan nǎiyóu* | 酸奶油

■ steak sauce | *níupái jiàng* | 牛排酱

What kind of soup do you have? | *Nǐmén yǒu shénme yàng de tāng?*
你们有什么样的____汤？

■ beef | *níuròu* | 牛肉

■ chicken | *jī* | 鸡

■ French onion | *Fǎshì yángcōng* | 法式洋葱

■ potato | *tǔdòu* | 土豆

■ vegetable | *shūcài* | 蔬菜

Please let me see the dessert menu. | *Qǐng géi wǒ kàn tiándian dān.*
请给我看甜点单。

■ cookies	*bǐnggān*	饼干
■ fruit	*shúiguǒ*	水果
■ ice cream	*bīngqīlín*	冰淇淋
■ pie	*pài*	排
■ pudding	*bùdīng*	布丁

What kind of cake do you have?	*Nǐmén yǒu shénme yàng de dàngāo?*	
	你们有什么样的蛋糕？	
■ cheese	*nǎilào*	奶酪
■ chocolate	*qiǎokèlì*	巧克力
■ sponge	*sōnggāo*	松糕

SPECIAL CIRCUMSTANCES

Many travelers have special dietary requirements, so here are a few phrases that might help you get what you need or avoid what you don't want or can't eat. There are also some phrases you might need to voice your complaints.

I don't want anything _____.	*Wǒ bú yào _____ cài.*	
	我不要___菜。	
■ fried	*chǎo de*	炒的
■ sweet	*tián de*	甜的
■ spicy	*là de*	辣的

I cannot eat anything made with _____.	*Wǒ bù néng chī yǒu _____ de cài.*	
	我不能吃有___的菜。	
■ monosodium glutamate	*wèijīng*	味精
■ salt	*yán*	盐
■ sugar	*táng*	糖

c = ts; *q* = ch; *x* = sh; *z* = dz; *zh* = j

I don't want any dishes with meat.	*Wǒ bú yào yǒu ròu de cài.*	我不要有肉的菜。
I'm a vegetarian.	*Wǒ chī sù.*	我吃素。
I don't eat ____.	*Wǒ bù chī ____.*	我不吃____。
■ eggs	*dàn*	蛋
■ pork	*zhūròu*	猪肉
■ shellfish	*yǒu ké de yú xiā*	有壳的鱼虾
This food is undercooked.	*Zhège tài shēngle.*	这个太生了。
The table isn't clean.	*Zhūozi bù gānjìng.*	桌子不干净。
Please wipe off the table.	*Qǐng cā zhūozi.*	请擦桌子。
This is dirty.	*Zhège zāng le.*	这个脏了。
I am missing ____.	*Wǒ chà ____.*	我差____。
■ one chopstick	*yī zhī kùaizi*	一只筷子
■ a napkin	*yī zhāng cānjīn*	一张餐巾
■ a glass	*yīge bēizi*	一个杯子
The food is ____.	*Cài ____.*	菜____。
■ cold	*lěng le*	冷了
■ not hot enough	*bú gòu rè*	不够热
There is too much fat.	*Féiròu tài dūo.*	肥肉太多。
This is too ____.	*Zhège tài ____.*	这个太____。
■ salty	*xián*	咸
■ sour	*sūan*	酸
■ bitter	*kǔ*	苦

■ dry   *gān*   干

■ oily   *yóunì*   油腻

This isn't fresh.	*Zhèige bù xīnxiān.* 这个不新鲜。	
We have been waiting a long time.	*Wǒmén děng le hén jǐu le.* 我们等了很久了。	
Please bring our drinks.	*Qǐng bá yǐnlìao sòng lái.* 请把饮料送来。	

SETTLING UP

The check, please.	*Qǐng jíe zhàng.*	请结帐。
Separate checks, please.	*Qǐng fēnkāi sùan.*	请分开算。
I didn't order this.	*Wǒ méi jìao zhèige.*	我没叫这个。
I don't think the bill is correct.	*Wó xiǎng zhàngdān yǒu cùo.*	我想帐单有错。
Where should we pay?	*Dào náli fù zhàng?*	在哪里付帐？
May I use a credit card?	*Wǒ kéyǐ yòng xìnyòng kǎ ma?*	我可以用信用卡吗？
Is a service charge included?	*Bāokùo fúwùfèi ma?*	包括服务费吗？
How much is the service charge?	*Fúwùfèi dūoshǎo?*	服务费多少？
May I have a receipt?	*Qǐng kāi shōujù.*	请开收据。

c = ts; *q* = ch; *x* = sh; *z* = dz; *zh* = j

REGIONAL CHINESE SPECIALTIES

Just as the Chinese spoken language varies from province to province, so does Chinese cuisine. Each province has its own specialties, its own styles of cooking, and its own local ingredients. Be sure to ask for local specialties in each place you visit in China; you won't be disappointed.

The four major schools of Chinese cooking correspond to the four major geographic areas of this vast country—north, south, east, and west. Below is a general description of their special features.

Northern Chinese cuisine, also referred to as Mandarin cuisine, is the cooking of the provinces north of the Yangzi (Yangtse) River, including Hebei (which surrounds Beijing), Henan, Shandong, Shanxi, and Liaoning. Northerners eat a lot of beef, lamb, and duck and use garlic and scallions in abundance. Their grain intake is largely in wheat products, and they prefer relatively bland cooking, eschewing seasonings that are overly salty, sweet, or spicy.

Western Chinese cuisine is best known as the cooking of Sichuan and Hunan Provinces. The climate of this area is hot and humid a good deal of the year, and the hot peppers that grow in abundance are used liberally in cooking, giving the cuisine a well-deserved, fiery reputation. The people in this area also tend to use more salt in their cooking than do people in other regions.

Eastern Chinese cuisine, the cooking of the Shanghai, Jiangsu, and Zhejiang area, takes maximum advantage of the region's proximity to the sea and its large number of lakes—it is known far and wide for its many varieties of seafood. Eastern cuisine features a cornucopia of fresh vegetables, including many types of bamboo, as well as the liberal use of soy sauce and sugar.

Southern Chinese cuisine features the cooking of Guangdong Province as well as that of Fujian and Taiwan. Like Eastern cooking, it relies heavily on seafood, fresh fruit, and vegetables. To preserve the natural flavors of the food, the cooks in this area prefer not to use strong seasonings.

Due to this region's traditional contact with the outside world, foreign ingredients have slowly crept in, so that cream sauces and baked pastries are not unknown. Barbecued meats are popular, and soups are prominently featured.

Cantonese cuisine is also known for a subspecialty called **dim sum**, which is described in the next section.

DIM SUM

Dim sum, pronounced **diǎn xīn** in Mandarin, merits a separate section because of its popularity and its special nature. It is native to southern China; however, it is widely available in Hong Kong, Southeast Asia, North America, and pretty much anywhere where there are large numbers of Cantonese people.

Dim sum consists of very small portions of snack foods, served with tea from late morning until early afternoon. In the most traditional restaurants the food is pushed along on carts, and you simply signal the waiter or waitress when you want a dish of whatever is on the cart. The whole idea of dim sum is to nibble on many different types of delicacies in a single sitting. Chinese also use dim sum brunches as an opportunity to catch up with friends, since the whole meal can last for hours.

Here are some of the most popular types of dim sum, plus some useful vocabulary for ordering it.

Where can I go to eat dim sum?	*Dào nálǐ qù chī Guǎngdōng diǎnxīn?* 到哪里去吃广东点心？
Please write down the address of the restaurant.	*Qǐng bǎ fànguǎn dìzhǐ xiě xìalài.* 请把饭馆地址写下来。

c = ts; *q* = ch; *x* = sh; *z* = dz; *zh* = j

We are a party of six.	*Wǒmén yǒu lìu wèi.* 我们有六位。	
Please bring us a pot of ____ tea.	*Qǐng géi wǒmén ____ chá.* 请给我们___茶。	
■ 红	*hóng*	black
■ 菊花	*júhūa*	chrysan- themum
■ 清	*qīng*	green
■ 茉莉花；香片	*mòlìhūa;* *xīangpìan*	jasmine
■ 乌龙	*wūlóng*	oolong
请来一碟____。	*Qǐng lái yī* *díe ____.*	Please give me a plate of ____.
■ 牛肉丸	*níuròu wán*	beef balls
■ 牛肚	*níudǔ*	beef tripe
■ 椰塔	*yétǎ*	coconut tarts
■ 芋角	*yùjǐao*	deep-fried taro root
■ 蛋塔	*dàntǎ*	egg tarts
■ 锅贴	*gūotīe*	fried pork dumplings
■ 烧卖	*shāomài*	open-topped steamed pork dumplings
■ 虾丸	*xīa wán*	shrimp balls
■ 虾饺	*xīa jǐao*	shrimp dumplings
■ 小笼包	*xǐaolóng bāo*	small steamed pork buns

■ 排骨	*páigǔ*	spareribs
■ 春卷	*chūnjuǎn*	spring rolls (egg rolls)
■ 肠粉	*cháng fěn*	steamed stuffed rice crêpes
■ 马拉糕	*mǎlā gāo*	steamed sponge cake
■ 叉烧包	*chāshāo bāo*	steamed roast pork buns
■ 酿豆腐	*nìang dòufu*	stuffed bean curd
■ 鸭掌	*yāzhǎng*	stuffed duck feet
■ 酿青椒	*nìang qīngjīao*	stuffed peppers
■ 豆沙包	*dòushā bāo*	sweet bean buns
■ 糯米鸡	*nùomǐ jī*	sweet rice with meat stuffed in lotus leaves
■ 萝卜糕	*lúobo gāo*	turnip cake
■ 馄饨	*húndùn*	wontons

c = ts; *q* = ch; *x* = sh; *z* = dz; *zh* = j

GETTING TO KNOW PEOPLE

MEETING PEOPLE

The Chinese much prefer formal introductions to striking up casual conversations as a means to making new friends. When a mutual friend introduces you to someone, you are automatically someone worthy of friendship and respect. Also, many Chinese are shy by nature and find it difficult to make the first move in uncertain social situations. If there is no one to make the introduction for you, it is all right to present yourself. As a rule, you will find the Chinese people to be extremely friendly to foreigners, and it's not at all uncommon for a Chinese to approach a foreigner on the street and begin to practice a little English.

If you want to engage someone in conversation, a smile and a **Ní hǎo?** (Hello) is often all that is necessary to begin. Areas of easy conversation include your nationality, the length of your intended stay in China, cities you hope to visit, your profession, and your family.

Cultural differences are many and are fun to discover. A basic one is Chinese group-consciousness, a marked contrast to the individual-centeredness common to many Western societies. Chinese are encouraged to conform, to accept authority, and to subordinate their individual wills and desires to those of the greater group to which they belong—whether their family, class at school, or work unit. Chinese often expect their foreign guests to behave in similar ways, and difficulties can occur, for example, when many members of a tour group begin to give different signals to the guide about what they want to do or where they want to go. The Chinese expect groups to have designated leaders and to speak with one voice, and they are sometimes disoriented when this is not the case.

Another cultural difference—not so surprising, perhaps, given the overcrowding and overpopulation in China—occurs over the notion of privacy. There is no good translation for the word *privacy* in Chinese, and your affairs are not necessarily presumed to be your own. Chinese people may innocently ask you questions you consider to be embarrassing—such as how much money you make or how much you paid for something—or occasionally a hotel service person may come bounding into your room without the courtesy of knocking first.

The concept of "face" is also central to any understanding of the differences between East and West. This is a subtle, intangible commodity related to one's dignity and prestige. To cause a person to "lose face" is a major affront. Be careful of criticizing a Chinese person in front of other people, or of insulting or making fun of someone. And understand that sometimes when you fail to get a direct answer to a question you pose to a Chinese, the reason may not be that he or she is being evasive, but that he or she is trying to spare you the loss of face that saying no to you would bring on.

No discussion of why the Chinese act as they do would be complete without mention of what the Chinese call **guānxi**. This term literally means "relationship," but is actually far better translated as "connections." Guanxi is sort of a tit-for-tat, "you-scratch-my-back, I'll-scratch-yours" arrangement, whereby favors are done and rules are bent and sometimes even broken for friends. It is a reciprocal obligation, and someone with whom you have established guānxi may well expect your aid in solving a problem.

Sometimes foreigners are approached to do things that are illegal, such as changing money; presumptuous, such as sponsoring someone they hardly know for study abroad; or impossible, such as securing a foreign visa for someone. It's important to communicate as best you can that something is out of your control or very difficult for you to do in situations such as this; if your Chinese friend believes that you are simply unwilling to help, he or she will think that you have failed to discharge an obligation.

c = ts; q = ch; x = sh; z = dz; zh = j

As a general rule, Chinese are less likely to express emotions publicly than their Western counterparts. Negative feelings, in particular, such as jealousy, anger, disappointment, or unhappiness, are considered private matters, and letting such emotions run free is regarded as ill-mannered. When you come up against a frustrating situation in China—and it's likely that you will—try at all costs to keep your cool. You can of course convey anger or dissatisfaction with a particular set of circumstances, but try to do so without appearing visibly agitated. To do so will earn you more respect and will increase the likelihood of achieving your goal.

This section includes some basic vocabulary for breaking the ice with people you have not met before.

Hello. How do you do?	*Nǐ hǎo?*	你好？
My name is ____.	*Wǒ jiào ____.*	我叫____。
What is your name?	*Nǐ jiào shénme míngzì?*	你叫什么名字？
I'm an American.	*Wǒ shì Měiguó rén.*	我是美国人。
Do you live here?	*Nǐ zhù zhèlǐ ma?*	你住这里吗？
I am from ____.	*Wǒ cóng ____ lái de.*	我从____来的。
■ the United States	*Měiguó*	美国
■ the U.K.	*Yīngguó*	英国
■ Canada	*Jiānádà*	加拿大
■ Australia	*Aòzhōu*	澳洲
■ New Zealand	*Xīnxīlán*	新西兰
I like China very much.	*Wǒ hén xǐhuān Zhōngguó.* 我很喜欢中国。	

I would like to go there.	*Wǒ hén xǐang dào nàli qù.*	我很想到那里去。
How long will you be staying?	*Nǐ yào dāi dūojǐu?*	你要呆多久？
I'll stay for ____.	*Wǒ yào dāi ____.*	我要呆____。
■ a few days	*jǐ tīan*	几天
■ a week	*yí xīngqī*	一个星期
Where are you living now?	*Nǐ xìanzài zhù náli?*	你现在住哪里？
What hotel are you staying at?	*Nǐ zhù něige fàndìan?*	你住哪个饭店？
I am staying at the ____ Hotel.	*Wǒ zhù ____ Fàndìan.*	我住____饭店。
What do you think of ____?	*Nǐ dùi ____ júede zěnmeyàng?*	你对____觉得怎么样？
I don't like it very much.	*Wǒ bú tài xǐhūan.*	我不太喜欢。
I think it's very ____.	*Wǒ júede hěn ____.*	我觉得很____。
■ interesting	*yǒu yìsi*	有意思
■ beautiful	*měi*	美
■ wonderful	*bàng*	棒

GREETINGS AND INTRODUCTIONS

May I please introduce my ____.	*Qǐng ràng wǒ jìeshào wǒ de ____.*	请让我介绍我的____。
■ boss	*láobǎn*	老板

c = ts; *q* = ch; *x* = sh; *z* = dz; *zh* = j

■ boyfriend	*nán péngyou*	男朋友
■ classmate	*tóngxúe*	同学
■ colleague	*tóngshì*	同事
■ elder brother	*gēge*	哥哥
■ elder sister	*jǐejie*	姐姐
■ father	*bàba*	爸爸
■ friend	*péngyou*	朋友
■ girlfriend	*nǔ péngyou*	女朋友
■ husband	*zhàngfu*	丈夫
■ mother	*māma*	妈妈
■ staff member	*gōngzuò rényúan*	工作人员
■ student	*xúeshēng*	学生
■ teacher	*lǎoshī*	老师
■ wife	*tàitai*	太太
■ younger brother	*dìdi*	弟弟
■ younger sister	*mèimei*	妹妹

Glad to meet you.	*Hěn gāoxìng jiàndào nǐ.*	
	很高兴见到你。	
I'm honored.	*Wó hěn róngxìng.*	
	我很荣幸。	
Please allow me to introduce myself.	*Qǐng ràng wǒ jièshào wǒ zìjǐ.*	
	请让我介绍我自己。	
My name is ____. And yours?	*Wǒ jìao ____.* *Ní ne?*	我叫____。 你呢？
I am a (an) ____.	*Wǒ shì ____.*	我是____。
■ accountant	*kùaijì shī*	会计师
■ artist	*yìshù jīa*	艺术家
■ athlete	*yùndòng yúan*	运动员

■ banker	*yínháng jiā*	银行家
■ businessperson	*shāngrén*	商人
■ college professor	*dàxué jiàoshòu*	大学教授
■ computer scientist	*jìsuànjī zhuānjiā*	计算机专家
■ dancer	*wúdǎo jiā*	舞蹈家
■ dentist	*yáyī*	牙医
■ designer	*shèjì jiā*	设计家
■ doctor	*yīshēng*	医生
■ editor	*biānjì*	编辑
■ engineer	*gōngchéng shī*	工程师
■ farmer	*nóngmín*	农民
■ government official	*zhèngfǔ guānyuán*	政府官员
■ insurance salesman	*báoxiǎn yèzhě*	保险业者
■ lawyer	*lǜshī*	律师
■ musician	*yīnyuè jiā*	音乐家
■ reporter	*jìzhě*	记者
■ retired person	*tùixiū rényuán*	退休人员
■ scientist	*kēxué jiā*	科学家
■ soldier	*jūnrén*	军人
■ student	*xuéshēng*	学生
■ teacher	*jiàoshī*	教师
■ technician	*jìshù rényuán*	技术人员
■ writer	*zuòjiā*	作家

c = ts; *q* = ch; *x* = sh; *z* = dz; *zh* = j

SOCIALIZING

You will find most Chinese people very curious about people from other countries, and quite open to making friends with foreigners. Most of the time, all it takes to start a friendship is some small talk to break the ice.

Where are you from?	*Nǐ cóng nálǐ lài?* 你从哪里来？
Where is your original home?	*Nǐ de lǎojiā zài nálǐ?* 你的老家在哪里？
How long have you lived here?	*Nǐ zài zhèlǐ zhùle dūojǐu?* 你在这里住了多久？
How many people are in your family?	*Nǐ de jiā yóu jǐge rén?* 你的家有几个人？
Are you married?	*Nǐ jíehūn le ma?* 你结婚了吗？
Do you have any children?	*Nǐ yóu xǐaohái ma?* 你有小孩吗？
What are their ages?	*Tāmen dūo dà?* 他们多大？
We have children the same age.	*Wǒmén de xǐaohái yǐyàng dà.* 我们的小孩一样大。
What is your work unit?	*Nǐ zài něige dānwèi gōngzùo?* 你在哪个单位工作？
Have you ever traveled abroad?	*Nǐ dào gùo gúowài ma?* 你到过国外吗？
To which countries?	*Dàogùo něixīe gúojiā?* 到过哪些国家？

Can you give me your telephone number?	*Nǐ néng gàosu wó nǐ de diànhùa hàomǎ ma?* 你能告诉我你的电话号码吗？
What is your telephone number?	*Nǐ de diànhùa hàomǎ dūoshǎo?* 你的电话号码多少？
What is your address?	*Nǐ de dìzhǐ shì shénme?* 你的地址是什么？
Do you have a fax number?	*Nǐ yǒu chúanzhēnjī hàomǎ ma?* 你有传真机号码吗？
What is your e-mail address?	*Nǐde diànzǐ yóujìan xìnxiāng shìshénme?* 你的电子邮件信箱是什么？
Here's my address.	*Zhè shì wǒ de dìzhǐ.* 这是我的地址。
Here's my telephone number.	*Zhè shì wǒ de diànhùa hàomǎ.* 这是我的电话号码。
May I write to you?	*Wǒ kéyǐ géi ní xiě xìn ma?* 我可以给你写信吗？
Will you write back?	*Nǐ hùi húi xìn ma?* 你会回信吗？
May I take a picture of you?	*Wǒ géi nǐ zhàoxìang hǎo ma?* 我给你照相好吗？
Please stand here.	*Qǐng zhàn zài zhèli.* 请站在这里。
Don't move.	*Bíe dòng le.* 别动了。
Smile!	*Xìao!* 笑！

c = ts; *q* = ch; *x* = sh; *z* = dz; *zh* = j

Will you take a picture of me (us)?	*Qǐng bāng wǒ (wǒmén) zhào ge xiàng hǎo ma?* 请帮我（我们）照个相好吗？
Are you doing anything tomorrow?	*Nǐ míngtiān yǒu shì ma?* 你明天有事吗？
Are you free this evening?	*Nǐ jīnwán yǒu kòng ma?* 你今晚有空吗？
Would you like to go together?	*Ní xiǎng yīqǐ qù ma?* 你想一起去吗？
I'll wait for you in front of the hotel.	*Wǒ zài fàndiàn ménkǒu déng nǐ.* 我在饭店门口等你。
I'll pick you up at ____.	*Wǒ zài ____ jīe nǐ.* 我在____接你。

SAYING GOOD-BYE

I'm happy to have met you.	*Hěn gāoxìng rènshi nǐ.* 很高兴认识你。
I hope to see you again sometime.	*Xīwàng yǐhòu zài jiàndào nǐ.* 希望以后再见到你。
I wish you a safe trip.	*Zhù nǐ yī lù píng ān.* 祝你一路平安。
Please send my regards to ____.	*Qǐng wènhòu ____.* 请问候____。
This was a very nice evening.	*Jīnwán hěn yúkùai.* 今晚很愉快。
You must come to visit us.	*Nǐ yīdìng yào lái kàn wǒmén.* 你一定要来看我们。
Good-bye.	*Zàijian.* 再见。

GESTURES

Some of your most natural gestures may not evoke the same responses from a Chinese that they would from another Westerner. A shoulder shrug signifying "I don't know" or an erect index finger signaling "just one moment," for example, aren't readily understood in China. Some gestures, on the other hand, are very easily interpreted and occasionally even shared by the Chinese. Giving the "thumbs up" sign, for example, is read in both cultures to be a positive evaluation of something; nodding a Chinese that they head for yes or no are also understood. And, unlike the Japanese, shaking hands as a form of greeting is quite normal to the Chinese. You may notice a slight nodding of the head together with the handshake—but you'll never see a Chinese bow at the waist in Japanese fashion.

You may also experience some gestures that are peculiarly Chinese. "Come here" is communicated with a palm-down hand outstretched toward the listener, waving up and down—the Chinese don't use their fingers to motion toward themselves. And the numbers from one to ten all are signified by special hand motions.

Be aware that the Chinese find some postures and movements offensive. It isn't polite, for example, to show someone the bottoms of your feet. It's also not appropriate to give an enthusiastic bear hug or a slap on the back to a Chinese you don't know well. Above all, be careful not to come into physical contact with a Chinese of the opposite sex you do not know extremely well. This could easily be misconstrued.

The Chinese, for their part, may surprise or even offend you with some of their habits. Belching, expelling mucus, and even passing gas in public are common, and little is thought of spitting on the street, though the government has been trying to discourage this habit. Chinese smokers are indiscriminate as to location; there is little recognition that smoke may be considered offensive by a nonsmoker. And pointing to people—even staring at them—is not considered a breach of etiquette.

The concept of personal distance also differs among cultures, and in China someone may jar you a bit by standing or sitting at a distance you consider to be too close. You may also be surprised if a Chinese of the same sex is quite physical around you. It's common in China for someone of the same sex to put his arm around a friend, or lean on him, or gently nudge him through a doorway, or even hold hands. You should be aware that there are generally no sexual overtones to same-sex touching in China.

SHOPPING

GOING SHOPPING

There are many wonderful things to buy in China, and many types of places that sell them. Whether you visit a small specialty store, a large department store, an outdoor market, or a street vendor, shopping can be a lot of fun. The Chinese themselves love to shop, and for this reason markets are often extremely crowded.

Large, state-run stores are usually fixed-price establishments, but bargaining is the rule elsewhere. When goods are not marked, the price quoted to a foreign visitor may sometimes be quite a bit inflated over that charged to local residents. You can usually get a merchant to shave 5 to 10 percent off any quoted price; hard bargaining can often result in even larger discounts.

Specialty shops exist side by side with large department stores in China. There are bookstores, clothing stores, shoe stores, hat shops, jewelry stores, souvenir stores, camera and photographic stores, antique stores, stationery stores, arts and crafts shops, music and electronics stores, toy stores, opticians, barber and beauty shops, newsstands, and pharmacies. For certain merchandise such as electrical appliances, housewares, and toiletries, your best bet may be the local department stores, where the selection is often quite good. Food can be purchased at supermarkets as well as open-air fruit and vegetable markets.

I'd like to go shopping today.	*Wǒ jīntiān xiǎng qù mǎi dōngxi.* 我今天想去买东西。
Where is there a(n) ____?	*Náli yǒu* ____? 哪里有____?

c = ts; *q* = ch; *x* = sh; *z* = dz; *zh* = j

■ antique shop	*gúdǒng diàn*	古董店
■ appliance store	*jiāyòng diànqì háng*	家用电器行
■ bakery	*gāobǐng diàn*	糕饼店
■ barbershop	*lǐfà guǎn*	理发馆
■ beauty parlor	*měiróng yuàn*	美容院
■ bookstore	*shūdiàn*	书店
■ camera shop	*zhàoxiàng qìcái háng*	照相器材行
■ candy store	*tánggǔo diàn*	糖果店
■ coffee shop	*kāfēi diàn*	咖啡店
■ clothing store	*fúzhuāng diàn*	服装店
■ department store	*bǎihùo shāngdiàn*	百货商店
■ drugstore	*yàofáng*	药房
■ fabric store	*bù diàn*	布店
■ florist	*hūadiàn*	花店
■ furrier	*píhùo diàn*	皮货店
■ food market	*cài shìchǎng*	菜市场
■ gift shop	*lípǐn diàn*	礼品店
■ hardware store	*wǔjīn háng*	五金行
■ hat shop	*màozi diàn*	帽子店
■ Internet café	*Yīngtèwǎng kāfēitīng*	英特网咖啡厅
■ jewelry store	*zhūbǎo diàn*	珠宝店
■ laundry	*xǐyī diàn*	洗衣店
■ leather goods store	*píhùo diàn*	皮货店
■ liquor store	*mài jǐu de diàn*	卖酒的店

■ newsstand	*bàotān*	报摊
■ optician	*yǎnjìng háng*	眼镜行
■ pawnshop	*dàng pù*	当铺
■ photographer	*zhàoxiàng gǔan*	照相馆
■ record store	*chàngpiàn háng*	唱片行
■ second-hand store	*jiùhùo dìan*	旧货店
■ shoe repair shop	*xīu xíe dìan*	修鞋店
■ shoe store	*xíedìan*	鞋店
■ snack shop	*xǐaochī dìan*	小吃店
■ stationery store	*wénjù dìan*	文具店
■ supermarket	*cháojī shìchǎng*	超级市场
■ tailor (for Western-style clothing)	*xīzhūang dìan*	西装店
■ tobacco shop	*yāncǎo dìan*	烟草店
■ toy store	*wánjù dìan*	玩具店
■ variety store	*záhùo dìan*	杂货店
■ watch repair shop	*xīu bǐao dìan*	修表店
Sir!	*Shīfu!*	师傅！
Miss!	*Xíaojǐe!*	小姐！
Young man! (service person)	*Fúwùyúan!*	服务员！
Can you help me?	*Nǐ néng bāng wǒ ma?*	你能帮我吗？

c = ts; *q* = ch; *x* = sh; *z* = dz; *zh* = j

How much is this?	*Zhèige duōshǎo qián?* 这个多少钱?
I would like three of them.	*Wó xiǎngyào sāngè.* 我想要三个。
Is the price negotiable?	*Kéyí jiǎng jià mā?* 可以讲价吗?
Can you give me a discount?	*Qǐng dá yīgè zhékòu.* 请打一个折扣。
How much of a discount can you give me?	*Ni néng géi wǒ dūodà de zhékòu?* 你能给我多大的折扣?
I would like to return this.	*Wǒ yào tùi hùo.* 我要退货。
It doesn't fit me.	*Bù héshēn.* 不合身。
It was broken when I bought it.	*Mǎilái jìu hùaile.* 买来就坏了。
I don't like it.	*Wǒ bù xǐhūan.* 我不喜欢。
It's the wrong color.	*Yánsè búdùi.* 颜色不对。
It's the wrong size.	*Dàxǐao búdùi.* 大小不对。
The quality is poor.	*Zhìliàng tài chà.* 质量太差。
I want my money back.	*Wǒ yāoqíu tùikǔan.* 我要求退款。
I want you to credit my credit card account.	*Wǒ xīwàng ní bǎ qían jìrù wǒde xìnyòng kǎ.* 我希望你把钱记入我的信用卡。

I want to see the general manager.	*Wó xǐang jiàn zǒngjīnglǐ.* 我想见总经理。

BOOKS

Where is the biggest bookstore here?	*Zùi dà de shūdìan zài náli?* 最大的书店在哪里？
I'm looking for a copy of ____.	*Wǒ yào zhǎo yī běn ____.* 我要找一本___。
The title of the book is ____.	*Shū míng shì ____.* 书名是___。
The author of the book is ____.	*Zùozhé shì ____.* 作者是___。
I'm looking for a book about ____.	*Wó zhǎo yī bén yǒu gūan ____ de shū.* 我找一本有关___的书。
I'm just looking.	*Wó zhǐ shì kànkan.* 我只是看看。
Do you have any books (novels) in English?	*Ní yǒu Yīngwén de shū (xǐaoshūo) ma?* 你有英文的书（小说）吗？

I would like ____.	*Wó xǐangyào*	我想要___。
■ a Chinese-English dictionary	*yī běn Hàn-Yīng zìdǐan*	一本汉英字典
■ an English-Chinese dictionary	*yī běn Yīng-Hàn zìdǐan*	一本英汉字典

c = ts; *q* = ch; *x* = sh; *z* = dz; *zh* = j

■ a guidebook	*yī běn lǚyóu xiǎocè*	一本旅游小册
■ a tourist map	*yī zhāng lǚyóu tú*	一张旅游图
Where can I find ____?	*Náli yǒu ____?*	哪里有____?
■ art books (Chinese paintings)	*huàcè (Zhōngguó huà)*	画册（中国画）
■ calligraphy books	*zìtiē*	字帖
■ books about China	*jièshao Zhōngguó de shū*	介绍中国的书
■ Chinese language texts	*xué Zhōngwén de shū*	学中文的书
■ children's books	*xiǎohái de shū*	小孩的书
■ fiction	*xiǎoshūo*	小说
■ history books	*lìshǐ shū*	历史书
I'd like these books.	*Wǒ yào mǎi zhèixiē shū.* 我要买这些书。	
Will you wrap them, please?	*Qǐng bāo qǐlái hǎo ma?* 请包起来好吗？	

CLOTHING

Would you please show me ____.	*Qǐng géi wǒ kànkan ____.* 请给我看看____。

- a belt · *pídài* · 皮带
- a blouse · *nǚ chènshān* · 女衬衫
- a dress · *yī tào yīfu* · 一套衣服
- a Chinese jacket · *zhōngshān fú* · 中山服
- a chipao (cheongsam; traditional Chinese women's formal wear) · *qípáo* · 旗袍
- leather (suede) gloves · *pí (yángpí) shǒutào* · 皮（羊皮）手套
- handkerchiefs · *shǒujuàn* · 手绢
- a hat · *màozi* · 帽子
- a jacket · *wàitào* · 外套
- an overcoat · *dàyī* · 大衣
- a pair of pajamas · *shùiyī* · 睡衣
- pants · *kùzi* · 裤子
- a raincoat · *yǔyī* · 雨衣
- a robe · *páozi* · 袍子
- a scarf · *wéijīn* · 围巾
- a shirt · *chènshān* · 衬衫
- a pair of shoes · *yī shuāng xié* · 一双鞋
- short pants · *dǔan kù* · 短裤
- a skirt · *qúnzi* · 裙子
- slippers · *tūoxié* · 拖鞋

c = ts; *q* = ch; *x* = sh; *z* = dz; *zh* = j

■ socks	*wàzi*	袜子
■ a suit (Western-style)	*xīzhuāng*	西装
■ a sweater	*máoyī*	毛衣
■ a sweatshirt	*yùndòng shān*	运动衫
■ a sweatsuit	*yùndòng yī*	运动衣
■ a tie	*lǐngdài*	领带
■ a pair of underpants	*nèikù*	内裤
■ an undershirt	*nèiyī*	内衣

I'd like it with ____ sleeves.	*Wǒ yào ____ xiù de.* 我要____袖的。	
■ short	*duǎn*	短
■ long	*cháng*	长
■ no	*méi*	没

Do you have anything ____?	*Yǒu méi yǒu ____ de?* 有没有____的？	
■ better	*hǎo yīdiǎn*	好一点
■ cheaper	*piányi yīdiǎn*	便宜一点
■ else	*qítā*	其他
■ larger	*dà yīdiǎn*	大一点
■ longer	*cháng yīdiǎn*	长一点
■ shorter	*duǎn yīdiǎn*	短一点
■ smaller	*xǐao yūdiǎn*	小一点

COLORS

| I don't like the color. | *Wǒ bù xǐhūan zhèige yánsè.* |
| | 我不喜欢这个颜色。 |

| Do you have anything in ____? | *Ní yǒu méi yǒu ____ sè de?* |
| | 你有没有___色的？ |

■ black	*hēi*	黑
■ blue	*lán*	蓝
■ brown	*kāfēi*	咖啡
■ green	*lǜ*	绿
■ gray	*hūi*	灰
■ orange	*júhóng*	橘红
■ pink	*fěnhóng*	粉红
■ purple	*zǐ*	紫

c = ts; *q* = ch; *x* = sh; *z* = dz; *zh* = j

■ red	*hóng*	红
■ white	*bái*	白
■ yellow	*huáng*	黄

Do you have a lighter (darker) shade?

Yǒu méi yǒu dàn (shēn) yīdiǎn de?

有没有淡（深）一点的？

MATERIALS

cashmere	*kāishìmǐ*	开士米
cotton	*mianbù*	棉布
denim	*xíewén chū míanbù*	斜纹粗棉布
lace	*huābīan*	花边
leather	*pígé zhìpǐn*	皮革制品
nylon	*nílóng*	尼龙
polyester	*huàxīan*	化纤
satin	*dùanzi*	缎子
silk	*sīchóu*	丝绸
wool	*yángmáo*	羊毛

FIT, ALTERATIONS

It doesn't fit me.

Dùi wǒ bù héshēn.

对我不合身。

It fits very well.

Héshēn jíle.

合身极了。

Please take my measurements.	*Qǐng liáng wǒ de chǐcùn.* 请量我的尺寸。
My size is ____.	*Wǒ de chǐcùn shì ____.* 我的尺寸是____。
May I try it on?	*Wǒ kéyǐ shì yī shì ma?* 我可以试一试吗？
Can you alter it?	*Nǐ néng gǎi yī gǎi ma?* 你能改一改吗？
Can you let it out?	*Nǐ néng fàng dà yīdian ma?* 你能放大一点吗？
May I return this?	*Zhèige néng bù néng tùi?* 这个能不能退？
Do you have something handmade?	*Yóu shǒugōng zùo de ma?* 有手工做的吗？
The zipper is broken.	*Lālìan hùai le.* 拉链坏了。
I'll buy this one.	*Wó mǎi zhèi jìan.* 我买这件。
Please wrap it up.	*Qǐng bāo qǐlái.* 请包起来。

SHOES

| I'd like to see a pair of shoes (boots). | *Wó xiǎng kànkan yī shūang xíe (xūe).*
我想看看一双鞋（靴）。 |
| I'd like to try the pair in the window. | *Wó xiǎng shì chúchūang lǐ de nèi shūang.*
我想试橱窗里的那双。 |

c = ts; *q* = ch; *x* = sh; *z* = dz; *zh* = j

I take size ____.	*Wǒ de chǐcùn shì* ____.	
	我的尺寸是____。	

This pair is ____.	*Zhèi shuāng* ____.	这双____。
■ exactly right	*gāng hǎo*	刚好
■ too loose	*tài sōng*	太松
■ too narrow	*tài zhǎi*	太窄
■ too tight	*tài jǐn*	太紧
■ too wide	*tài kuān*	太宽

I also need ____.	*Wǒ hái yào* ____.	我还要____。
■ shoelaces	*xíedài*	鞋带
■ shoe polish	*xieyoú*	鞋油

AT THE SUPERMARKET

Where is (are) ____?	____ *zài nálǐ?*	____在那里？
■ beverages	*yǐnliào*	饮料
■ canned goods	*gùantóu shípǐn*	罐头食品
■ dairy foods	*nǎizhì pǐn*	奶制品
■ frozen foods	*lěngdòng shípǐn*	冷冻食品
■ fruits	*shúigǔo*	水果
■ grains	*liángshí lèi*	粮食类
■ hardware	*xíao wǔjīn*	小五金
■ meat	*ròu*	肉
■ oils	*yóu lèi*	油类
■ snacks	*xǐaochī lèi*	小吃类
■ soaps and detergents	*féizào yú qīngjié jì*	肥皂与清洁剂
■ spices	*tiáowèi liào*	调味料

| ■ vegetables | *shūcài* | 蔬菜 |
| ■ wines and liquors | *jiŭ lèi* | 酒类 |

| Where can I find a shopping cart? | *Nálí yóu shŏu tūi chē?* 哪里有手推车？ |
| May I have another shopping bag? | *Qĭng zài géi wŏ yīgè gòuwù dài?* 请再给我一个购物袋？ |

JEWELRY

I'd like to see ____.	*Wó xĭang kànkan*	我想看看____。
■ a bracelet	*shŏuzhúo*	手镯
■ a brooch	*xīongzhēn*	胸针
■ a chain	*liànzi*	链子
■ a charm	*xĭao shīwù*	小饰物
■ some earrings	*ěrhúan*	耳环
■ a necklace	*xìanglìan*	项链
■ a pin	*bíezhēn*	别针
■ a ring	*jìezhi*	戒指
■ a watch	*shóubĭao*	手表
Is this ____?	*Zhè shì ____ de ma?*	这是____的吗？
■ cloisonné	*jĭngtàilán*	景泰蓝
■ gold	*jīn*	金
■ platinum	*báijīn*	白金
■ silver	*yín*	银
■ stainless steel	*búxìugāng*	不锈钢

c = ts; *q* = ch; *x* = sh; *z* = dz; *zh* = j

Is it solid gold or gold-plated?	*Shì chúnjīn de háishì dùjīn de?* 是纯金的还是镀金的？	
How many carats is it?	*Yǒu duōshao kèlā?* 有多少克拉？	
What is that stone?	*Nà shì shénme bǎoshí?* 那是什么宝石？	
I would like ____.	*Wó xiǎngyào ____.* 我想要____。	
■ an amethyst	*zǐjīn*	紫晶
■ an aquamarine	*hǎilán bǎoshí*	海蓝宝石
■ a diamond	*zhùanshí*	钻石
■ an emerald	*lǜ bǎoshí*	绿宝石
■ ivory	*xiàngyá*	象牙
■ jade	*yù*	玉
■ pearls	*zhēnzhū*	珍珠
■ a ruby	*hóng bǎoshí*	红宝石
■ a sapphire	*lán bǎoshí*	蓝宝石
■ turquoise	*lǜsōng shí*	绿松石
I like this ring.	*Wó xǐhuān zhèige jièzhi.* 我喜欢这个戒指。	
How much is it?	*Duōshǎo qián?* 多少钱？	

MUSIC AND ELECTRONICS

Do you sell ____?	*Nǐmén mài ____ ma?* 你们卖____吗？	
■ cassettes	*héshì lùyīndài*	盒式录音带
■ CDs	*guāngpán*	光盘

■ VCRs	*shìpín gāomì guāng pán*	视频高密光盘
■ videocassettes	*lùxìang dài*	录像带
■ records	*chàngpiàn*	唱片
I want to buy ____.	*Wó xiáng mǎi ____.*	我想买____。
■ a computer	*jìsùanjī*	计算机
■ computer hardware	*yìngjìan*	硬件
■ computer software	*rǔanjìan*	软件
■ a video game	*dìanzǐ yóuxì*	电子游戏
I need a ____.	*Wǒ xūyào yígè ____.*	我需要一个____。
■ CD-ROM	*guāng qū*	光驱
■ cord	*dìanxìan*	电线
■ disk holder	*cípǎn jìa*	磁片架
■ floppy disk	*rǔan cípán*	软磁盘
■ hard disk	*yìngpán*	硬盘
■ modem	*tiáozhì jǐetiáo qì*	调制解调器
■ monitor (CRT)	*yīnjí shèxìang gǔan*	阴极射像管
■ mouse	*láoshǔ*	老鼠
■ printer	*dǎyìn jī*	打印机
Where can I find ____ software?	*Nálí yǒu ____ rǔanjìan?* 哪里有____软件？	
■ business	*shāngyòng*	商用
■ Chinese word processing	*Zhōngwén wénzì chùlí*	中文文字处理

c = ts; *q* = ch; *x* = sh; *z* = dz; *zh* = j

■ English word processing	*Yīngwén wénzì chùlí*	英文文字处理
■ game	*yóuxì*	游戏
■ graphic design	*tú xiàng shèjì*	图像设计
■ spreadsheet	*kōngbái biǎogé chéngxù*	空白表格程序
■ system	*xìtǒng*	系统
■ telecommunications	*dìanxùn*	电讯

NEWSSTAND

Do you carry ____ in English?	*Nǐmén yǒu Yīngwén ____ ma?* 你们有英文____吗？	
■ newspapers	*baozhǐ*	报纸
■ magazines	*zázhì*	杂志
■ books	*shū*	书
I'd like to buy some postcards.	*Wó xíang mǎi míngxìnpìan.* 我想买明信片。	
Do you have stamps?	*Yǒu yóupìao ma?* 有邮票吗？	
How much is it?	*Dūoshǎo qían?* 多少钱？	

PHOTOGRAPHIC SUPPLIES

Where can I have some film developed?	*Náli kéyí xǐ zhàopìan?* 哪里可以洗照片？

How much does it cost to develop a roll of ____?	*Xǐ yī juǎn ____ yào duōshǎo?* 洗一卷____要多少？	
■ prints	*xiàngpiàn*	相片
■ slides	*huàndēng piàn*	幻灯片

I want ____.	*Wǒ yào ____.*	我要____。
■ an enlargement	*fàng dà*	放大
■ a glossy finish	*guāngmiàn de*	光面的
■ a matte finish	*bù guānghúa de*	不光滑的
■ a print of each	*měi yígè dǐpiàn yì zhāng*	每一个底片一张
■ two prints of each	*měi yígè dǐpiàn liǎng zhāng*	每一个底片两张

Can you develop my pictures on a disk?	*Nǐ néng bǎ zhàopiàn fàng zái pánshàng ma?* 你能把照片放在盘上吗？	

I want a roll of 24 (36) exposures of ____.	*Wǒ yào yī juǎn èrshí sì (sānshílìu) zhāng de ____.* 我要一卷二十四（三十六）张的____。	
■ color film	*cǎisè jīao juǎn*	彩色胶卷
■ black-and-white film	*hēibái jīao juǎn*	黑白胶卷

I would like ____ film.	*Wǒ yào ____ jīao juǎn.*	我要____胶卷。
■ Chinese	*Zhōngguó*	中国
■ American	*Měiguó*	美国
■ Japanese	*Rìběn*	日本

What is the film speed?	*Jiāojuǎn de sùdù shì duōshǎo?* 胶卷的速度是多少？	

c = ts; *q* = ch; *x* = sh; *z* = dz; *zh* = j

When can I pick up the pictures?	*Shénme shíhòu qǔ zhàopiàn?* 什么时候取照片？
Do you sell cameras?	*Nǐmén mài zhàoxiàng jī ma?* 你们卖照相机吗？
I want an inexpensive one.	*Wǒ yào yīge piányi de.* 我要一个便宜的。
I want a better one.	*Wǒ yào hǎo yīdiǎn de.* 我要好一点的。
I want a completely automatic one.	*Wǒ yào quán zìdòng de.* 我要全自动的。
Do you sell disposable cameras?	*Nǐmén mài yí cì xìng de zhàoxiàngjī mǎ?* 你们卖一次性的照相机吗？
I need a special kind of battery.	*Wǒ yào tèzhǒng diànchí.* 我要特种电池。
Do you have this kind?	*Nǐmén yǒu zhèizhǒng de ma?* 你们有这种的吗？
Where can I find a battery to fit this camera?	*Zài nálí mǎidedào pèi zhèige zhàoxiàngjī de diànchí?* 在哪里买得到配这个照相机的电池？
Do you fix cameras?	*Nǐmén xiū zhàoxiàng jī ma?* 你们修照相机吗？
Mine is broken.	*Wǒ de huàile.* 我的坏了。

SOUVENIRS

China offers a vast array of handicrafts that are often welcome gifts to your friends at home and that serve as excellent souvenirs of the country. Among the most popular

items are cloisonné ware, porcelain ware, jewelry, lacquer
ware, pottery, fabrics, embroidery, bamboo and cane
products, paper cuts, furniture, rugs, and wooden articles.
One can also purchase Chinese scrolls, calligraphy, seals,
brushes and inks, and other art supplies.

Would you please show me some ____?	*Qǐng géi wǒ kànkan ____.* 请给我看看____。	
■ calligraphy	*shūfǎ*	书法
■ carpets	*dìtǎn*	地毯
■ carved objects	*dīaokè pǐn*	雕刻品
■ cloisonné	*jǐngtàilán*	景泰蓝
■ dolls	*wáwa*	娃娃
■ embroidery	*xìuhūa zhìpǐn*	绣花制品
■ fabrics	*bùlìao*	布料
■ fans	*shànzi*	扇子
■ furs	*pímáo*	皮毛
■ furniture	*jīajù*	家具
■ glass	*bōlí zhìpǐn*	玻璃制品
■ jewelry	*zhūbǎo; shǒushī*	珠宝；首饰
■ lace	*hūabīan*	花边
■ lacquer ware	*qīqì*	漆器
■ leather goods	*pígé zhìpǐn*	皮革制品
■ musical instruments	*yùeqì*	乐器
■ paintings	*hùa*	画
■ paper cuts	*jíanzhǐ*	剪纸
■ porcelain	*cíqì*	瓷器
■ pottery	*táoqì*	陶器

c = ts; *q* = ch; *x* = sh; *z* = dz; *zh* = j

■ silks   *sīzhī pǐn*   丝织品

■ snuff bottles   *bí yān hú*   鼻烟壶

■ stone rubbings   *mó tuōběn*   摹拓本

I don't want to spend more than ____ yuan.	*Wó xǐang zùi dūo hūa ____ yúan.* 我想最多花____元。

ANTIQUES

There are fabulous antiques to be had in China. Vintage clocks, metalware, porcelains, silks, paintings, calligraphy, wood and lacquer ware, and furniture are sold everywhere. Some are quite beautiful, rare, and valuable.

You should be aware, however, that some Chinese antiques are subject to export restrictions. In general, objects of art such as porcelains may not be exported if they are more than about 200 years old. In the case of wood products, it is the type of wood from which an object is made rather than its age that governs whether its export is restricted. Products made from three different types of rare wood may not currently leave the country.

Antiques, whether obtained from state-run stores or from private dealers, must bear a red wax seal in order to be legally removed from China. Chinese Customs is empowered to seize any suspect goods that do not have it. The seal must be applied by the local cultural artifacts bureau, whose experts are charged with determining the age and composition of the items. Reputable dealers can often arrange for the seal to be applied to goods you wish to purchase.

You won't find bargain basement prices on rare cultural treasures, but prices on Chinese antiques in China do tend to be better than they are elsewhere in the world. Bear in mind that haggling is quite acceptable when buying antiques.

What's the price of ____ ?	*____ yào dūoshǎo qían?* ____要多少钱？

■ this box	*Zhèige hézi*	这个盒子
■ this calligraphy	*Zhèi fù zì*	这幅字
■ this clock	*Zhèige zhōng*	这个钟
■ this painting	*Zhèi fù huà*	这幅画
■ this piece of jewelry	*Zhei jiàn shǒushī*	这件首饰
■ this rug	*Zhèi zhāng dìtǎn*	这张地毯
■ this vase	*Zhèige huāpíng*	这个花瓶

How old is it?
Zhèige dūoshǎo nián?
这个多少年？

Does it still work?
Zhèige hái néng yòng ma?
这个还能用吗？

Which dynasty does it come from?
Něige cháodài de?
哪个朝代的？

Where is your antique furniture?
Nǐde gúdǒng jiājù zài nálǐ?
你的古董家具在哪里？

■ altar table	*jìbài yòng de zhǔozi*	祭拜用的桌子
■ bed	*chúang*	床
■ Buddha	*Fóxìang*	佛像
■ carpet	*dìtǎn*	地毯
■ chair	*yǐzi*	椅子
■ chest	*gùizi*	柜子
■ idol	*shénxìang*	神像
■ lantern	*dēnglóng*	灯笼
■ picture	*hùaxìang*	画像

c = ts; *q* = ch; *x* = sh; *z* = dz; *zh* = j

■ portrait	*rénwù xiàng*	人物像
■ screen	*píngfēng*	屏风
■ statue	*diāoxiàng*	雕像
■ stool	*dèngzi*	凳子
■ table	*zhūozi*	桌子
■ window	*chūang*	窗

May I take it out of
China?

Néng dài chūgúo ma?
能带出国吗？

Can you have the export
seal put on for me?

*Nǐ néng jīa zhúnxǔ chūgúo de
hǔoqī yìn ma?*
你能加准许出国的火漆印吗？

Can you make it a little
cheaper?

Nǐ néng sùan píanyi yīdǐan ma?
你能算便宜一点吗？

TOBACCO SHOP

Please give me
a pack of ____
cigarettes.

*Qǐng géi wǒ yī bāo ____ de
xīangyān.*
请给我一包____的香烟。

■ filtered	*yǒu gùo lǜzǔi*	有过滤嘴
■ unfiltered	*bù jīa lǜzǔi*	不加滤嘴

Do you have American
cigarettes?

Yóu Měigúo yān ma?
有美国烟吗？

I would like a carton.

Wó xīangyào yī tíao.
我想要一条。

Do you have any
matches?

Yóu hǔochái ma?
有火柴吗？

TOILETRIES

Do you have ____ ?	Yǒu méi yǒu ____ ?	有没有____?
■ adhesive bandage	*bēngdài*	绷带
■ a brush	*shūazi*	刷子
■ cologne	*xiāngshǔi*	香水
■ a comb	*shūzi*	梳子
■ cotton balls	*míanhūa qíu*	棉花球
■ cotton swabs	*míanhūa qīan*	棉花签
■ deodorant	*chúchòu jì*	除臭剂
■ hairpins	*fàjīa*	发夹
■ mouthwash	*shùkóu shǔi*	漱口水
■ makeup	*hùazhūang pǐn*	化妆品
■ a mirror	*jìngzi*	镜子
■ nail clippers	*jǐan zhǐjia dāo*	剪指甲刀
■ nail polish	*zhíjǐa yóu*	指甲油
■ a prophylactic (condom)	*bìyùntào*	避孕套
■ a razor	*gūahú dāo*	刮胡刀
■ razor blades	*dāopìan*	刀片
■ sanitary napkins	*yùe jīng dài*	月经带
■ scissors	*jǐandāo*	剪刀
■ shampoo	*xǐfà jì*	洗发剂
■ soap	*féizào*	肥皂
■ a soap dish	*féizào díe*	肥皂碟

c = ts; *q* = ch; *x* = sh; *z* = dz; *zh* = j

■ tampons	*yuèjīng yòng míansāi*	月经用棉塞
■ tissues	*huàzhūang yòng zhǐ*	化妆用纸
■ toilet paper	*wèishēng zhǐ*	卫生纸
■ a toothbrush	*yáshūa*	牙刷
■ toothpaste	*yágāo*	牙膏

ELECTRICAL APPLIANCES/AUDIOVISUAL EQUIPMENT

I need a _____.	*Wǒ xuyao yīgě _____.* 我需要一个___。	
■ adaptor	*zhǔanjīe qì*	转接器
■ air conditioner	*kōngtíao jī*	空调机
■ alarm clock	*nàozhōng*	闹钟
■ answering machine	*liúyán jī*	留言机
■ blender	*jiǎo bàn qì*	搅拌器
■ calculator	*jìsùan qì*	计算器
■ camcorder	*shèxiàng jī*	摄像机
■ camera	*zhàoxiàng jī*	照相机
■ can opener	*kāi gùan qì*	开罐器
■ CD player	*jígūang chàngjī*	激光唱机
■ coffeemaker	*zìdòng kāfēi jī*	自动咖啡机
■ computer	*jìsùan jī*	计算机
■ dehumidifier	*jiǎnshī qì*	减湿器
■ dryer	*hōnggān jī*	烘干机
■ electric fan	*diàn fēngshàn*	电风扇

■ electric grill	*dìan kǎo jìa*	电烤架
■ electric knife	*dìandōng càidāo*	电动菜刀
■ electric razor	*dìandōng gūahú dāo*	电动刮胡刀
■ electric steamer	*dìan zhēng gǔo*	电蒸锅
■ electric wok	*dìan chǎo gǔo*	电炒锅
■ fax machine	*chúanzhēn jī*	传真机
■ food processor	*shípǐn jǐagōngqì*	食品加工器
■ freezer	*lěngdòng jī*	冷冻机
■ hair dryer	*chūi fēng jī*	吹风机
■ heater	*nǔanqì jī*	暖气机
■ humidifier	*zēngshī qì*	增湿器
■ iron	*yùndǒu*	熨斗
■ juicer	*dá gǔozhī jī*	打果汁机
■ karaoke machine	*kǎlāoukèi jī*	卡拉OK机
■ lamp	*dēng*	灯
■ microwave oven	*wēibō lú*	微波炉
■ modem	*tiáozhì jiětiáo qì*	调制解调器
■ outlet	*dìanyúan chāzùo*	电源插座
■ plug	*chātóu*	插头
■ printer	*dǎyìn jī*	打印机
■ radio	*shǒuyīn jī*	收音机
■ refrigerator	*bīngxiāng*	冰箱
■ rice cooker	*dìan fàn gǔo*	电饭锅
■ slide projector	*hùandēng jī*	幻灯机

c = ts; *q* = ch; *x* = sh; *z* = dz; *zh* = j

■ smoke detector	*yānwù bàojǐng qì*	烟雾报警器
■ stereo system	*zǔhé yīnxiǎng xìtǒng*	组合音响系统
■ switch	*kāigūan qì*	开关器
■ tape recorder	*lùyīn jī*	录音机
■ telephone	*diànhùa*	电话
■ television	*diànshì jī*	电视机
■ toaster	*kǎo mìanbāojī*	烤面包片机
■ toaster oven	*dìan hōngxīang*	电烘箱
■ transformer	*bìanyā qì*	变压器
■ vacuum cleaner	*xīchén qì*	吸尘器
■ videocassette recorder	*lùxìangjī*	录像机
■ videodisc player	*yǐngdié jī*	影碟机
■ washing machine	*xǐyī jī*	洗衣机
■ wire	*diàn xìàn*	电线

HOUSEWARES

■ ashtray	*yānhūi gāng*	烟灰缸
■ basket	*lánzi*	篮子
■ bowl	*wǎn*	碗
■ candy dish	*gǔopán*	果盘
■ chair	*yǐzi*	椅子
■ chopsticks	*kùaizi*	筷子
■ cooking pot	*gūozi*	锅子

■ cup	*bēizi*	杯子
■ cutting board	*zhēn bǎn*	砧板
■ dish towel	*mā bù*	抹布
■ fork	*chāzi*	叉子
■ frying pan	*chǎocài guō*	炒菜锅
■ kettle	*kāishuǐ hú*	开水壶
■ knife	*dāozi*	刀子
■ plate; dish	*pánzi*	盘子
■ sofa	*shāfā*	沙发
■ spatula	*guāchǎn*	刮铲
■ sponge	*hǎimían*	海绵
■ spoon	*tiáogēng*	调羹
■ steamer	*zhēnglóng*	蒸笼
■ trash can	*lājī tǒng*	垃圾筒

c = ts; *q* = ch; *x* = sh; *z* = dz; *zh* = j

PERSONAL CARE AND SERVICES

AT THE BARBER

Where is there a good barbershop?	*Nǎli yóu hǎo de lǐfà guǎn?* 哪里有好的理发馆？	
May I make an appointment?	*Wǒ kéyǐ yùyuē lǐfà ma?* 我可以预约理发吗？	
Do I have to wait long?	*Yào děng hén jǐu ma?* 要等很久吗？	
I want a shave.	*Wǒ yào guā liǎn.* 我要刮脸。	
I want a haircut.	*Wǒ yào lǐfà.* 我要理发。	
I'd like a trim, please.	*Qíng bǎ tóufa jiǎnqí.* 请把头发剪齐。	
Don't cut it too short.	*Bíe jiǎn tài dǔan.* 别剪太短。	
Please cut it a little shorter.	*Qíng jiǎn dǔan yīdian.* 请剪短一点。	
Please cut a little more ____.	*Qíng zài ____ zài jiǎn yīdian.* 请在____再剪一点。	

▪ here	*zhèli*	这里
▪ in back	*hòumiàn*	后面
▪ in front	*qíanmìan*	前面
▪ off the sides	*lǐang páng*	两旁
▪ off the top	*dǐngshàng*	顶上

That's enough.	*Gòu le.*	够了。
Please thin it out.	*Qǐng dǎbáo.*	请打薄。
I (don't) want ____.	*Wǒ (bú) yào ____.*	我（不）要____。

■ a shampoo	*xǐ tóu*	洗头
■ tonic	*fàyóu*	发油

Please trim my ____.	*Qǐng xīu wǒ de ____.*	请修我的____。

■ beard	*húxū*	胡须
■ mustache	*xǐao húzi*	小胡子
■ sideburns	*líanbìng húzi*	连鬓胡子

Can you give me a massage?	*Kéyǐ wèi wǒ ànmó ma?* 可以为我按摩吗？
Please massage my head only.	*Qǐng zhǐ ànmó wǒ de tóubù.* 请只按摩我的头部。
Please massage my whole body.	*Qǐng wèi wǒ quánshēn ànmó.* 请为我全身按摩。
How much do I owe you?	*Wǒ gāi fù nǐ dūoshǎo?* 我该付你多少？

AT THE BEAUTY PARLOR

Is there a beauty parlor at the hotel?	*Fàndìan yóu měiróng yùan ma?* 饭店有美容院吗？
Is there one nearby?	*Fùjìn yǒu yīge ma?* 附近有一个吗？

c = ts; *q* = ch; *x* = sh; *z* = dz; *zh* = j

I'd like to make an appointment for ____.	*Wó xiǎng yùdìng zài* ____.	我想预定在____。
■ this afternoon	*jīntīan xiàwǔ*	今天下午
■ tomorrow	*míngtīan*	明天

Please give me ____.	*Qǐng wèi wǒ* ____.	请为我____。
■ electrolysis	*diànshí chú máo*	电蚀除毛
■ a facial massage	*mìanbù ànmó*	面部按摩
■ a haircut	*lǐfà*	理发
■ a manicure	*xīu zhǐjia*	修指甲
■ a pedicure	*xīu jǐao zhǐjia*	修脚指甲
■ a permanent	*tàng tóufa*	烫头发

■ a shampoo	*xǐ tóu*	洗头
■ a wash and blow dry	*xǐ hòu chūigān.*	洗后吹干

I need to color my hair.   *Wǒ xūyào rǎn tóufa.*
我需要染头发。

What colors do you have?   *Nǐmén yǒu nǎxīe yánsè?*
你们有哪些颜色？

Don't apply any hair spray, please.   *Qǐng búyào pēn jīaoshǔi.*
请不要喷胶水。

Not too much hair spray, please.   *Bú yào pēn tài dūo jīaoshǔi.*
不要喷太多胶水。

LAUNDRY AND DRY CLEANING

Does the hotel offer laundry service?   *Fàndìan yóu xǐyī de fúwù ma?*
饭店有洗衣的服务吗？

How about dry cleaning?   *Yǒu gānxǐ ma?*
有干洗吗？

I have a lot of clothes to be ____.   *Wó yóu xǔdūo yīfu yào ____.*
我有许多衣服要____。

■ dry-cleaned	*gānxǐ*	干洗
■ ironed	*tàng*	烫
■ mended	*bǔ*	补
■ washed	*xǐ*	洗

Please don't use any starch.   *Qǐng bú yào shàng jīang.*
请不要上浆。

c = ts; *q* = ch; *x* = sh; *z* = dz; *zh* = j

| Light starch, please. | *Qǐng shàng yīdiǎn jiāng.* 请上一点浆。 | |

| Here's the laundry list: | *Zhè shì xǐyī dān:* 这是洗衣单： | |

■ three men's shirts	*sān jiàn nán chènshān*	三件男衬衫
■ twelve handkerchiefs	*shíèr tiáo shǒujuàn*	十二条手绢
■ six pairs of socks	*liù shuāng wàzi*	六双袜子
■ one blouse	*yī jiàn nǚ chènshān*	一件女衬衫
■ four panties	*sì tiáo nǚ nèikù*	四条女内裤
■ two pajamas	*liǎng jiàn shùiyī*	两件睡衣
■ two suits	*liǎng tào xīzhuāng*	两套西装
■ three ties	*sān tiáo lǐngdài*	三条领带
■ two dresses	*liǎng jiàn yīfu*	两件衣服
■ one sweater	*yī jiàn máoyī*	一件毛衣
■ one pair of gloves	*yī shuāng shǒutào*	一双手套

| I need them for | *Wǒ ____ jiù xūyào yòng.* | 我____就需要用。 |

■ tonight	*jīnwǎn*	今晚
■ tomorrow	*míngtīan*	明天
■ the day after tomorrow	*hòutīan*	后天
■ next week	*xià xīngqī*	下星期

| I'm leaving soon. | *Wó hěn kùai jiù yào zǒu.* 我很快就要走。 | |

I'm leaving tomorrow morning.	*Wǒ míngtīan zǎoshàng jìu yào zǒu.*	我明天早上就要走。
When will you bring it back?	*Nǐ shénme shíhòu kéyǐ jīao géi wǒ?*	你什么时候可以交给我？
When will it be ready?	*Shénme shíhòu hǎo?*	什么时候好？
Can you guarantee that I will have it back on time?	*Nǐ néng bǎozhèng zhǔnshí jīao géi wǒ ma?*	你能保证准时交给我吗？
There's a button ____.	*Yīge kòuzi ____.*	一个扣子____。
■ missing	*dīu le*	丢了
■ loose	*sōng le*	松了
Please sew it back on.	*Qǐng bāng wǒ féng hǎo.*	请帮我缝好。
This isn't my laundry.	*Zhèixīe búshì wǒ de yīfu.*	这些不是我的衣服。

SHOE REPAIRS

Can you fix these ____?	*Nǐ néng xīu zhèi shūang ____ma?*	你能修这双____吗？
■ shoes	*xíe*	鞋
■ boots	*xūe*	靴
The heel is broken.	*Hòugēn dùanle.*	后跟断了。

c = ts; *q* = ch; *x* = sh; *z* = dz; *zh* = j

Please give me ____ soles.	*Qǐng wèi wǒ huàn ____ xiédǐ.* 请为我换____鞋底。	
▪ full	*qúan*	全
▪ half	*bàn*	半

I'd like rubber heels.	*Wǒ yào xiàngpí hòugēn.* 我要橡皮后跟。
Please shine them.	*Qǐng wèi wǒ cā xié.* 请为我擦鞋。
When will they be ready?	*Shénme shíhòu hǎo?* 什么时候好？
I need them by Saturday without fail.	*Wǒ Xīngqīliù yīdìng děi yào.* 我星期六一定得要。

MEDICAL CARE

AT THE PHARMACY

Is there a pharmacy nearby?	*Fùjìn yǒu yàofáng ma?*	附近有药房吗？
At what time does the pharmacy open (close)?	*Yàofáng jídiǎn kāi (guān)?*	药房几点开（关）？
Do you sell Western medicine?	*Yǒu mài Xīyào ma?*	有卖西药吗？
I don't want any traditional Chinese medicine.	*Wǒ búyào Zhōngyào.*	我不要中药。
I need something for ____.	*Wǒ yào zhì ____ de yào.*	我要治____的药。
▪ an allergy	*gùomǐn*	过敏
▪ a cold	*shāngfēng*	伤风
▪ constipation	*bìanmì*	便秘
▪ a cough	*késòu*	咳嗽
▪ diarrhea	*xìe dùzi*	泻肚子
▪ a fever	*fāshāo*	发烧
▪ the flu	*líuxíngxìng gǎnmào*	流行性感冒
▪ hay fever	*hūafěn rè*	花粉热
▪ a headache	*tóutòng*	头痛
▪ insomnia	*shīmían*	失眠
▪ nausea	*zùo ǒu*	作呕

c = ts; *q* = ch; *x* = sh; *z* = dz; *zh* = j

■ sunburn	*pífū shàijiāo*	皮肤晒焦
■ a toothache	*yá tòng*	牙痛
■ an upset stomach	*dùzi tòng*	肚子痛
It's an emergency.	*Zhè shì jízhěn.*	这是急诊。
How long will it take?	*Yào duōjiǔ?*	要多久？
When can I pick it up?	*Shénme shíhòu qǔ yào?*	什么时候取药？
I would like ____.	*Wó xiǎngyào ____.*	我想要___。
■ adhesive tape	*jiāobù*	胶布
■ alcohol	*jiǔjīng*	酒精
■ an antacid	*kàngsuān yào*	抗酸药
■ an antiseptic	*xiāodú jì*	消毒剂
■ aspirin	*āsīpǐlín*	阿司匹林
■ bandages	*bēngdài*	绷带
■ corn plasters	*jīyǎn gāoyào*	鸡眼膏药
■ absorbent cotton	*míanhūa*	棉花
■ cough drops	*késòu yào*	咳嗽药
■ cough syrup	*késòu tángjīang*	咳嗽糖浆
■ eardrops	*ěr yàoshuǐ*	耳药水
■ eyedrops	*yǎn yàoshuǐ*	眼药水
■ a (mild) laxative	*(qīng de) xièyào*	(轻的) 泻药
■ milk of magnesia	*yǎnghùaméi rǔyè*	氧化镁乳液
■ suppositories	*zùoyào*	坐药
■ a thermometer	*wēndù jì*	温度计
■ tincture of iodine	*díanjiǔ*	碘酒

■ tranquilizers	*zhènjìng jì*	镇静剂
■ vitamins	*wéishēng sù*	维生素

DOCTORS

You never know when you might need a doctor while you are on vacation. In China you are likely to run into physicians with a wide range of skills and training. Many are schooled in traditional Chinese remedies as well as Western medicine.

Larger Chinese cities usually have one or more state-run hospitals designated for the care of foreigners where English is spoken. These may sometimes have equipment that is quite modern, though in general, standards lag behind the West. There are other alternatives as well. Several large cities have modern joint-venture clinics that are staffed with foreign doctors and other health professionals.

Medical evacuation can be arranged in emergency situations through foreign embassies and international health organizations.

If your doctor does not speak English, the following phrases and expressions will help you communicate.

I don't feel well.	*Wǒ bú tài shūfu.* 我不太舒服。
I'm sick.	*Wǒ bìng le.* 我病了。
I want to see a doctor.	*Wǒ yào kàn yīshēng.* 我要看医生。
Is there a doctor who speaks English?	*Yǒu néng shuō Yīngwén de yīshēng ma?* 有能说英文的医生吗？
Where is his office?	*Tā de zhěnsuǒ zài nálǐ?* 他的诊所在哪里？

c = ts; *q* = ch; *x* = sh; *z* = dz; *zh* = j

I'm dizzy.	*Wǒ tóuyūn.*	我头晕。
I feel weak.	*Wó gǎndào shūairùo wúlì.* 我感到衰弱无力。	
I want to sit down for a while.	*Wó xǐang zùo xìalái.* 我想坐下来。	
My temperature is normal (37°C).	*Wǒ de tǐwēn zhèngcháng (Shèshì sānshíqī dù).* 我的体温正常（摄氏三十七度）。	

PARTS OF THE BODY

abdomen	*dùzi*	肚子
ankle	*jǐaohúai*	脚踝
appendix	*lánwěi*	阑尾
arm	*shǒubei*	手臂
back	*bèi*	背
breast	*rǔfáng*	乳房
chest	*xīongqīang*	胸腔
chin	*xìaba*	下巴
ear	*ěrdūo*	耳朵
elbow	*shóuzhǒu*	手肘
eye	*yǎnjīng*	眼睛
face	*lǐan*	脸
finger	*shóuzhǐ*	手指
foot	*jǐao*	脚
forehead	*tóu é*	头额
groin	*shǔxībù*	鼠蹊部
gums	*yáyín*	牙龈
hand	*shǒu*	手

head	*tóu*	头
heart	*xīnzàng*	心脏
heel	*jǐao hòugēn*	脚后跟
hip	*túnbù*	臀部
knee	*xī*	膝
leg	*tǔ*	腿
lips	*chún*	唇
mouth	*zǔiba*	嘴巴
neck	*bózi*	脖子
nipple	*rǔtóu*	乳头
nose	*bízi*	鼻子
penis	*yīnjīng*	阴茎
shoulder	*jīanbǎng*	肩膀
skin	*pífū*	皮肤
testicle	*gǎowán*	睾丸
throat	*hóulóng*	喉咙
toe	*jíaozhǐ*	脚趾
tonsils	*bǐantáo xìan*	扁桃腺
tooth	*yáchǐ*	牙齿
vagina	*yīndào*	阴道
waist	*yāo*	腰
wrist	*shóuwǎnzi*	手腕子

TELLING THE DOCTOR

I have ____.	*Wǒ ____.*	我____。
■ an abscess	*yǒu nóngzhǒng*	有脓肿
■ a broken bone	*gǔtóu dùanle*	骨头断了

c = ts; *q* = ch; *x* = sh; *z* = dz; *zh* = j

■ a bruise	*cāshāng le*	擦伤了
■ a burn	*shāoshāng le*	烧伤了
■ the chills	*fā lěng*	发冷
■ a cold	*gǎnmào le*	感冒了
■ cramps	*chōujīn le*	抽筋了
■ a cut	*bèi gēshāng le*	被割伤了
■ diarrhea	*xiè dùzi le*	泻肚子了
■ dysentery	*yǒu lìji*	有痢疾
■ a fever	*fāshāo le*	发烧了
■ a fracture	*gǔtóu zhédùan le*	骨头折断了
■ a headache	*tóutòng*	头痛
■ an infection	*fāyán le*	发炎了
■ something in my eye	*yán lǐtóu yǒu dōngxi*	眼里头有东西
■ a sore throat	*hóulóng tòng*	喉咙痛
■ a stomachache	*dùzi tòng*	肚子痛
■ a wound	*shòushāng le*	受伤了

I am constipated.	*Wó yǒu biànmì.*	我有便秘。
I have swollen glands.	*Wǒ de xiàntǐ zhǒng le.* 我的腺体肿了。	
It hurts me here.	*Wǒ zhèli tòng.*	我这里痛。
My whole body hurts.	*Wǒ quánshēn tòng.*	我全身痛。
My ____ hurts.	*Wǒ de ____ tòng.*	我的____痛。
■ back	*bèi*	背
■ buttocks	*pìgu*	屁股
■ leg	*tǔi*	腿
■ shoulder	*jiānbǎng*	肩膀

■ throat	*hóulóng*	喉咙
■ thumb	*dà múzhǐ*	大拇指

I've had this pain since yesterday.	*Wǒ cóng zuótiān jiù tòng le.*	我从昨天就痛了。

There's (no) history of _____ in my family.	*Wǒ jiā (méi) yǒu _____ de bìnglì.*	我家（没）有_____的病历。

■ asthma	*qìchuǎn bìng*	气喘病
■ diabetes	*tángniào bìng*	糖尿病

I'm allergic to antibiotics (penicillin).	*Wǒ duì kàngshēng sù (pánníxīlín) guòmǐn.*	我对抗生素（盘尼西林）过敏。

I have a pain in my chest.	*Wó gǎndào xiōngqiāng tòng.*	我感到胸腔痛。

I had a heart attack _____ years ago.	*Wǒ _____ nían qían fāguò xīnzàng bìng.*	我_____年前发过心脏病。

I have never been vaccinated against _____.	*Wǒ hái méiyóu dǎ _____ yùfángzhēn.*	我还没有打_____预防针。

■ cholera	*huòlùan*	霍乱
■ diphtheria	*báihóu*	白喉
■ hepatitis A	*jiǎxíng gānyán*	甲型肝炎
■ hepatitis B	*yǐxíng gānyán*	乙型肝炎
■ hepatitis C	*bǐngxíng gānyán*	丙型肝炎
■ polio	*xiǎoér mábìzhèng*	小儿麻痹症
■ smallpox	*tiānhuā*	天花
■ tetanus	*pò shāngfēng*	破伤风

c = ts; *q* = ch; *x* = sh; *z* = dz; *zh* = j

■ typhoid fever	*shānghán*	伤寒
■ yellow fever	*hùangrè bìng*	黄热病

My blood type is ____.	*Wǒde xǐexíng shì ____.*	我的血型是____。

I have never had ____.	*Wǒ cónglái méiyǒu déguò ____.*	我从来没有得过____。
■ chicken pox	*shǔidòu*	水痘
■ German measles	*Déguo mázhěn*	德国麻疹
■ measles	*mázhěn*	麻疹
■ mumps	*liúxíngxìng sāixìanyán*	流行性腮腺炎

I'm currently taking this medicine.	*Wǒ xìanzài yòng zhèige yào.*	我现在用这个药。
I'm pregnant.	*Wǒ húaiyùn le.*	我怀孕了。
I feel all right now.	*Wǒ xìanzài hǎoxīe le.*	我现在好些了。
I feel a lot better.	*Wó hǎo dūo le.*	我好多了。
I feel worse.	*Wó gǎndào gèng bù shūfu.*	我感到更不舒服。

Do I have ____?	*Wó yǒu ____ ma?*	我有____吗？
■ appendicitis	*lánwěi yán*	阑尾炎
■ the flu	*liúxíngxìng gǎnmào*	流行性感冒
■ tonsilitis	*bǐantáoxìan yán*	扁桃腺炎
■ AIDS	*aìzībìng*	爱滋病
■ diabetes	*tángnìao bìng*	糖尿病
■ a fever	*fāshāo*	发烧

■ gonorrhea	*línbìng*	淋病
■ hemorrhoids	*zhìchuāng*	痔疮
■ high blood pressure	*gāo xuěyā*	高血压
■ low blood pressure	*dī xuěyā*	低血压
■ syphillis	*méidú*	梅毒
■ tuberculosis	*fèibìng*	肺病
■ an ulcer	*kùiyáng*	溃疡
■ venereal disease	*xìngbìng*	性病

Is it serious?	*Yánzhòng ma?*	严重吗？
Is it contagious?	*Chúanrǎn ma?* 传染吗？	
Do I have to go to the hospital?	*Wǒ xūyào shàng yīyuàn ma?* 我需要上医院吗？	
When can I continue my trip?	*Wǒ shénme shíhòu kéyǐ jìxù lǚxíng?* 我什么时候可以继续旅行？	

DOCTOR'S INSTRUCTIONS

Please open your mouth.	*Qíng bá zǔi zhāngkāi.* 请把嘴张开。
Please stick out your tongue.	*Qíng bǎ shétóu shēn chūlái.* 请把舌头伸出来。
Cough.	*Késòu.* 咳嗽。
Breathe deeply.	*Shēn hūxī.* 深呼吸。

c = ts; *q* = ch; *x* = sh; *z* = dz; *zh* = j

Please take off your clothing.	*Qǐng bǎ yīfu tuōdiào.*	请把衣服脱掉。
Lie down.	*Tǎngxià.*	躺下。
Stand up.	*Zhàn qǐlái.*	站起来。
Please get dressed.	*Qǐng chuān yī.*	请穿衣。

PATIENT

Are you going to give me a prescription?	*Nǐ yào géi wǒ kāi yàofāng ma?*	你要给我开药方吗？
What's the dosage for this medicine?	*Zhèige yào zěnme yòngfǎ?*	这个药怎么用法？
How long do I have to stay in bed?	*Wǒ zài chuángshàng yào tǎng dūojǐu?*	我在床上要躺多久？
I don't wish to take Chinese traditional medicine.	*Wǒ bú yào chī Zhōngyào.*	我不要吃中药。
Can you prescribe some Western medicine, please?	*Nǐ néng géi wǒ kāi Xīyào ma?*	你能给我开西药吗？
I don't wish to undergo acupuncture.	*Wǒ bù xǐang yòng zhēnjǐu zhì.*	我不想用针灸治。
Thank you very much.	*Fēicháng xièxie nǐ.*	非常谢谢你。
What is the fee?	*Fèiyòng dūoshǎo?*	费用多少？
I wish to be evacuated to Hong Kong.	*Wǒ xīwàng bèi sòng dào Xīanggǎng qù.*	我希望被送到香港去。

Please inform the U.S. Embassy (Consulate) to make arrangements.	*Qǐng tōngzhī Měiguó Dàshíguǎn (Lǐngshìguǎn) zuòchū ānpái.* 请通知美国大使馆（领事馆）作出安排。

IN THE HOSPITAL (ACCIDENTS)

Help!	*Jiùmìng!*	救命！
Call a doctor, quickly!	*Gǎnkùai jìao yīshēng!* 赶快叫医生！	
Call an ambulance, quickly!	*Gǎnkùai jìao jìuhù chē!* 赶快叫救护车！	
Take me (him, her) to the hopsital.	*Sòng wǒ (tā) dào yīyùan qù.* 送我（他）到医院去。	
I need first aid.	*Wǒ xūyào jíjìu.* 我需要急救。	

c = ts; *q* = ch; *x* = sh; *z* = dz; *zh* = j

I've fallen.	*Wǒ diējīao le.* 我跌交了。	
I was ____ by a car.	*Wǒ bèi qìchē ____.*	我被汽车____。
▓ knocked down	*chùangdǎo le*	撞倒了
▓ run over	*nǐangùo le*	碾过了
I've had a heart attack.	*Wǒ xīnzàng bìng fāle.*	我心脏病发了。
I ____ myself.	*Wǒ bèi ____ le.*	我被____了。
▓ burned	*shāoshāng*	烧伤
▓ cut	*gēshāng*	割伤
I'm bleeding.	*Wǒ zài líu xǐe.*	我在流血。
I think the bone is ____.	*Wó xíang gǔtóu ____ le.* 我想骨头____了。	
▓ broken	*dùan*	断
▓ dislocated	*tūojìu*	脱臼
▓ fractured	*zhédùan*	折断
My leg is swollen.	*Wǒ de tǔi fāzhǒng.* 我的腿发肿。	
My ankle (wrist) is sprained.	*Wǒ de jǐaohúai (shóuwǎnzi) nǐule.* 我的脚踝（手腕子）扭了。	
I can't move my elbow (knee).	*Wǒ de shóuzhǒu (xīgài) bù néng dòng.* 我的手肘（膝盖）不能动。	

AT THE DENTIST

Chinese dentistry is somewhat behind that of the West. Few foreign residents of China go to local dentists for other than emergency care; for extensive dental work most prefer to see a dentist outside of China.

I have to go to the dentist.	*Wǒ yào qù kàn yáyī.* 我要去看牙医。
Can you recommend a dentisty?	*Nǐ jièshào yīge yáyī hǎo ma?* 你介绍一个牙医好吗？
My tooth hurts a great deal.	*Wǒ de yáchǐ hěn tòng.* 我的牙齿很痛。
I've lost a filling.	*Wǒ de yáchōngtián diūle.* 我的牙充填丢了。
I've broken a tooth.	*Wǒ de yáchǐ duànle.* 我的牙齿断了。
I can't chew.	*Wǒ bù néng yǎo.* 我不能咬。
My gums hurt me.	*Wǒ de yáyíng tòng.* 我的牙龈痛。
Is there an infection?	*Yǒu méi yǒu fāyán?* 有没有发炎？
Can the tooth still be repaired?	*Yá hái néng bǔ ma?* 牙还能补吗？
Must you extract the tooth?	*Yīdìng yào bǎ yá bádiào ma?* 一定要把牙拔掉吗？
I won't have it pulled.	*Wǒ bú yuànyì bádiào.* 我不愿意拔掉。

c = ts; *q* = ch; *x* = sh; *z* = dz; *zh* = j

I will wait and ask my dentist at home.	Wǒ yào huíjiā wèn wǒ de yáyī. 我要回家问我的牙医。	
Can you fill it ____?	Nǐ néng ____ tián ma?	你能____填吗？
■ with amalgam	yòng gǒnghéjīn	用汞合金
■ with gold	yòng jīn	用金
■ with silver	yòng yín	用银
■ temporarily	zhànshí de	暂时的
Can you fix ____?	Nǐ néng bǔ zhèige ____ ma?	你能补这个____吗？
■ this bridge	chǐqiáo	齿桥
■ this crown	chǐguàn	齿冠
■ this denture	jiǎyá	假牙
When should I come back?	Shénme shíhòu zài lái? 什么时候再来？	
What is your fee?	Fèiyòng duōshǎo? 费用多少？	

AT THE EYE DOCTOR/OPTICIAN

My eye ____.	Wǒde yán ____.	我的眼____。
■ hurts	tòng	痛
■ is red	fā hóng	发红
■ is swollen	fā zhǒng	发肿
■ itches	fā yǎng	发痒
My vision is blurred.	Wǒ de yán móhu. 我的眼模糊。	
I lost my glasses.	Wǒde yǎnjìng diūle. 我的眼镜丢了。	

I need a pair of glasses.	*Wǒ yào pèi yīfù yǎnjìng.* 我需要配一副眼镜。
I need a pair of contact lenses.	*Wǒ yào pèi yǐngxíng yǎnjìng.* 我需要配隐形眼镜。
I don't have my prescription.	*Wǒ méiyǒu chǔfāng.* 我没有处方。
Would you examine me, please?	*Qǐng géi wó jǐanchá yíxià.* 请给我检查一下。
I would like a pair of bifocals.	*Wǒ yào yīfù shuānggūang yǎnjìng.* 我要一副双光眼镜。
How long will it take?	*Yào děng dūojǐu?* 要等多久？

COMMUNICATIONS

POST OFFICE

You probably won't have to visit the post office while you are in China, since the majority of major hotels have postal counters that offer most services. Here are some useful phrases.

I want to mail a letter.	*Wǒ yào jì yī fēng xìn.* 我要寄一封信。	
Where's the post office?	*Yóujú zài nálǐ?* 邮局在哪里？	
Where's a mailbox?	*Yóutǒng zài nálǐ?* 邮筒在哪里？	
What is the postage for ____ to the United States?	*Jì ____ dào Měiguó yào dūoshǎo qián?* 寄____到美国要多少钱？	
■ this aerogram	*zhèi zhāng yóujiǎn*	这张邮简
■ this airmail letter	*zhèi fēng hángkōng xìn*	这封航空信
■ this express letter	*zhèi fēng kùai xìn*	这封快信
■ this insured letter	*zhèi fēng bǎojià xìn*	这封保价信
■ this letter	*zhèi fēng xìn*	这封信
■ this registered letter	*zhèi fēng gùahào xìn*	这封挂号信
■ this special delivery letter	*zhèi fēng xìanshí zhūansóng xìn*	这封限时专送信

■ this package	*zhèige bāoguǒ*	这个包裹
■ this postcard	*zhèi zhāng míngxìnpìan*	这张明信片

When will it arrive?	*Shénme shíhòu jìdào?* 什么时候寄到？	
Where can I purchase stamps?	*Nǎli kéyí mǎidào yóupìao?* 哪里可以买到邮票？	
Are there any letters for me?	*Yǒu méi yóu wǒ de xìn?* 有没有我的信？	
My name is ____.	*Wǒ jìao ____.*	我叫____。
I'd like ____.	*Wó xǐangyào ____.*	我想要____。
■ five airmail stamps	*wǔ zhāng hángkōng yóupìao*	五张航空邮票
■ four aerogram	*sì zhāng yóujiǎn*	四张邮简

Need I fill out a customs declaration?	*Wǒ yào tían bàogūan dān ma?* 我要填报关单吗？	
Must I open this for inspection?	*Xūyào dǎkāi jiǎnchá ma?* 需要打开检查吗？	
I didn't bring my passport.	*Wǒ méi dài hùzhào.* 我没带护照。	
I collect stamps.	*Wǒ jī yóupìao.* 我集邮票。	
Do you have any pretty stamps?	*Ní yǒu méi yóu hěn pìaolìang de yóupìao?* 你有没有很漂亮的邮票？	

c = ts; *q* = ch; *x* = sh; *z* = dz; *zh* = j

TELECOMMUNICATIONS

The Chinese government has been moving very quickly in recent years to install new telephone lines. While phone calls can still sometimes be plagued by bad connections, busy signals, and busy circuits, these problems are increasingly becoming things of the past.

You can't make an international or even a domestic long-distance call from just any phone in China; the line must be specially designated for international direct dialing (IDD) or domestic direct dialing (DDD) service. For international calls, it is usually cheaper when the billing is done outside of China, so calling home collect may save you some money. Note, however, that "call-back" services—through which you place a call and automatically receive a call back from another country—are illegal in China.

Recent years have seen a proliferation of cell phones and paging devices in China. Included in the following section is vocabulary for leaving a message with a paging service.

While most Chinese families still do not own computers, this has not stopped the Internet from making extensive inroads into China. Helping this process along is a proliferation of Internet cafés where you can rent the use of a computer and an Internet connection by the hour. This is also useful for travelers who are far from home but still wish to receive e-mail. At the end of this section you will find basic vocabulary for logging in.

Where is a public telephone?	*Nǎli yǒu gōngyòng diànhuà?*	哪里有公用电话？
May I use your phone?	*Wǒ kéyǐ yòng nǐ de diànhùa ma?*	我可以用你的电话吗？
I want to make a(n) ____.	*Wǒ yào dǎ yīge ____ diànhùa.*	我要打一个___电话。
■ international call	*guójì chángtú*	国际长途
■ local call	*běndì*	本地

■ long-distance call	*chángtú*	长途
■ person-to-person call	*jìaorén de chángtú*	叫人的长途
Can I dial direct?	*Néng zhíjīe bō ma?* 能直接拨吗？	
Does this phone have ____?	*Zhèige dìanhùa yǒu ____ ma?* 这个电话有___吗？	
■ domestic direct dialing (DDD)	*gúonèi zhíjīe chángtú bōhào* 国内直接长途拨号	
■ international direct dialing (IDD)	*gúojì zhíjīe chángtú bōhào* 国际直接长途拨号	
How do I get the operator?	*Zǒngjī zěnme dǎ?* 总机怎么打？	
Operator, please connect me with number 6500-2231.	*Zǒngjī, qǐng jīe lìuwǔ línglíng èrèr sānyī hào.* 总机，请接六五零零二二三一号。	
My telephone number is ____.	*Wǒ de dìanhùa hàomǎ shì ____.* 我的电话号码是___。	
Hello?	*Wèi!* 喂！	
Please ____.	*Qǐng ____.* 请___。	
■ connect me with extension 46	*jīe sìlìu hào fēnjī* 接四六号分机	
■ connect me with Mr. Wang	*zhǔan Wáng Xīansheng* 转王先生	

c = ts; *q* = ch; *x* = sh; *z* = dz; *zh* = j

I'd like to speak with ____.	*Wó zhǎo ____.*	我找____。
Is ____ in?	*____ zài ma?*	____在吗？
When will he be back?	*Tā shénme shíhòu húilái?*	他什么时候回来？
It is I.	*Wǒ jiù shì.*	我就是。
Who is calling?	*Qǐng wèn něiwèi?*	请问哪位？
I can't hear.	*Wǒ tīng bù qīng.*	我听不清。
Please speak louder.	*Qǐng dà shēng yīdǐan.*	请大声一点。
Don't hang up.	*Bíe guàdiào.*	别挂掉。
This is ____.	*Wǒ shì ____.*	我是____。
Operator, there is no answer.	*Zǒngjī, méi rén jīe.*	总机，没人接。

The line is busy.	*Zhàn xìan.*	占线。
The number you gave me was wrong.	*Nǐ géi wǒ de hàomǎ cùole.*	你给我的号码错了。
I was cut off.	*Dùanle.*	断了。
I want to leave a message for ____.	*Wó xiǎng líuhùa géi ____.*	我想留话给____。
Where can I go to send a fax?	*Dào nálǐ qù fā chúanzhēn?*	到哪里去发传真？
What is your beeper number?	*Nǐ de hūjǐ hàomǎ shì dūoshǎo?*	你的呼机号码是多少？
I would like to page number 443628.	*Wó xiǎng hū sìsì sānlìu èrbā hào.*	我想呼四四三六二八号。
My surname is ____.	*Wǒ xìng ____.*	我姓____。
My telephone number is ____.	*Wǒ de dìanhùa shì ____.*	我的电话是____。
My extension is ____.	*Wǒ de fēnjī hàomǎ shì ____.*	我的分机号码是____。
Please tell him (her) to call me back.	*Qǐng jìao tā húi wǒ dìanhùa.*	请叫他回我电话。
Please tell him (her) to wait for my call.	*Qǐng jìao tā déng wǒde dìanhùa.*	请叫他等我的电话。
Where can I rent a cell phone?	*Zài nálǐ kéyǐ zūdào shǒujī?*	在哪里可以租到手机？
How much does it cost?	*Yào dūoshǎo qían?*	要多少钱？

c = ts; *q* = ch; *x* = sh; *z* = dz; *zh* = j

Do you charge by the minute?	*Nǐ shì àn shíjīan sùan ma?* 你是按时间算吗？
When must I return it?	*Shénme shíhòu húan?* 什么时候还？
Where can I get on the Internet?	*Dào nǎlǐ qù shàng yīngtèwǎng?* 到哪里去上英特网？
Where is an Internet café?	*Nǎlǐ yǒu yīngtèwǎng kāfēi dìan?* 哪里有英特网咖啡店？
May I use a computer?	*Wǒ kéyǐ yòng jìsùanjī ma?* 我可以用计算机吗？
How much for an hour?	*Yígè xǐaoshí dūoshǎo qían?* 一个小时多少钱？
How do I get on-line?	*Zěnmeyàng shàng wǎng?* 怎么样上网？
I would like to check my e-mail.	*Wó xǐang chá wǒ de dìanzǐ yóujìan.* 我想查我的电子邮件。
I would like to search the Internet.	*Wó xǐang chá Yīngtèwǎng.* 我想查英特网。
How can I find that homepage?	*Zěnmeyàng cái zhǎodédào nèige Wǎngyè?* 怎么样才找得到那个网页？
How fast is this modem?	*Zhèige tíaozhì jǐetíaoqì de sùdù shì dūoshǎo?* 这个调制解调器的速度是多少？
This computer is broken.	*Zhèige jìsùanjī hùaile.* 这个计算机坏了。
I lost my connection.	*Wǒde xìan dùanle.* 我的线断了。

How can I reconnect?	*Zěnmeyàng zài jīeshàng?*
	怎么样再接上？
Where can I print?	*Nálǐ kéyí dǎyìn?*
	哪里可以打印？

GENERAL INFORMATION

TELLING TIME

When the Chinese tell time, they generally state the period of the day before the exact hour. The period between midnight and dawn is the early morning, or **qīngzǎo**. From about 6:00 A.M. to noon is the morning, **zǎoshàng**. Noon to 6:00 P.M. is **xiàwǔ**, the afternoon. And from 6:00 P.M. until midnight is **wǎnshàng**. So 7:00 P.M. is expressed as **wǎnshàng qīdiǎn**, and 11:30 A.M. is **zǎoshàng shíyīdiǎn bàn**. Only when the time of day isn't specified does one say, simply, **liùdiǎn bàn** (6:30).

Official time is sometimes expressed according to the 24-hour clock. You will find that trains and planes are often scheduled using these terms. The 24-hour clock is never used in normal conversation, however, so a plane departing at 15:00 is still said to leave at **xiàwǔ sāndiǎn**, or "three in the afternoon."

Remember that all of China is officially in one time zone. There are not different zones for different regions as there are elsewhere in the world, so when it is six in the morning in Beijing, it is six in Sichuan Province, even though it may be quite dark there.

What time is it?	*Jídiǎn zhōng?*	几点钟？
■ hour	*xiǎoshí; zhōngtóu*	小时；钟头
■ half an hour	*bàn xiǎoshí*	半小时
■ an hour and a half	*yī xiǎoshí bàn*	一小时半
■ quarter (15 minutes)	*kè*	刻
■ minute	*fēn*	分
■ second	*miǎo*	秒

It is now ____.	*Xiànzài shì____.*	现在是____。
■ noon	*zhōngwǔ*	中午
■ 1:05	*yīdiǎn língwǔ fēn*	一点零五分
■ 2:10	*liángdiǎn shí fēn*	两点十分
■ 3:15	*sāndiǎn shíwǔ fēn; sāndiǎn yīkè*	三点十五分；三点一刻
■ 4:20	*sìdiǎn èrshí fēn*	四点二十分
■ 5:25	*wúdiǎn èrshíwǔ fēn*	五点二十五分
■ 6:30	*liùdiǎn sānshí fēn; liùdiǎn bàn*	六点三十分；六点半
■ 7:35	*qīdiǎn sānshíwǔ fēn*	七点三十五分
■ 8:40	*bādiǎn sìshí fēn*	八点四十分

c = ts; *q* = ch; *x* = sh; *z* = dz; *zh* = j

■ 9:45	*jiŭdian sìshíwŭ fēn; jiŭdiǎn jiān sānkè*	九点四十五分； 九点三刻
■ 10:50	*shídian wǔshí fēn*	十点五十分
■ 11:55	*shíyīdiǎn wǔshíwǔ fēn*	十一点五十五分
■ 8:00	*bādiǎn zhōng*	八点钟
■ midnight	*wǔyè*	午夜

EXPRESSIONS OF TIME

When?	*Shénme shíhòu?*	什么时候？
At what time?	*Jídiǎn?*	几点？
■ at ____ o'clock	*zài ____ diǎn zhōng*	在____点钟
■ at noon	*zài zhōngwǔ*	在中午
■ at 4:00 P.M. sharp	*zài xìawǔ sìdiǎn zhěng* 在下午四点正	
■ an hour from now	*zài yīge zhōngtóu* 再一个钟头	
■ not before 2:00 A.M.	*bú yào zài zǎoshàng líangdiǎn yǐqían* 不要在早上两点以前	
■ after 3:00 P.M.	*xìawǔ sāndiǎn yǐhòu* 下午三点以后	
■ at about 9:00 P.M.	*dàyuē wǎnshàng jíudiǎn* 大约晚上九点	
■ between six and seven o'clock	*zài lìudiǎn hé qīdiǎn zhījīan* 在六点和七点之间	

■ until five   *yīzhí dào wúdiǎn*
  o'clock   一直到五点

Since what time ____?	*Cóng jídiǎn kāishǐ ____?* 从几点开始____?	
per hour	*méi xiǎoshí*	每小时
three hours ago	*sānge siǎoshí yǐqián* 三个小时以前	
early	*zǎo*	早
late	*wǎn*	晚
late in arriving	*chídào le*	迟到了
on time	*zhǔnshí*	准时
in the morning	*zài zǎoshàng*	在早上
in the afternoon	*zài xiàwǔ*	在下午
in the evening	*zài wǎnshàng*	在晚上

---

c = ts; *q* = ch; *x* = sh; *z* = dz; *zh* = j

DAYS OF THE WEEK

What day is today?	*Jīntīan xīngqī jǐ?*	今天星期几？
Today is ____.	*Jīntīan shì ____.*	今天是____。
■ Monday	*Xīngqīyī*	星期一
■ Tuesday	*Xīngqīèr*	星期二
■ Wednesday	*Xīngqīsān*	星期三
■ Thursday	*Xīngqīsì*	星期四
■ Friday	*Xīngqīwǔ*	星期五
■ Saturday	*Xīngqīliù*	星期六
■ Sunday	*Xīngqītīan*	星期天
last Monday	*shàngge Xīngqīyī*	上个星期一
this Wednesday	*zhèige Xīngqīsān*	这个星期三
next Tuesday	*xìage Xīngqīèr*	下个星期二

NOTE: Use the above expressions and similar ones carefully. The Chinese use **zhèige** to describe days within the current week, beginning this past Monday and ending this coming Sunday. Any day before this past Monday is considered part of last week, and is described with **shàngge**. And similarly, a day after this coming Sunday is not part of this week and can't be described with the expression "zhèige"; as part of next week it is properly spoken of as **xìage**.

birthday	*shēngrì*	生日
the day after tomorrow	*hòutīan*	后天
the day before	*qían yī tīan*	前一天
the day before yesterday	*qíantīan*	前天

during the day	*zài báitīan*	在白天
during the evening	*zài wǎnshàng*	在晚上
during the week	*zài zhōunèi*	在周内
every day	*měitīan*	每天
in five days	*wǔtīan yǐhòu*	五天以后
from this day on	*cóng jīntīan qǐ*	从今天起
holiday	*jíerì*	节日
last week	*shàngge xīngqī*	上个星期
the next day	*dìèr tīan*	第二天
next week	*xìage xīngqī*	下个星期
six days ago	*lìutīan yǐqián*	六天以前
this week	*zhèige xīngqī*	这个星期
today	*jīntīan*	今天
tomorrow	*míngtīan*	明天
two days ago	*dà qíantīan;* *lǐang tīan qían*	大前天；两天前
two days from now	*dà hòutīan*	大后天
vacation day	*jìarì*	假日
within five days	*wǔtīan yǐnèi*	五天以内
yesterday	*zúotīan*	昨天
the week after next	*xìaxìage xīngqī*	下下个星期
the weekend	*zhōumò*	周末
a week from today	*xìa xīngqī de* *tóng yī tīan*	下星期的同一天

c = ts; *q* = ch; *x* = sh; *z* = dz; *zh* = j

MONTHS OF THE YEAR

January	*Yīyuè*	一月
February	*Èryuè*	二月
March	*Sānyuè*	三月
April	*Sìyuè*	四月
May	*Wǔyuè*	五月
June	*Liùyuè*	六月
July	*Qīyuè*	七月
August	*Bāyuè*	八月
September	*Jiuyuè*	九月
October	*Shíyuè*	十月
November	*Shíyīyuè*	十一月
December	*Shíèryuè*	十二月
last month	*shàngge yuè*	上个月
next month	*xiage yuè*	下个月
this month	*zhèige yuè*	这个月
two months ago	*liǎngge yuè yǐqián*	两个月以前
in two months	*liǎngge yuè yǐhòu*	两个月以后
the month after next	*xiaxiage yuè*	下下个月
the month before last	*qiange yuè*	前个月
during the month of ____	*zài ____ yuè yǐnèi*	在____月以内

since the month of ____	*cóng ____ yùe kāishǐ*	从____月开始
every month	*měige yùe*	每个月
What is today's date?	*Jīntīan jǐhào?*	今天几号？
Today is ____.	*Jīntīan shì ____*	今天是____。
■ Monday, May 11	*Wǔyùe shíyī rì, Xīngqīyī* 五月十一日，星期一	
■ Tuesday, June 1	*Lìuyùe yī rì, Xīngqīèr* 六月一日，星期二	

NOTE: When weekdays and dates are given together, as in the two examples above, the date precedes the day of the week. It is expressed just the opposite of the way it is in English.

all year	*qúannían*	全年
during the year	*zài yīnían yǐnèi*	在一年以内
last year	*qù nían*	去年
next year	*míngnían*	明年
per year; every year	*měinían*	每年
the year after next	*hòunían*	后年
the year before last	*qíannían*	前年

THE FOUR SEASONS

spring	*chūnjì*	春季
summer	*xìajì*	夏季

c = ts; *q* = ch; *x* = sh; *z* = dz; *zh* = j

fall	*qiūjì*	秋季
winter	*dōngjì*	冬季
in the springtime	*zài chūntīan*	在春天
in the summertime	*zài xìatīan*	在夏天
before the fall	*qiūjì yǐqián*	秋季以前
after the winter	*dōngjì yǐhòu*	冬季以后

WEATHER

What is the weather like?	*Tīanqì zěnmeyàng?*	天气怎么样？
It is bad.	*Bùhǎo.*	不好。
It is beautiful.	*Hǎo jíle.*	好极了。
It is cold.	*Mán lěng de.*	蛮冷的。
It is very cold.	*Hén lěng.*	很冷。
It is comfortable.	*Hěn shūfu.*	很舒服。
It is cool.	*Hěn líangkùai.*	很凉快。
It is foggy.	*Yǒu wù.*	有雾。
It is hot.	*Mán rè de.*	蛮热的。
It ls very hot.	*Hěn rè.*	很热。
It is raining.	*Xìa yǔ le.*	下雨了。
It is snowing.	*Xìa xǔe le.*	下雪了。
It is sunny.	*Yǒu tàiyàng.*	有太阳。
It is windy.	*Fēng dà.*	风大。

It's too hot to go out.	*Tài rè le, bù chūqù ba.*	太热了， 不出去吧。
Is it going to rain today?	*Jīntiān huì xià yǔ ma?*	今天会下雨吗？
It's very dry.	*Hěn gānzào.*	很干燥。
It's very humid.	*Hěn mēnrè.*	很焖热。
Today's temperature is ____.	*Jīntiān de wēndù shì ____.*	今天的温度是____。

■ 75 degrees Fahrenheit   *qīshíwǔ Huáshì dù*
七十五华氏度

■ 20 degrees Centigrade   *èrshí Shèshì dù*
二十摄氏度

TEMPERATURE CONVERSIONS

To change Fahrenheit to **Centigrade**: subtract 32 and multiply by $\frac{5}{9}$.

To change **Centigrade** to Fahrenheit: multiply by $\frac{9}{5}$ and add 32.

DIRECTIONS

above	*zài shàngmiàn de*	在上面的
back	*hòumiàn*	后面
below	*zài xiàmiàn de*	在下面的
down	*xiàmiàn*	下面
east	*dōngfāng*	东方
front	*qiánmiàn*	前面

c = ts; *q* = ch; *x* = sh; *z* = dz; *zh* = j

left	*zuǒbiān*	左边
middle	*zhōngjiān*	中间
north	*běifāng*	北方
right	*yòubiān*	右边
south	*nánfāng*	南方
up	*shàngmiàn*	上面
west	*xīfāng*	西方

IMPORTANT SIGNS

小心	*xiǎoxīn*	be careful
非营业时间	*fēi yíngyè shíjiān*	closed for business
危险	*wéixiǎn*	danger
不许进入	*bùxǔ jìnrù*	do not enter
紧急出口	*jǐnjí chūkǒu*	emergency exit
闲人免入	*xiánrén miǎnrù*	employees only
入口	*rùkǒu*	entrance
出口	*chūkǒu*	exit
医院	*yīyuàn*	hospital
询问处	*xúnwèn chù*	information desk
女厕所	*nǚ cèsuǒ*	ladies' room
男厕所	*nán cèsuǒ*	men's room
不许停车	*bùxǔ tíng chē*	no parking
请勿吸烟	*qǐng wù xīyān*	no smoking

请勿吐痰	*qǐng wù tǔtán*	no spitting
非饮用水	*fēi yǐnyòng shuǐ*	nonpotable water
开	*kāi*	open
月台	*yùetái*	platform
请勿动手	*qǐng wù dòngshǒu*	please don't touch
拉	*lā*	pull
推	*tūi*	push
停止	*tíngzhǐ*	stop
厕所	*cèsǔo*	toilets
休息室	*xīuxi shì*	waiting room

STANDARD MEASUREMENTS

centimeter	*límǐ; gōngfēn*	厘米；公分
foot	*yīngchǐ*	英尺
inch	*yīngcùn*	英寸
kilometer	*gōnglǐ*	公里
meter	*mǐ; gōngchǐ*	米；公尺
mile	*yīnglǐ*	英里
millimeter	*háomǐ*	毫米
yard	*mǎ*	码

NOTE: Linear measurements are easily converted into square or cubic measurements in Chinese. For square

c = ts; q = ch; x = sh; z = dz; zh = j

measurements, simply attach the prefix **píngfāng** (平方), as in **píngfāng mǐ**, square meters. For cubic measurements, the prefix is **lìfāng** (立方).

acre	*yīngmǒu*	英亩
gallon	*jīalún*	加仑
gram	*gōngkè*	公克
hectare	*gōngqǐng*	公顷
kilogram	*gōngjīn*	公斤
liter	*shēng*	升
metric ton	*gōngdùn*	公吨
milligram	*háokè*	毫克
milliliter	*háoshēng*	毫升
ounce	*àngsī*	盎斯
pint	*pǐntūo*	品脱
pound	*bàng*	磅
quart	*kūatūo*	夸脱
ton	*dùn*	吨

CENTIMETERS/INCHES

The Chinese use the metric system for measurement, and they probably won't understand you if you talk in feet and inches. For many situations you'll probably want to use the following conversion tables.

CONVERSION TABLES

Inches		Millimeters	Cu. Feet		Cu. Meters
0.039	1	25.40	35.315	1	0.028
0.079	2	50.80	70.629	2	0.057
0.118	3	76.20	105.943	3	0.085
0.157	4	101.60	141.258	4	0.113
0.197	5	127.00	176.572	5	0.142

Feet		Meters	Cu. Yards		Cu. Meters
3.281	1	0.305	1.308	1	0.765
6.562	2	0.610	2.616	2	1.529
9.843	3	0.914	3.924	3	2.294
13.123	4	1.219	5.232	4	3.058
16.404	5	1.524	6.540	5	3.823

Yards		Meters	Pints		Liters
1.094	1	0.914	1.761	1	0.568
2.187	2	1.829	3.521	2	1.136
3.281	3	2.743	5.282	3	1.704
4.375	4	3.658	7.043	4	2.272
5.468	5	4.572	8.804	5	2.840

Miles		Kilometers	Gallons		Liters
0.621	1	1.609	0.220	1	4.546
1.243	2	3.219	0.440	2	9.092
1.864	3	4.828	0.660	3	13.638
2.485	4	6.437	0.880	4	18.184
3.107	5	8.047	1.101	5	22.730

Sq. Feet		Sq. Meters	Ounces		Grams
10.764	1	0.093	0.035	1	28.350
21.528	2	0.186	0.071	2	56.699
32.292	3	0.279	0.106	3	85.049
43.056	4	0.372	0.141	4	113.398
53.819	5	0.465	0.176	5	141.748

c = ts; q = ch; x = sh; z = dz; zh = j

Sq. Yards		Sq. Meters	Pounds		Kilograms
1.196	1	0.836	2.205	1	0.454
2.392	2	1.672	4.409	2	0.907
3.588	3	2.508	6.614	3	1.361
4.784	4	3.345	8.819	4	1.814
5.980	5	4.181	11.023	5	2.268

To use this table, refer to the 1–5 numbers in the center columns. For example, 1 in the feet-meters section means that 1 foot equals 0.305 meter and that 1 meter equals 3.281 feet.

To convert centimeters to inches, multiply by .39. To convert inches to centimeters, multiply by 2.54.

Centimeters

Inches

LIQUID MEASUREMENTS

1 liter = 1.06 quarts
4 liters = 1.06 gallons

For quick, approximate conversions, multiply the number of gallons by 4 to get liters. Divide the number of liters by 4 to get gallons.

TEMPERATURE

°C	0	5	10	15	20	25	30	35	40	60	80	100
°F	32	40	50	60	70	75	85	95	105	140	175	212

SPEED

Kilometers/hour	30	40	45	50	60	80	90	110	150	160
Miles/hour		19	25	28	31	37	50	56	68	93	100

TIRE PRESSURES

lb/sq in	20	22	24	26	28	30	32	34
kg/sq cm	1.41	1.55	1.69	1.83	1.97	2.11	2.25	2.39

CHINESE TRADITIONAL MEASUREMENTS

Though China officially uses the metric system, some traditional measurements survive and you may come across them. Here are the most commonly used ones with their equivalents.

c = ts; q = ch; x = sh; z = dz; zh = j

UNIT	PRONUN-CIATION	CHINESE CHARACTER	EQUIVALENTS
Chinese inch	*cùn*	寸	3.33 centimeters 1.31 inches
Chinese foot	*chǐ*	尺	.33 meter 1.09 feet
10 Chinese feet	*zhàng*	丈	3.33 meters 3.65 yards
Chinese mile	*lǐ*	里	.5 kilometers .31 mile
Chinese ounce	*liǎng*	两	.05 kilogram 1.76 ounces
catty	*jīn*	斤	.5 kilogram 1.1 pounds
picul	*dàn*	担	50 kilograms
Chinese quart	*shēng*	升	1.76 pints .22 gallon
Chinese peck	*dǒu*	斗	10 liters
Chinese acre	*mǔ*	亩	.067 hectare .16 acre
Chinese hectare	*qǐng*	顷	6.67 hectares

PUBLIC HOLIDAYS AND TRADITIONAL CELEBRATIONS

There are only four official public holidays in the People's Republic of China, which, with three days off for Spring Festival and two days for National Day, total nine days of rest. Note that people in Hong Kong and Taiwan and other overseas Chinese do not necessarily celebrate all of these holidays.

PUBLIC HOLIDAYS

January 1	New Year's Day, or **Yúandàn** (元旦). Also called **Xīnnían** (新年).
January or February	Spring Festival, or **Chūnjíe** (春节). A three-day celebration marking the lunar new year. The exact dates change from year to year because the holiday is still set according to the lunar calendar.
May 1	International Socialist Labor Day, **Láodòngjíe** (劳动节). Also referred to as **Wǔyī** (五一), meaning the first of May.
October 1, 2	National Day, or **Gúoqìng** (国庆). Anniversary of the founding of the People's Republic of China in 1949.

In addition to the public holidays, there are also some traditional Chinese festivals that are widely observed. The dates of these holidays vary from year to year because they are set by the lunar calendar. The most important ones are listed below.

CELEBRATIONS

January or February	Lantern Festival, or **Yúanxīaojíe** (元宵节). This occurs on the fifteenth day of the lunar new year and marks the end of the Spring Festival. It is a colorful festival during which people, especially children, carry lanterns through the streets and marketplaces in the evening. It is also a time for eating boiled dumplings called **tāngyúan** (汤圆), which are small glutinous rice balls filled with sesame paste or red bean paste.
April	Pure Brightness Festival, or **Qīngmíngjíe** (清明节). This is a spring holiday to honor ancestors. Traditional activities include the burning of mock paper money (for use by the departed in the next world) and the sweeping off of the graves of one's ancestors. The holiday is no longer widely celebrated in the PRC.

c = ts; q = ch; x = sh; z = dz; zh = j

CELEBRATIONS

| June | Dragon Boat Festival, or **Dūanwǔjíe** (端午节). The fifth day of the fifth lunar month. Commemorates the death of Qū Yúan, a patriotic poet of the Warring States Period (475–221 B.C.). Festivities include dragon boat races and the eating of **zòngzi** (粽子), glutinous rice dumplings with various fillings, steamed in lotus leaves. |
| September | Mid-autumn Festival, or **Zhōngqīujíe** (中秋节). Celebrated on the fifteenth day of the eighth lunar month. Commemorates an unsuccessful rebellion against the Mongolian rulers of the Yuan Dynasty (A.D. 1271–1368), but is also a kind of harvest festival. Traditional activities include family reunions and the consumption of **yùebǐng** (月饼), or moon cakes, a round lotus-seed pastry. |

TIMELINE OF CHINESE HISTORY

B.C.

ca. 2697	Legendary Yellow Emperor, common ancestor of the Chinese race, assumes throne. Legend credits him with the invention of the compass.
1766–1066	Shang Dynasty. The Great Bronze Age.
1066–256	Zhou Dynasty. Age of the Great Philosophers.
ca. sixth or seventh century	Laozi (Lao Tzu), founder of Taoism, describes the harmonious relationship between human individuals and the universal order, and advocates pacifism.
551–479	Kongzi (Confucius), the great thinker and teacher, expounds theories of ethics and statecraft.
479–438	Mozi (Mo Tzu) puts forth theory of religious piety and universal love.

fourth to third century	Extensive well building and construction of canals and irrigation systems.
399–295	Zhuangzi (Chuang Tzu) describes theory of infinity and advocates intellectual and artistic freedom.
371–289	Mengzi (Mencius), the most famous disciple of Confucius, authors theory of the goodness of human nature.
360–290	Sunzi (Sun Tzu) writes of *The Art of War*.
221	Qin Shihuang unites China and becomes its first emperor. He unifies the measuring system and written language and builds a transportation network.
214	The Great Wall is completed.
ca. 90	Sima Qian (Ssu-ma Ch'ien) compiles *Grand Historical Records*, 130 volumes of Chinese history.
A.D.	
65	Buddhism is introduced into northern China.
105	Paper is invented by Cai Lun.
600	Block printing is invented by Bi Sheng.
405–972	The Golden Age of Buddhist Philosophy in China.
610	Canal system, including the Grand Canal linking Beijing to Yangzhou on the Changjiang (Yangtse River), is completed.
eighth century	Li Bai (Li Po, 701–761) and Du Fu (Tu Fu, 712–770), famous Tang Dynasty poets.
ca. tenth century	Gunpowder is invented.
960–1644	Revival of Confucianism.
1215	Beijing falls to Genghis Khan.
1271	Kublai Khan declares himself Emperor of China and establishes the Yuan (Mongol) Dynasty.

c = ts; q = ch; x = sh; z = dz; zh = j

1275	Marco Polo visits China.
1601	Jesuit Matteo Ricci arrives in Beijing.
1644	Manchus conquer China and establish the Qing Dynasty.
1745	*The Dream of the Red Chamber* is written by Cao Xueqin.
1839–1842	The Opium (Anglo-Chinese) War.
1842	Treaty of Nanking opens five Chinese ports, including Hong Kong, to the British.
1850–1864	The Taiping Rebellion, a peasant uprising.
1866	Sun Yat-sen, founder of modern China, is born.
1887	Chiang Kai-shek is born.
1893	Mao Zedong (Mao Tse-tung) is born.
1894–1895	First Sino-Japanese War.
1899	U.S. Secretary of State John Hay issues "Open Door Notes" seeking equal access to Chinese markets for American traders.
1900	The Boxer Rebellion, violent popular resistance against the foreign presence in China.
1905	Sun Yat-sen establishes the "Three Principles of the People" (Nationalism, Democracy, and Socialism).
1908	Death of Ci Xi (Tzu Hsi), the Empress Dowager, who dominated Chinese politics for nearly half a century.
1911	The Qing Dynasty is overthrown; the Republic of China is proclaimed.
1916	General Yuan Shikai fails in an attempt to reestablish the monarchy.
1919	The May Fourth Movement, a movement by Chinese intellectuals espousing a number of cultural and political reforms.
1921	The Communist Party is established.
1925	Sun Yat-sen dies.
1926	Nationalist Party (KMT, or Guomindang) begins Northern Expedition to fight

	powerful local warlords in an attempt to unify China.
1934–1935	Communist Party undertakes the Long March to flee the Nationalists' extermination campaign, then establishes party headquarters at Yan'an, Shaanxi Province.
1936	Xi'an Incident. Chiang Kai-shek is kidnapped and Nationalists and Communists form a United Front against the Japanese.
1937–1945	Second Sino-Japanese War.
1949	Nationalists withdraw to Taiwan; the People's Republic of China is founded.
1957	The Hundred Flowers Movement, in which intellectuals are encouraged to voice political opinions, followed by the Anti-Rightist Campaign in which dissenters are purged.
1958	The Great Leap Forward, an unsuccessful effort to accelerate industrial and agricultural development, and the establishment of people's communes, a move to collectivize agriculture.
1966–1976	The Great Proletarian Cultural Revolution, a ten-year mass campaign of repudiation of traditional values and reactionaries and radicalization of the party, the military, and the government.
1971	U.S. Secretary of State Henry Kissinger visits China. Nationalist regime is expelled from China's seat in the United Nations in favor of the Communist government.
1972	U.S. President Richard Nixon visits China and signs the Shanghai Joint Communiqué, setting the groundwork for normalization of bilateral relations.

c = ts; q = ch; x = sh; z = dz; zh = j

1975	Chiang Kai-shek dies.
1976	Mao Zedong dies; the Gang of Four falls.
1978	Deng Xiaoping ascends to power. The Four Modernizations program—modernizing agriculture, industry, national defense, and science and technology—and the new Open Door Policy, which opens China to the outside world, are implemented.
1979	Normalization of relations between China and the United States. Deng Xiaoping visits the United States.
1980	The trial of the Gang of Four.
1984	British Prime Minister Margaret Thatcher and Chinese Premier Zhao Ziyang sign a landmark agreement providing for the return of the British crown colony of Hong Kong to Chinese sovereignty in 1997.
1985	President Li Xiannian visits the United States, becoming the first PRC head of state ever to do so.
1988	Taiwan President Chiang Ching-kuo, son of Chiang kai-shek, dies. Lee Teng-hui assumes presidency.
1989	Protesters are killed by People's Liberation Army troops in Tian'anmen Square following months of peaceful demonstrations urging democratization and elimination of corruption in government. Premier Zhao Ziyang is removed from power.
1992	Jiang Zemin assumes the post of Communist Party secretary and the following year becomes president of the PRC.
1995	The U.S. government grants a visa to Taiwan President Lee Teng-hui to visit his alma mater, Cornell University. This provokes threatening military exercises in

1996	Lee Teng-hui is again chosen president of Taiwan in the first popular election for a senior leader in Chinese history.		
1997	The colony of Hong Kong is returned to Chinese sovereignty after more than 150 years of British rule. President Jiang Zemin pays a state visit to the United States and President Bill Clinton reciprocates the following year. Deng Xiaoping dies.		
1999	The Portuguese government returns the colony of Macao to Chinese sovereignty after ruling it for nearly 450 years.		

the Taiwan Strait early the following year by the People's Liberation Army.

THE CHINESE DYNASTIES

PINYIN	TRADITIONAL DESCRIPTION	CHINESE CHARACTER	YEARS
Xià	Hsia	夏	2205–1765 B.C.
Shāng	Shang	商	1766–1066 B.C.
Zhōu	Chou	周	1066–256 B.C.
Xī Zhōu	Western Chou	西周	1066–771 B.C.
Dōng Zhōu	Eastern Chou	东周	770–256 B.C.
Chūn Qīu	Spring and Autumn	春秋	770–476 B.C.
Zhàn Gúo	Warring States	战国	475–221 B.C.
Qín	Ch'in	秦	221–207 B.C.
Hàn	Han	汉	206 B.C.–220 A.D.
Xī Hàn	Western Han	西汉	206 B.C.–24 A.D.
Dōng Hàn	Eastern Han	东汉	25–220 A.D.
Sān Gúo	Three Kingdoms	三国	220–280 A.D.
Wèi	Wei	魏	220–265 A.D.
Shǔ Hàn	Shu Han	蜀汉	221–263 A.D.
Wú	Wu	吴	222–280 A.D.

c = ts; q = ch; x = sh; z = dz; zh = j

PINYIN	TRADITIONAL DESCRIPTION	CHINESE CHARACTER	YEARS
Jìn	Chin	晋	265–420 A.D.
Xī Jìn	Western Chin	西晋	265–316 A.D.
Dōng Jìn	Eastern Chin	东晋	317–420 A.D.
Liù Cháo	Six Dynasties	六朝	420–589 A.D.
Súi	Sui	隋	581–618 A.D.
Táng	T'ang	唐	618–907 A.D.
Wǔ Dài	Five Dynasties	五代	907–960 A.D.
Shí Gúo	Ten Kingdoms	十国	902–979 A.D.
Sòng	Sung	宋	960–1279 A.D.
Běi Sòng	Northern Sung	北宋	960–1127 A.D.
Nán Sòng	Southern Sung	南宋	1127–1279 A.D.
Jīn	Kin	金	1115–1234 A.D.
Yúan	Yuan	元	1271–1368 A.D.
Míng	Ming	明	1368–1644 A.D.
Hóng Wǔ	Hung Wu	洪武	1368–1398 A.D.
Jian Wén	Chien Wen	建文	1399–1402 A.D.
Yǒng Lè	Yung Lo	永乐	1403–1424 A.D.
Hóng Xī	Hung Hsi	洪熙	1425 A.D.
Xūan Dé	Hsuan Te	宣德	1426–1435 A.D.
Zhèng Tǒng	Cheng T'ung	正统	1436–1449 A.D.
Jǐng Tài	Ching T'ai	景泰	1450–1456 A.D.
Tian Shùn	T'ien Shun	天顺	1457–1464 A.D.
Chéng Hùa	Ch'eng Hua	成化	1465–1487 A.D.
Hóng Zhì	Hung Chih	弘治	1488–1505 A.D.
Zhèng Dé	Cheng Te	正德	1506–1521 A.D.
Jīa Jìng	Chia Ching	嘉靖	1522–1566 A.D.
Lóng Qìng	Lung Ch'ing	隆庆	1567–1572 A.D.
Wàn Lì	Wan Li	万历	1573–1619 A.D.
Tài Chāng	T'ai Ch'ang	泰昌	1620 A.D.
Tian Qǐ	T'ien Ch'i	天启	1621–1627 A.D.
Chóng Zhēn	Ch'ung Chen	崇祯	1628–1644 A.D.
Qīng	Ching	清	1644–1911 A.D.
Shùn Zhì	Shun Chih	顺治	1644–1661 A.D.
Kāng Xī	Kang Hsi	康熙	1662–1722 A.D.
Yōng Zhèng	Yung Cheng	雍正	1723–1735 A.D.
Qían Lóng	Chien Lung	乾隆	1736–1796 A.D.
Jīa Qìng	Chia Ch'ing	嘉庆	1796–1820 A.D.
Dào Gūang	Tao Kuang	道光	1821–1850 A.D.
Xían Fēng	Hsien Feng	咸丰	1851–1862 A.D.
Tóng Zhì	T'ung Chih	同治	1862–1874 A.D.
Gūang Xù	Kuang Hsu	光绪	1875–1908 A.D.
Xūan Tǒng	Hsuan T'ung	宣统	1908–1911 A.D.

MINI-DICTIONARY FOR THE BUSINESS TRAVELER

advisor	*gùwèn*	顾问
air freight	*kōng yùn*	空运
amount	*jīn é*	金额
appraise	*gūjià*	估价
arbiter	*zhòngcáizhe*	仲裁者
arbitration	*zhòngcái*	仲裁
assistant manager	*zhùlǐ jīnglǐ*	助理经理
authorize	*shòuchúan*	授权
bank	*yínháng*	银行
bankrupt	*pòchǎn*	破产
bargain (v.)	*táojià*	讨价
barter	*yǐhùo yìhùo*	以货易货
bill (noun)	*pìaojù*	票据
bill (verb)	*kāi zhàngdān*	开帐单
bill of lading	*tíhùo dān*	提货单
board of directors	*dǒngshì hùi*	董事会
bond	*zhài qùan*	债券
borrow	*jìe*	借
bribery	*hùilù*	贿赂
business hours	*yíngyè shíjiān*	营业时间
buy	*mǎi*	买

c = ts; *q* = ch; *x* = sh; *z* = dz; *zh* = j

cash (noun)	*xiànkuǎn*	现款
cash a check	*duìxiàn*	兑现
certified check	*bǎofù zhīpìao*	保付支票
chairman	*dǒngshìzhǎng*	董事长
C.I.F.	*dào àn jìagé*	到岸价格
claim	*sūopéi*	索赔
company; corporation	*gōngsī*	公司
compensation for damage	*sǔnshī péicháng*	损失赔偿
compensation trade	*bǔcháng màoyì*	补偿贸易
competition	*jìngzhēng*	竞争
competitive price	*jù yǒu jìngzhēnglì de jìagé*	具有竞争力的价格
conflict of interest	*lìyì chōngtù*	利益冲突
consulting company	*zīxún gōngsī*	咨询公司
contract	*hétong*	合同
contractual obligations	*hétong de yìwù*	合同的义务
co-owner	*gòngtóng yōngyóuzhě*	共同拥有者
coproduction	*hézùo shēngchǎn*	合作生产
corporate law	*gōngsī fǎ*	公司法

corruption	*fǔbài*	腐败
cost	*chéngběn*	成本
countertrade	*fǎnxīao màoyì*	反销贸易
court	*fǎyùan*	法院
credit	*xìndài*	信贷
currency	*hùobì*	货币
Customs	*Hǎigūan*	海关
director	*dǒngshì*	董事
discount	*zhékòu*	折扣
distributor	*xīaoshòuzhě*	销售者
distribution center	*xīaoshòu zhōngxīn*	销售中心
due	*dàoqī*	到期
duty free	*mǐanshùi*	免税
enforcement	*zhífǎ*	执法
enterprise	*qǐyè*	企业
exchange rate	*dùihùan lǚ*	兑换率
expedite delivery	*xùnsù jīaohùo*	迅速交货
expenses	*fèiyòng*	费用
export	*chūkǒu*	出口
F.O.B.	*chúanshàng jīaohùo*	船上交货
foreign exchange	*wàihùi*	外汇
general manager	*zǒngjīnglǐ*	总经理
goods	*hùowù*	货物

c = ts; *q* = ch; *x* = sh; *z* = dz; *zh* = j

import	jìnkǒu	进口
income	shōurù	收入
income tax	suǒdé shuì	所得税
installment	fēnqī fù kuǎn	分期付款
insurance	báoxīan	保险
interest	lìxī	利息
interest rate	lìlǜ	利率
international law	gúojì fǎ	国际法
investment	tóuzī	投资
joint venture	hézī qǐyè	合资企业
lawsuit	sùsòng	诉讼
lawyer	lǜshī	律师
lend	jìe gěi	借给
letter of credit	xìnyòng zhèng	信用证
letter of intent	yìxìang shū	意向书
liability	zhàiwù	债务
license	xúkě zhèng	许可证
loan	dàikuǎn	贷款
loss	kūi sǔn	亏损
manager	jīnglǐ	经理
market price	shìchǎng jìagé	市场价格
marketing	shìchǎng yíngxīao	市场营销
memorandum of understanding	liàngjǐe bèiwànglù	谅解备忘录

mortgage	*dǐyā*	抵押
ownership	*yōngyǒuqúan*	拥有权
partial payment	*bùfèn fù kuǎn*	部分付款
partner	*héhǔo rén*	合伙人
patent	*zhūanlì*	专利
payment	*fù kuǎn*	付款
president	*zǒngcái*	总裁
price	*jìagé*	价格
pricing	*bīaojìa*	标价
processing	*jīagōng*	加工
product	*chánpǐn*	产品
profit	*lìrùn*	利润
property	*cáichǎn*	财产
purchasing agent	*dàigòu rén*	代购人
representative	*dàilǐrén*	代理人
retail	*língshòu*	零售
sale	*xīaoshòu*	销售
salesperson	*shòuhùoyúan*	售货员
sales tax	*yíngyè shùi*	营业税
sea freight	*hǎi yùn*	海运
security	*zhèng quàn*	证券
sell	*shòumài*	售卖
send	*yùnsòng*	运送
send back	*sònghúi*	送回

c = ts; *q* = ch; *x* = sh; *z* = dz; *zh* = j

send C.O.D.	*huòdào fù kuǎn*	货到付款
share	*gǔfèn*	股份
shipment	*zhuāngyùn*	装运
shipping	*yùnsòng*	运送
store	*shāngdiàn*	商店
stock	*gǔpiào*	股票
tariff	*gūanshùi*	关税
tax	*shùi*	税
tax rate	*shùi lǜ*	税率
technology transfer	*jìshù zhǔanràng*	技术转让
trade	*màoyì*	贸易
transaction	*jīaoyì*	交易
transportation charges	*yùnshū fèiyòng*	运输费用
vice president	*fù zǒngcái*	副总裁
wages	*gōngzī*	工资
wholesale	*pīfā*	批发
wholly foreign-owned venture	*qúanzī yōngyǒu de wàiqǐ*	全资拥有的外企

QUICK GRAMMAR GUIDE

Compared to that of many other languages, including most European languages, Chinese grammar is not particularly difficult to master. More often than not, word order in Chinese is intuitive to English speakers. And in many instances Chinese is quite a bit simpler—for example, you don't have to conjugate verbs or learn verb tenses.

The synopsis of Chinese grammar that follows is by necessity oversimplified. Rather than employ the complicated terminology of the linguist, we have attempted to analyze Chinese grammar using parts of speech familiar to English speakers.

NOUNS AND PRONOUNS

Like most Chinese words, nouns can be one or more characters in length. No distinction is made between singular and plural nouns—there is no equivalent of adding *s* as is done in English. When it is necessary to distinguish plurals, this is done through the use of auxiliary measure words. There is also no distinction between subjects and objects; the same word can serve both purposes. And unlike nouns in the Romance languages, Chinese nouns are not assigned genders. Examples of nouns:

树	*shù*	tree
东西	*dōngxi*	thing
电视	*dìanshì*	television
桌子	*zhūozi*	table

c = ts; *q* = ch; *x* = sh; *z* = dz; *zh* = j

Pronouns stand in for nouns, just as they do in English. They also do not change whether used as subjects or objects.

Simple pronouns:

我	*Wǒ*	I; me
你	*nǐ*	you (singular)
他；她；它	*tā*	he; she; it (the written characters change for each of these three meanings, but their pronunciation is the same)
我们	*wǒmén*	we
你们	*nǐmén*	you (plural)
他们	*tāmén*	they

NOTE: The **mén** (们) character that is added to **wǒ**, **nǐ**, and **tā** to render them in the plural form (as above) may *not* be used to make plural nouns or pronouns representing inanimate objects.

POSSESSIVES AND MEASURE WORDS

To make a possessive out of a noun or pronoun, simply add the particle **de** (的). Thus "my" or "mine" is **wǒ de** in Chinese; "their" or "theirs" is **tāmén de**. Similarly,

老师的	*lǎoshī de*	the teacher's
车子的	*chēzi de*	of the car; the car's

Chinese nouns are counted by using measure words. We do this to some extent in English when we say "a ream of paper" or "a school of fish." But while in English we have the option of simply saying "a book" or "three tables," in Chinese you *must* use a measure word in order to specify number. So in Chinese "a book" is not "yī shū," ("one" + "book"), it is **yī běn shū** (一本书), or one volume of books. Similarly, three tables is **sān zhāng zhuōzi** (三张桌子).

There isn't one unique measure word for each noun; measure words describe classes of objects with similar characteristics. Thus the word **zhāng** (张) in the example above can be used to describe wide, flat objects of many types—not only tables, but also pieces of paper and sheets. **Tíao** (条), another measure word, is used for counting long, thin objects like sticks and poles.

The general-use measure word is **gè** (个). It is present throughout this volume is such combinations as **zhèige** and **nèige**. You can generally get away with using **gè** when you're not sure what the measure word of choice is for a particular noun. It may not be the exact word, but it will certainly be understood.

一棵树	*yī kē shù*	a tree
四支笔	*sì zhī bǐ*	four pens
一所房子	*yī suǒ fángzi*	a house
几个人	*jǐge rén*	some people

VERBS

Verbs are simple affairs in Chinese. They, too, may be one or more characters in length. Chinese verbs are not conjugated, but keep one simple form regardless of the subject and regardless of the tense. Thus the verb **qù** (去), meaning "to go," is the same whether the subject is I, you, he,

c = ts; *q* = ch; *x* = sh; *z* = dz; *zh* = j

we, or they, and whether the action took place yesterday or will happen three weeks from now. There are, of course, ways to indicate tense in Chinese sentences (see below), but auxiliaries do this job; the verb is never inflected.

Examples of verbs:

买	*mǎi*	to buy; also buy, buys, will buy, buying, bought, etc.
看	*kàn*	to see
来	*lái*	to come
学习	*xúexí*	to study

VERB TENSES

Since the verb form in Chinese doesn't change to reflect the time that an action takes place, helping words do the trick. To suggest that an action took place in the past, the particles **le** (了) and/or **gùo** (过) are employed, usually either directly after the verb or else at the end of the sentence. **Le** tends to imply that an action has recently been completed, whereas **gùo** can apply to one that took place either far in the past or at some unspecified time in the past.

我吃了。	*Wǒ chī le.*	I've eaten.
他买了书。 (他买书了。)	*Tā mǎi le shū.* (*Tā mǎi shū le.*)	He bought (a) book.
猫走了。	*Māo zǒu le.*	The cat has gone.
我看过。	*Wǒ kàn gùo.*	I've already seen (it).
我去过了。	*Wǒ qù gùo le.*	I've gone (there) before.

Future tense is generally expressed using the helping words **yào** (要) or **huì** (会). Since **yào** also means "to want," it can imply intention as well.

我要离开。	*Wǒ yào líkāi.*	I will (want to) leave.
东西会破。	*Dōngxi huì pò.*	The thing is going to break.

Specific time words can naturally add precision when it is called for. If you use the word **zúotīan**, meaning "yesterday," for example, you make it clear exactly when the action took place. Unlike English, time words generally follow the subject and precede the verb, as in the examples below.

她昨天走了。	*Tā zúotīan zǒu le.*	She left yesterday.
我明年要买。	*Wǒ míngnían yào mǎi.*	I'm going to buy (something) next year.
你们后天会看到。	*Nǐmén hòutīan huì kàndào.*	You'll see (it) the day after tomorrow.

ADJECTIVES

Adjectives in Chinese don't need to agree in gender or number with the nouns they modify, as they do in many languages. The adjective **hǎo** (好), which means "good," can be used with I, you, he, she, it, we, and they without changing its form. Adjectives also don't require the verb "to be" in the sentence; **Tā lèi**, which means "he is tired," is in fact literally

c = ts; *q* = ch; *x* = sh; *z* = dz; *zh* = j

just "he tired." Adding the verb "to be" to form "Tā shì lèi" would be incorrect in Chinese.

When adjectives modify nouns in phrases they generally precede the noun, often using the auxiliary **de** in between.

Some examples of adjectives and adjectival phrases:

红	*hóng*	red
聪明	*cōngmíng*	smart; intelligent
你聪明。	*Nǐ cōngmíng.*	You are smart.
我们矮。	*Wǒmén ǎi.*	We are short.
蓝的书	*lán de shū*	blue book
大的人	*dà de rén*	big person

ADVERBS

Adverbs modify verbs or adjectives. Examples are **yě** (也), meaning "also"; **hěn** (很), meaning "very"; and **zǒng** (总), meaning "always." They precede the verb or the adjective they modify.

弟弟也去。	*Dìdi yě qù.*	Younger brother is also going.
中国很大。	*Zhōngúo hěn dà.*	China is very large.
天总下雨。	*Tīan zǒng xìa yǔ.*	The heavens always rain.

NEGATIVES

The insertion of a single word will generally turn a Chinese declarative sentence into its negative. The most common negative is the word **bù** (不), and it is placed just before the verb in the sentence. (**Bù**, by the way, is normally said in the fourth tone; when it precedes another fourth tone, however, it is pronounced in the second tone, as **bú**).

王先生不来。	*Wáng Xiānsheng bù lái.*	Mr. Wang isn't coming.
桌子不平。	*Zhuōzi bù píng.*	The table isn't flat.
他们不累。	*Tāmén bú lèi.*	They aren't tired.

The word **méi** (没) may also be used to indicate negation. It *must* be used to negate the verb **yǒu**, "to have"—"bù" isn't acceptable here. **Méi** is used widely as well to indicate an action which has not been completed.

| 你没有书。 | *Nǐ méi yǒu shū.* | You don't have a book. |
| 她没去。 | *Tā méi qù.* | She hasn't gone. or She didn't go. |

One final note: there isn't one single way to say "not" in Chinese. To communicate disagreement or unwillingness, one simply negates whatever verb has just been used. So if someone asks a question with the verb "to be," for example, **Nǐ shì Měiguórén ma?** ("Are you American?"), the way to say no is **bú shì**. Similarly, questions with **yǒu méi yǒu** ("do you have any" or "did you") are negated with **méiyǒu**, and **Nǐ qù bú qù?** ("Are you going?") would be answered in the negative as **bú qù**.

INTERROGATIVES

There are three basic ways to form questions in Chinese. The simplest and most common way is to add the particle **ma**

c = ts; *q* = ch; *x* = sh; *z* = dz; *zh* = j

(吗), pronounced in the neutral tone, to the very end of a declarative sentence.

她累吗？	*Tā lèi ma?*	Is she tired?
李先生饿吗？	*Lǐ Xiānsheng è ma?*	Is Mr. Li hungry?

The second way to ask a question is to use the choice method. This presents the listener with two opposite alternatives and allows him or her to select one. For example, **zǒu** (走) means "to leave" and, of course, **bù zǒu** means "to not leave." So "Are you leaving?" which could be expressed as **Nǐ zǒu ma** (see above), can also be asked as **Nǐ zǒu bù zǒu?**

人高不高？	*Rén gāo bù gāo?*	Is the person tall?
你去不去北京？	*Nǐ qù bú qù Běijīng?*	Are you going to Beijing?
他有没有书？	*Tā yǒu méi yǒu shū?*	Does he have any books?

The third method is by employing an interrogative pronoun. Examples are **shéi** (谁) or "who," **zěnme** (怎么) or "how," **shénme** (什么) or "what," **wèishénme** (为什么) or "why," and **náli** (哪里) or "where." Thus **Nǐ shì shéi?**, literally "You are who?" is understood to be the question "Who are you?"

这是什么？	*Zhè shì shénme?*	What is this?
你为什么不来？	*Nǐ wèishénme bù lái?*	Why won't you come?
车站在哪里？	*Chēzhàn zài náli?*	Where is the station?

NOTE: In answering a question in Chinese, follow the grammar of the question. The answer to **Zhè shì shénme**, above, might be **Zhè shì yǐzi** ("This is a chair"). You just substitute the noun for the interrogative pronoun. Similarly, the answer to **Tā yǒu méi yǒu shū** should be either **Tā yǒu**

shū ("He has books") or else **Tā méi yǒu shū**, ("He doesn't have any books") and the answer to **Tā lèi ma?** is **Tā lèi** ("She is tired") or **Tā bú lèi** ("She isn't tired"). Just stick to the word order of the original question and you won't go too far wrong.

c = ts; q = ch; x = sh; z = dz; zh = j

ENGLISH-CHINESE DICTIONARY

A

a; an *yī; yīge* 一；一个

able *néng* 能

above *shàngmian* 上面

abroad *gúowài* 国外

according to *ànzhào* 按照

accountant *kuàijì zhī* 会计师

ache *tòng* 痛

  headache *tòu tòng* 头痛

  stomachache *dùzi tòng* 肚子痛

  toothache *yá tòng* 牙痛

actor *yǎnyúan* 演员

acupuncture *zhēnjiǔ* 针灸

adaptor (electrical) *zhǔanjīe qì* 转接器

add *jīa* 加

address *dìzhǐ* 地址

adult *chéngrén* 成人

advertisement *gùanggào* 广告

advice *jìanyì* 建议

aerogram *hángkōng yòujǐan* 航空邮简

airline *hángkōng gōngsī* 航空公司

afraid *pà* 怕

after *yǐhòu* 以后

afternoon *xìawǔ* 下午

again *zài* 再

agree *tòngyì* 同意

ahead *qíantóu* 前头

air conditioning *kōngtíao* 空调

airmail letter *hángkōng xìn* 航空信

airplane *fēijī* 飞机

airport *fēijī chǎng* 飞机场

à la carte *língdǐan* 零点

alcohol (ethyl) *jiǔjīng* 酒精

all *yúan dōu* 全；都

  all day *qúan tīan* 全天

  all over (ended) *qúanbù jíeshù* 全部结束

  all together (in all) *zǒnggòng* 总共

allergy *gùomǐn* 过敏

almost *jīhū* 几乎

alone *dāndú* 单独

already *yǐjīng* 已经

also *yě* 也

always *zǒngshì* 总是

ambulance *jìuhù chē* 救护车

America *Měigúo* 美国

American (n) *Měigúorén* 美国人

American (adj) *Měigúo de* 美国的

among *zài . . . zhōng* 在…中

and *hé* 和

answer *húidá* 回答

antique *gúdǒng* 古董

any *rènhé* 任何

anybody *rènhé rén* 任何人

anyplace *rènhé dìfang*
任何地方

anything *rènhé dōngxi*
任何东西

anytime *rènhé shíjīan*
任何时间

appendicitis *lánwěi yán*
阑尾炎

appetizer *kāiwèi xǐaocài*
开胃小菜

apple *píngguǒ* 苹果

appliance *jīayòng dìanqì*
家用电器

appointment *yūehùi* 约会

approximately *dàyūe* 大约

argument *zhēnglùn* 争论

arm *shǒubei* 手臂

arrive *dàodá* 到达

artist *yìshù jīa* 艺术家

ask (a question) *wèn* 问

asthma *qìchuǎn bìng* 气喘病

at *zài* 在

athlete *yùndòng yúan* 运动员

auditorium *lǐtáng* 礼堂

August *Bāyùe* 八月

Australia *Aòdàlìyà* 澳大利亚

author *zuòzhé* 作者

automatic teller machine
(ATM) *tíkǔan jī* 提款机

automobile *qìchē* 汽车

avoid *bìmìan* 避免

awaken *xǐng* 醒

B

back (body) *bèi* 背

back (location) *hòumìan*
后面

backward *lùohòu* 落后

bacon *xūnròu* 熏肉

bad *hùai* 坏

baggage *xínglǐ* 行李

bake *kǎo* 烤

bakery *gāobǐng dìan* 糕饼店

bamboo shoot *zhúsǔn* 竹笋

banana *xiāngjīao* 香蕉

bandage *bēngdài* 绷带

bank *yínháng* 银行

bar *jǐubā* 酒吧

barber *lǐfà shī* 理发师

barbershop *lǐfà gǔan* 理发馆

bargain (v) *jǐangjìa* 讲价

bargain (v) *tǎojìa* 讨价

baseball *bàngqíu* 棒球

basket *lánzi* 篮子

basketball *lánqíu* 篮球

bathe *xǐzǎo* 洗澡

bathing suit *yóuyǒng yī*
游泳衣

bathroom (for bathing) *xǐzǎo
jīan* 洗澡间

bathroom (lavatory) *cèsǔo*
厕所

bathtub *zǎopén* 澡盆

battery *dìanchí* 电池

be *shì* 是

beach *hǎitān* 海滩

bean curd *dòufu* 豆腐

beautiful *měilì* 美丽

beauty parlor *měiróng yùan*
美容院

because *yīnwèi* 因为

become *chéngwéi* 成为

bed *chúang* 床

bedroom *wòfáng* 卧房

beef *níuròu* 牛肉

c = ts; *q* = ch; *x* = sh; *z* = dz; *zh* = j

beer *píjiǔ* 啤酒

before *yǐqián* 以前

begin *kāishǐ* 开始

behind *zài hòumian* 在后面

believe *xiāngxìn* 相信

below *zài dǐxià* 在底下

belt *pídài* 皮带

beside *zài pángbiān* 在旁边

better *gèng hǎo* 更好

between *zài . . . zhījiān* 在…之间

beverage *yǐnliào* 饮料

bicycle *zìxíng chē* 自行车

big *dà* 大

bill (currency note) *chāopiào* 钞票

bill (invoice) *zhàngdān* 帐单

settle a bill *jié zhàng* 结帐

birthday *shēngrì* 生日

bitter *kǔ* 苦

black *hēi* 黑

blanket *tǎnzi* 毯子

bleed *liú xiě* 流血

blood *xiě* 血

blood type *xiěxíng* 血型

blouse *nǚ chèn shān* 女衬衫

blue *lán* 蓝

boat *chuán* 船

body *shēntǐ* 身体

bone *gǔ* 骨

book (n) *shū* 书

bookstore *shūdiàn* 书店

boot *xuē* 靴

borrow *jiè* 借

boss (n) *lǎobǎn* 老板

bottle *píngzi* 瓶子

bowl *wǎn* 碗

box (n) *hézi* 盒子

boy *nán háizi* 男孩子

boyfriend *nán péngyou* 男朋友

bracelet *shǒuzhuó* 手镯

brandy *báilándì* 白兰地

bread *miànbāo* 面包

break (v) *dǎpò* 打破

breakfast *zǎocān* 早餐

bright *liàng* 亮

bring *dàilái* 带来

broccoli *xīlánhuā* 西蓝花

brother *xiōngdì* 兄弟

elder brother *gēge* 哥哥

younger brother *dìdi* 弟弟

brown *kāfēi sè* 咖啡色

brush *shuāzi* 刷子

toothbrush *yáshuā* 牙刷

Buddha *Fó* 佛

building (n) *dàlóu* 大楼

bulb *dēngpào* 灯泡

burn (injury) *shāoshāng* 烧伤

bus *gōnggòng qìchē* 公共汽车

bus stop *chē zhàn* 车站

business class *gōngwù cāng* 公务舱

businessman *shāngrén* 商人

busy *máng* 忙

but *dànshì* 但是

butter *huángyóu* 黄油

button (n) *kòuzi* 扣子

buy *mǎi* 买

C

cake *dàngāo* 蛋糕

calculator *jìsuàn qì* 计算器

call (v) *jiào* 叫

camcorder *shèxiàng jī* 摄像机

camera *zhàoxiàng jī* 照相机

can (be able to) *néng* 能

can (tin of food) *guàntóu* 罐头

Canada *Jīanádá* 加拿大

cancel *qǔxiāo* 取消

candy *tángguǒ* 糖果

can opener *kāi guàn qì* 开罐器

Cantonese dialect
Guǎngdōnghùa 广东话

car *qìchē* 汽车

card *kǎpiàn* 卡片

care for *zhàogu* 照顾

careful *xiǎoxīn* 小心

carpet *dìtǎn* 地毯

carrot *hú lúobo* 胡萝卜

carry *dài* 带

cash (n) *xìankuǎn* 现款

cash a check *dùixìan* 兑现

cashew *yāoguǒ* 腰果

cashier *chūnàyuán* 出纳员

cassette *héshì lùyīndài* 盒式录音带

cat *māo* 猫

cauliflower *càihūa* 菜花

CD *guāngpán* 光盘

CD-ROM *guāngqū* 光驱

celery *qíncài* 芹菜

cell phone *shǒu jī* 手机

cemetery *mùdì* 基地

Centigrade *shèshì* 摄氏

centimeter *gōngfēn* 公分

chair *yǐzi* 椅子

Champagne *xīangbīnjǐu* 香槟酒

change (coins) *língqián* 零钱

change (alter, vary) *gǎibìan* 改变

change (switch, as planes)
hùan 换

change money *hùan qían* 换钱

charge (expense, cost) *fèiyòng* 费用

cheap *píanyi* 便宜

cheat *qīpìan* 欺骗

check (an order for money)
zhīpìao 支票

　　traveler's check *lǚxíng zhīpìao* 旅行支票

check (restaurant bill)
zhàngdān 帐单

check (examine) *chá* 查

check (consign, as baggage)
tūoyùn 托运

cheers (toast) *gānbēi* 干杯

cheese *nǎilào* 奶酪

chicken *jī* 鸡

child *xiǎohái* 小孩

China *Zhōngguó* 中国

Chinese (person)
Zhōngguórén 中国人

Chinese language *pǔtōnghùa; gúoyǔ; hànyǔ; hǔayǔ; also Zhōngwén and Zhōngguóhua* 普通话；国语；汉语；华语；中文；中国话

chocolate *qiǎokèlì* 巧克力

choice *xuǎnzé* 选择

choose *xuǎn* 选

chopsticks *kuàizi* 筷子

church *jìaotáng* 教堂

cigarette *xīangyān* 香烟

city *chéngshì* 城市

classmate *tóngxúe* 同学

clean (adj) *gānjìng* 干净

clean (v) *nòng gānjìng* 弄干净

c = ts; *q* = ch; *x* = sh; *z* = dz; *zh* = j

clock *zhōng* 钟
  alarm clock *nào zhōng*
  闹钟

cloisonné *jǐngtàilán* 景泰蓝

close (v) *guān* 关

closed (store, bank, etc.)
  guānle 关了

closet *yī guì* 衣柜

cloth *bù* 布

clothing *yīfu* 衣服

coat *dà yī* 大衣

coffee *kāfēi* 咖啡

cognac *shàngděng báilándì*
  上等白兰地

cold (adj) *lěng* 冷

cold (n) *shāngfēng* 伤风

collar *lǐngzi* 领子

colleague *tóngshì* 同事

color *yánsè* 颜色

comb (n) *shūzi* 梳子

come *lái* 来

comfortable *shūfu* 舒服

compact disc *guāngpán* 光盘

company (business) *gōngsī*
  公司

complain *bàoyuàn* 抱怨

computer *jìsuàn jī; diànnǎo*
  计算机；电脑

concert *yīnyuè huì* 音乐会

conference *huìyì* 会议

confirm *quèrèn* 确认

congratulations *gōngxǐ* 恭喜

consulate *lǐngshìguǎn*
  领事馆

contact lens *yǐnxíng yǎnjìng*
  隐形眼镜

contagious *chuánrǎn de*
  传染的

contest *bǐsài* 比赛

contract (n) *hétong* 合同

convenient *fāngbiàn* 方便

cook (n) *chúshī* 厨师

cook (v) *zuò cài* 做菜

cookie *bǐnggān* 饼干

cool *liángkuai* 凉快

corn *yùmǐ* 玉米

cost (of production) *chéngběn*
  成本

cost (price) *jiàgé* 价格

costly *guì* 贵

cotton *miánhuā* 棉花

cough *késòu* 咳嗽

count (v) *suàn* 算

country *guójiā* 国家

countryside *xiāngxià* 乡下

court of law *fǎyuàn* 法院

courtyard *yuànzi* 院子

cover *gài* 盖

cover charge *rùchǎng fèiyòng*
  入场费用

crab *pángxiè* 螃蟹

cream *nǎiyóu* 奶油

credit card *xìnyòng kǎ*
  信用卡

cry (v) *kū* 哭

cucumber *huángguā* 黄瓜

cup *bēizi* 杯子

curtain *chuānglián* 窗帘

custom *fēngsú* 风俗

customer *gùkè* 顾客

Customs *hǎiguān* 海关

Customs official *hǎiguān*
  guānyuán 海关官员

cut (v) *gē* 割

D

daily *měitiān* 每天

dance (n) *wǔhuì* 舞会

dance (v) *tiàowǔ* 跳舞

dangerous *wēixiǎn* 危险

dark *àn* 暗

date (calendar) *rìqī* 日期

date (appointment) *yuēhùi* 约会

daughter *nǚér* 女儿

day *tiān* 天

  yesterday *zuótiān* 昨天

  day after tomorrow *hòutiān* 后天

deceive *qīpiàn* 欺骗

decide *juédìng* 决定

delegation *dàibiǎotúan* 代表团

deliver *yùnsòng* 运送

deliver *sòng* 送

dentist *yáyī* 牙医

deodorant *chúchòujì* 除臭剂

depart *líkāi* 离开

department store *bǎihùo shāngdiàn* 百货商店

detergent *qīngjiéjì* 清洁剂

diamond *zhùanshí* 钻石

diaper *niàobù* 尿布

diarrhea *xiè dùzi* 泻肚子

dictionary *zìdiǎn* 字典

different *bùtóng* 不同

difficult *nán* 难

difficulty *kùnnán* 困难

dine *chī* 吃

dining car *cānchē* 餐车

dining room *cāntīng* 餐厅

dinner *wǎncān* 晚餐

direct flight *zhífēi de hángbān* 直飞的航班

direction *fāngxiàng* 方向

dirty *zāng* 脏

disappointment *shīwàng* 失望

discount *zhékòu* 折扣

dish *pánzi* 盘子

distance *jùlí* 距离

district *dìqū* 地区

disturb *dárǎo* 打扰

dizzy *tóuyūn* 头晕

do *zùo* 做

doctor *yīshēng* 医生

dog *gǒu* 狗

doll *wáwa* 娃娃

dollar (U.S.) *měiyúan* 美元

door *mén* 门

doorbell *ménlíng* 门铃

down *xià* 下

  to go down *xiàqù* 下去

downstairs *lóuxià* 楼下

downtown *shì zhōngxīn* 市中心

drain (n) *páishúigǔan* 排水管

dress (n) *yī tào yīfu* 一套衣服

dress (v) *chūan* 穿

dress up *dǎbàn* 打扮

drink (n) *yǐnliao* 饮料

drink (v) *hē* 喝

driver *sījī* 司机

drugstore *yàofáng* 药房

drunk (adj) *zùi* 醉

dry (adj) *gān* 干

dry (v) *nòng gān* 弄干

dry-clean *gānxi* 干洗

duck (n) *yā* 鸭

dumpling *jiǎozi* 饺子

during *zài . . . zhōng* 在…中

dynasty *cháodài* 朝代

---

c = ts; *q* = ch; *x* = sh; *z* = dz; *zh* = j

E

each *měige* 每个

each other *hùxiāng* 互相

ear *ěrduo* 耳朵

early *zǎo* 早

earn *zhuàn* 赚

earrings *ěrhúan* 耳环

East (Orient) *Dōngfāng* 东方

easy *róngyì* 容易

eat *chī* 吃

economy class *pǔtōng cāng* 普通舱

egg *dàn* 蛋

eight *bā* 八

eighteen *shíbā* 十八

eighty *bāshí* 八十

electricity *diàn* 电

electronic game *diànzǐ yóuxì* 电子游戏

elevator *diàntī* 电梯

eleven *shíyī* 十一

e-mail *diànzǐ yóujiàn* 电子邮件

embassy *dàshí guǎn* 大使馆

embroidery *xiùhūa* 绣花

emergency *jízhěn* 急诊

empty *kōng* 空

end (v) *wán* 完

engineer *gōngchéng shī* 工程师

English (adj) *Yīnggúo de* 英国的

English (language) *Yīngwén* 英文

English (person) *Yīnggúo rén* 英国人

enough *gòu* 够

enter *jìnrù* 进入

entire *quánbù* 全部

entrance *jìnkǒu* 进口

envelope *xìnfēng* 信封

especially *tèbié* 特别

evening *wǎnshàng* 晚上

every *měi* 每

every day *měitiān* 每天

everybody *měige rén* 每个人

everywhere *měige dìfāng* 每个地方

examine *jiǎnchá* 检查

example *lìzi* 例子

exchange (money) *dùihùan* 兑换

exchange rate *dùihùan lǜ* 兑换率

Excuse me (apologizing) *Dùibuqǐ.* 对不起。

Excuse me. (getting attention) *Láojià.* 劳驾。

exhibition *zhǎnlǎn* 展览

exit *chūkǒu* 出口

expensive *gùi* 贵

export *chūkǒu* 出口

eye (n) *yǎnjīng* 眼睛

F

fabric *bùlìao* 布料

face (n) *liǎn* 脸

factory *gōngchǎng* 工厂

Fahrenheit *Húashì* 华氏

fall (season) *qiūjì* 秋季

fall (v) *diào* 掉

false *jǐade* 假的

family *jiātíng* 家庭

fan (n) *shànzi* 扇子

far *yǔan* 远

farmer *nòngmín* 农民

fast (adv) *kùai* 快

fat *pàng* 胖

father *fùqīn* 父亲

dad *bàba* 爸爸

faucet *shuǐlóngtóu* 水龙头

fax *chúanzhēn* 传真

fax machine *chúanzhēn jī* 传真机

February *Èryuè* 二月

fee *fèiyòng* 费用

feel *gǎndào* 感到

festival *jiérì* 节日

fever *fāshāo* 发烧

few *shǎo* 少

a few *jǐge* 几个

fifteen *shíwǔ* 十五

fifty *wǔshí* 五十

film (rolls, for camera) *jiāojuǎn* 胶卷

film (movie) *diànyǐng* 电影

finger *shóuzhǐ* 手指

finished *wánchéng* 完成

fire (n) *huǒ* 火

first *dìyī* 第一

first aid *jíjiù* 急救

first class *tóuděng cāng* 头等舱

fish (n) *yú* 鱼

fish (v) *diào yú* 钓鱼

five *wǔ* 五

fix *xīu* 修

flashlight *shǒudiàntǒng* 手电筒

flat (adj) *píng* 平

flavor *wèidao* 味道

flight (airline) *hángbān* 航班

flight attendant *chéngwùyuán* 乘务员

floor (ground) *dìmiàn* 地面

floor (story) *lóu* 楼

floppy disk *ruǎn cípán* 软磁盘

flower *huā* 花

fly (v) *fēi* 飞

fog *wù* 雾

follow *gēnzhe* 跟着

food *shípǐn* 食品

foot (anatomy) *jiǎo* 脚

foot (measurement) *yīngchǐ* 英尺

foreign *wàiguó de* 外国的

foreign exchange *wàihuì* 外汇

forget *wàngjì* 忘记

fork (n) *chāzi* 叉子

former *yǐqián de* 以前的

forty *sìshí* 四十

forward *xiàng qián* 向前

four *sì* 四

fourteen *shísì* 十四

free (without cost) *miǎnfèi* 免费

freedom *zìyóu* 自由

fresh *xīnxiān* 新鲜

freezer *lěngdòng jī* 冷冻机

Friday *Xīngqīwǔ* 星期五

friend *péngyou* 朋友

Friendship Store *Yǒuyì Shāngdiàn* 友谊商店

front *qiánmiàn* 前面

fruit *shúiguǒ* 水果

fur *pímáo* 皮毛

furniture *jiājù* 家具

G

garbage *lājī* 垃圾

garden *huāyuán* 花园

---

c = ts; *q* = ch; *x* = sh; *z* = dz; *zh* = j

garlic *dà suàn* 大蒜

gas station *jiāyóu zhàn* 加油站

gasoline *qìyóu* 汽油

general manager *zǒngjīnglǐ* 总经理

get up *qǐlái* 起来

gift *lǐpǐn* 礼品

ginger *jiāng* 姜

girl *nǚ háizi* 女孩子

girlfriend *nǚ péngyou* 女朋友

give *gěi* 给

glass (material) *bōli* 玻璃

glass (cup) *bēizi* 杯子

glasses (spectacles) *yǎnjìng* 眼镜

glove *shǒutào* 手套

glue *jiāoshuǐ* 胶水

go (leave) *zǒu* 走

go down *xià qù* 下去

gold *jīn* 金

good *hǎo* 好

Good-bye. *Zàijiàn.* 再见。

goose *é* 鹅

gram *kè* 克

grape *pútáo* 葡萄

gray *huī sè* 灰色

green *lǜ* 绿

ground (n) *dìmiàn* 地面

guide (lead sightseeing) *dǎoyóu* 导游

guidebook *lǚyóu shǒucè* 导游手册

H

hair *tóufa* 头发

haircut *lǐfà* 理发

half *bàn* 半

ham *huǒtuǐ* 火腿

hamburger *hànbǎo bāo* 汉堡包

hand *shǒu* 手

handicapped person *cánjí rén* 残疾人

handkerchief *shǒujuàn* 手绢

handsome *hǎokàn* 好看

hanger (clothes) *yījià* 衣架

happy *gāoxìng* 高兴

hat *màozi* 帽子

have *yǒu* 有

have just *gāngcái* 刚才

have to *bìxū* 必需

he *tā* 他

head *tóu* 斗

healthy *jiànkāng* 健康

hear *tīngjiàn* 听见

heart *xīnzàng* 心脏

heart attack *xīnzàng bìng* 心脏病

heat (n) *nuǎnqì* 暖气

heater *nuǎnqì jī* 暖气机

height *gāodù* 高度

Hello. *Ní hǎo.* 你好。

help (assist) *bāng máng* 帮忙

help (for emergencies) *jiù mìng* 救命

here *zhèlǐ* 这里

high *gāo* 高

high school *gāo zhōng* 高中

highway *gōnglù* 公路

hire *gùyòng* 雇用

hit *dǎ* 打

hold *ná* 拿

holiday *jiérì* 节日

homepage *Wǎng yè* 网页

honey *fēngmì* 蜂蜜

hope *xīwàng* 希望

horse *mǎ* 马

hospital *yīyuàn* 医院
host (n) *zhǔrén* 主人
host (v) *zhāodài* 招待
hot *rè* 热
hot dog *rè gǒu* 热狗
hotel *lǘguǎn* 旅馆
  fàndiàn 饭店
hot pepper sauce *làjīao jìang* 辣椒酱
hour *xǐaoshí* 小时
house (n) *fángzi* 房子
how *zěnme* 怎么
how many (for a few) *jǐgè* 几个
how many (any number) *dūoshǎo* 多少
humid *mēnrè* 焖热
hundred *bǎi* 百
  one hundred *yībǎi* 一百
  two hundred *liángbǎi* 两百
hungry *è* 饿
hurry (quickly) *kùai* 快
  in a hurry (pressed) *jí* 急
husband *zhàngfu* 丈夫

in *zài . . . lǐ* 在…里
inch *yīngcùn* 英寸
include *bāokùo* 包括
income *shōurù* 收入
infection *fāyán* 发炎
information *xìnxī* 信息
information desk *xúnwèn chù* 询问处
inside *zài . . . lǐmìan* 在…里面
instead of *dàitì* 代替
insurance *báoxiǎn* 保险
intelligent *cōngmíng* 聪明
interesting *yǒu yìsi* 有意思
international *gúojì* 国际
Internet *Yīngtèwǎng* 英特网
interpreter *fānyì* 翻译
introduce *jìeshào* 介绍
investment *tóuzī* 投资
invite *yāoqǐng* 邀请
iron (v) *tàng* 烫
iron (n) *yùndǒu* 熨斗
island *dǎo* 岛
it *tā* 它
itch *yǎng* 痒
itinerary *rìchéng* 日程

I

I (me) *wǒ* 我
ice *bīng* 冰
ice cream *bīngqīlín* 冰淇淋
if *jǐarú* 假如
ill (get sick) *bìngle* 病了
immediately *mǎshàng* 马上
import (trade goods) *jìnkǒu* 进口
important *zhòngyào* 重要
impossible *bù kěnéng* 不可能

J

jacket *wàitào* 外套
jade *yù* 玉
jam *gúojìang* 果酱
January *Yīyùe* 一月
jewelry *zhūbǎo* 珠宝
jewelry shop *zhūbǎo dìan* 珠宝店
joke *xìaohua* 笑话
journey *lǚxíng* 旅行

c = ts; *q* = ch; *x* = sh; *z* = dz; *zh* = j

juice (n) *guǒzhī* 果汁
July *Qīyuè* 七月
June *Lìuyuè* 六月
just (very recently) *gāngcái* 刚才
just (only) *zhǐ* 只

K

karaoke *kǎlāōukèi* 卡拉OK
keep *líu* 留
ketchup *fānqié jiàng* 番茄酱
key *yàoshi* 钥匙
kilogram *gōngjīn* 公斤
kilometer *gōnglǐ* 公里
kitchen *chújáng* 厨房
knife (n) *dāozi* 刀子
know (facts) *zhīdào* 知道
know (people) *rènshi* 认识

L

lake *hú* 湖
lamb (mutton) *yángròu* 羊肉
lamp *dēng* 灯
land (n) *dì* 地
landscape (n) *fēngjǐng* 风景
language *yǔyán* 语言
laptop computer *biànxíe shì
dìannǎo* 便携式电脑
large *dà* 大
last (final) *zùihòu* 最后
late *wǎn* 晚
late in arriving *chídào* 迟到
laugh *xìao* 笑
launder (clothing) *xǐyī* 洗衣
lawyer *lǜshī* 律师
learn *xúexí* 学习
least *zùi shǎo* 最少
　　at least *zhìshǎo* 至少

leather *pígé* 皮革
leave (v) *líkāi* 离开
left (direction) *zuǒbiān* 左边
leg *tǔi* 腿
lemon *níngméng* 柠檬
lend *jìe* (*gěi*) 借（给）
less *shǎo* 少
letter (correspondence) *xìn*
信
lettuce *shēng cài* 生菜
library *túshūguǎn* 图书馆
light (weight) *qīng* 轻
　　lighter *qīng dǐan* 轻点
lighter (cigarette) *dá huǒ jī*
打火机
like (similar to) *xìang* 像
like (v) *xǐhuān* 喜欢
lipstick *kǒuhóng* 口红
liquor *jǐu* 酒
list *dānzi* 单子
listen *tīng* 听
liter *shēng* 升
little (adj) *xǐao* 小
little (adv) *shǎo* 少
live (exist) *húo* 活
live (reside) *zhù* 住
loan *dàikuǎn* 贷款
lobby *dàtīng* 大厅
lobster *lòngxīa* 龙虾
local *běndì* 本地
lock *sǔo* 锁
long *cháng* 长
long distance *chángtú* 长途
look at *kàn* 看
look for *zhǎo* 找
lose (misplace) *dīu* 丢
lose (not win) *shū* 输
lose your way *mí lù* 迷路
lots (many) *hěn dūo* 很多
love *ài* 爱

low (in height) *dī* 低
luck *yùnqì* 运气
luggage *xíngli* 行李
lunch (n) *wǔcān* 午餐

M

magazine *zázhì* 杂志
mail (v) *jì xìn* 寄信
mailbox *yóutǒng* 邮筒
mailman *yóuchāi* 邮差
make *zuò* 做
makeup *huàzhuāng pǐn*
　化妆品
man *nán rén* 男人
manager *jīnglǐ* 经理
　general manager
　zǒngjīnglǐ 总经理
Mandarin (dialect) *Pǔtōnghùa*
　普通话
manicure *xiū zhǐjia* 修指甲
many *hěn duō* 很多
　too many *tài duō* 太多
map *dìtú* 地图
March *Sānyuè* 三月
market *shìchǎng* 市场
marry *jiéhūn* 结婚
massage *ànmó* 按摩
matches (lighter) *huǒchái*
　火柴
material (cloth) *bùliào* 布料
matter (affair) *shìqíng* 事情
　It doesn't matter. *Méi yǒu*
　guānxi. 没有关系
　What's the matter? *Zěnme*
　le? 怎么了？
mattress *chúang diàn* 床垫
May *Wǔyuè* 五月

maybe *kěnéng* 可能
mayonnaise *dànhuáng jiàng*
　蛋黄酱
me *wǒ* 我
meal *cān* 餐
meaning *yìsi* 意思
measure (v) *liáng* 量
meat *ròu* 肉
medicine *yào* 药
medium (cooking) *bú nèn bù*
　lǎo 不嫩不老
meet with *huìjiàn* 会见
meeting *huìyì* 会议
menu *càidān* 菜单
merchant *shāngrén* 商人
meter *gōngchǐ* 公尺
meter *biāo* 表
microwave oven *wēibō lú*
　微波炉
middle *zhōngjiān* 中间
　in the middle of *zài . . .*
　zhōngjiān 在…中间
midnight *wǔyè* 午夜
milk *niúnǎi* 牛奶
million *bǎi wàn* 百万
minute (time) *fēn* 分
mirror (n) *jìngzi* 镜子
miss (think of, remember)
　xiǎngniàn 想念
Miss *Xiáojiě* 小姐
mistake (n) *cuòwù* 错误
misunderstanding *wùhùi*
　误会
money *qián* 钱
month *yuè* 月
morning *zǎoshàng* 早上
　good morning *zǎoshàng*
　hǎo 早上好

mother *mǔqīn* 母亲
  mom *māma* 妈妈
mountain *shān* 山
mouth *zǔibā* 嘴吧
movie *diànyǐng* 电影
Mr. *Xiānsheng* 先生
Mrs. *Fūren* 夫人
museum *bówùguǎn* 博物馆
mushroom *mògù* 蘑菇
music *yīnyuè* 音乐
musician *yīnyuè jiā* 音乐家
mustard *jièmò* 芥末
my *wǒde* 我的

N

name *míngzì* 名字
  surname *xìng* 姓
  My name is *wǒ jiào* 我叫
  What's your name?
    Nǐ jiào shénme míngzì
    你叫什么名字？
napkin *cānjīn* 餐巾
napkin, sanitary *yuèjīng dài*
  月经带
near (to) *lí . . . jìn* 离…近
necessary *bìxū* 必需
neck *bòzi* 脖子
necklace *xiàngliàn* 项链
need *xūyào* 需要
needle *zhēn* 针
negative (film) *dǐpiàn* 底片
neighbor *línjū* 邻居
never *yǒngbù* 永个
new *xīn* 新
news *xīnwén* 新闻
newspaper *bàozhǐ* 报纸
New Zealand *Xīn Xīlán*
  新西兰
next *xià yīge* 下一个

night *wǎnshàng* 晚上
nine *jiǔ* 九
nineteen *shíjiǔ* 十九
ninety *jiǔshí* 九十
no (not true) *bú shì* 不是
noisy *chǎo* 吵
nonstop flight *zhídá de*
  hángbān 直达的航班
noodle *miàntiáo* 面条
noon *zhōngwǔ* 中午
north *běifāng* 北方
nose *bízi* 鼻子
notebook *bǐjì běn* 笔记本
novel (story) *xiǎoshuō* 小说
now *xiànzài* 现在
number (numeral) *hàomǎ*
  号码
  room number *fángjiān*
    hàomǎ 房间号码
number (quantity) *shùzì* 数字
nurse *hùshi* 护士

O

obtain *dédào* 得到
ocean *hǎiyáng* 海洋
of course *dāngrán* 当然
offer (proffer) *tígòng* 提供
office *bàngōngshì* 办公室
  box office *shòupiào chù*
    售票处
  post office *yóujú* 邮局
often *jīngcháng* 经常
oil *yóu* 油
O.K. *kéyǐ* 可以
old *lǎo* 老
  How old are you? *Nǐ duō*
    dà le? 你多大了？
on (top of) *zài . . . shàng*
  在…上

one (number) *yī* 一

one (item) *yīge* 一个

onion *yángcōng* 洋葱

on-line *shàngwǎng* 上网

only (sole) *wéiyī* 惟一

only have *zhǐyǒu* 只有

open *kāi* 开

opera *gējù* 歌剧

operator (switchboard) *zǒngjī* 总机

opportunity *jīhuì* 机会

opposite *xiāngfǎn* 相反

or (conjunctive) *huòzhe* 或者

or (disjunctive) *háishì* 还是

orange (fruit) *júzi* 橘子

orange (color) *júhóng sè* 橘红色

orchestra *yuèduì* 乐队

other (those left out) *qítā* 其他

other (alternative) *lìngwài* 另外

outside *wàimiàn* 外面

over (finished) *wánle* 完了

over (on top of) *zài . . . shàngmiàn* 在…上面

overcoat *dàyī* 大衣

overseas *hǎiwài* 海外

owe *qiàn* 欠

P

package *bāoguǒ* 包裹

pager *hūjī* 呼机

pain *tòng* 痛

painting *huà* 画

pair (n) *shuāng* 双 *duì* 对

pajamas *shuìyī* 睡衣

pants *kùzi* 裤子

paper *zhǐ* 纸

  toilet paper *wèishēng zhǐ* 卫生纸

  wrapping paper *bāozhuāng zhǐ* 包装纸

  writing paper *xiězì zhǐ* 写字纸

park (n) *gōngyuán* 公园

passport *hùzhào* 护照

pay (v) *fù* 付

peach *táozi* 桃子

peanuts *huāshēngmǐ* 花生米

pear *lí* 梨

pen (ballpoint) *yuánzhū bǐ* 圆珠笔

pencil *qiānbǐ* 铅笔

pepper *hújiāo* 胡椒

perfect (adj) *wánměi* 完美

perfume *xiāngshuǐ* 香水

permit (n) *xǔkězhèng* 许可证

permit (v) *ràng* 让

person *rén* 人

pharmacy *yàofáng* 药房

photograph (n) *zhàopiàn* 照片

photograph (v) *zhàoxiàng* 照相

picnic *yěcān* 野餐

picture (painting) *huà* 画

pie *pài* 排

piece *kuài; jiàn* 块；件

pigeon *gēzi* 鸽子

pillow *zhěntou* 枕头

pilot *jiàshǐ* 驾驶

pin (safety pin or brooch) *biézhēn* 别针

c = ts; *q* = ch; *x* = sh; *z* = dz; *zh* = j

pin (straight) *dàtóu zhēn* 大头针

pineapple *bōluó* 菠萝

pink *fěnhóng sè* 粉红色

pizza *bǐsà bǐng* 比萨饼

place (n) *dìfāng* 地方

plan *jìhuà* 计划

plate *pánzi* 盘子

platform *yuètái* 月台

play (drama) *huàjù* 话剧

play (v) *wán* 玩

please *qǐng* 请

plug (electrical) *chātóu* 插头

pocketbook *qiánbāo* 钱包

police *jǐngchá* 警察

police station *jǐngchá jú* 警察局

poor (not rich) *qióng* 穷

poor (pitiful) *kělián* 可怜

porcelain *cíqì* 瓷器

pork *zhūròu* 猪肉

porter *fúwùyuán* 服务员

post office *yóujú* 邮局

postage *yóufèi* 邮费

postcard *míngxìngpiàn* 明信片

pot *guōzi* 锅子

potato *tǔdòu* 土豆

pottery *táoqì* 陶器

pound (weight) *bàng* 磅

pound sterling, British *Yīng bàng* 英磅

practice (v) *liànxí* 练习

pregnant *huáiyùn* 怀孕

prepare *zhǔnbèi* 准备

prescription *yàofāng* 药方

pretty *piàoliàng* 漂亮

price (n) *jiàgé* 价格

printer *dǎyìn jī* 打印机

private *sīrén* 私人

problem *wèntí* 问题

processing fee *shǒnxù fèi* 手续费

profession *zhíyè* 职业

profit *lìrùn* 利润

program (n) *jiemù* 节目

promise (v) *yǔnnuò* 允诺

pronounce (sound) *fāyīn* 发音

protect *bǎohù* 保护

public (adj) *gōnggòng* 公共

pudding *bùdīng* 布丁

pull *lā* 拉

purchase *mǎi* 买

purple *zǐsè* 紫色

purse *qiánbāo* 钱包

push *tuī* 推

put *fàng* 放

Q

quality *zhìliàng* 质量

quantity *shùliàng* 数量

quarter (fraction) *sì fēn zhī yī* 四分之一

three quarters *sì fēn zhī sān* 四分之三

question (n) *wèntí* 问题

quiet *ānjìng* 安静

quick *kuài* 快

quilt *míanbèi* 棉被

R

radio (n) *shōuyīnjī* 收音机

railroad *tiělù* 铁路

railroad station *huǒchē zhàn* 火车站

rain (n) *yǔ* 雨

rain (v) *xià yǔ* 下雨

raincoat *yŭyī* 雨衣
rare (cooking) *nèn* 嫩
rate of exchange *duìhùan lǜ* 兑换率
raw *shēng de* 生的
razor *dāopiàn* 刀片
read *dú* 读
ready *zhŭnbèi hăole* 准备好了
really *zhēn de* 真的
rear *hòumiàn* 后面
reason (n) *lǐyóu* 理由
receipt *shōujù* 收据
receive *shōudào* 收到
recently *zùijìn* 最近
recommend *tūijiàn* 推荐
record (disk) *chàngpiàn* 唱片
red *hóng* 红
refrigerator *bīngxīang* 冰箱
refund *tùi qían* 退钱
refuse (v) *jùjué* 拒绝
regret *yíhàn* 遗憾
regular *píngcháng* 平常
regulation *gūizé* 规则
remember *jìde* 记得
remote control *yáokòng qí* 遥控器
rent (v) *zū* 租
repair *xīulǐ* 修理
repeat *chóngfù* 重复
representative *dàibĭao* 代表
resemble *xìang* 像
reservation (booking) *yùdìng* 预定
responsible for *fùzé* 负责
rest (v) *xīuxi* 休息
restaurant *fàngŭan* 饭馆
retail *língshòu* 零售

return (come back) *húilái* 回来
return (give back) *gūihúan* 归还
rice *mĭfàn* 米饭
　rice cooker *dìan fàn gūo* 电饭锅
right (direction) *yòubīan* 右边
right (correct) *dùi* 对
ring (jewelry) *jìezhi* 戒指
river *hé* 河
road *lù* 路
roof *wūdĭng* 屋顶
room *fángjīan* 房间
rug *xĭao dìtăn* 小地毯
rule (regulation) *gūidìng* 规定
ruler (straightedge) *chĭ* 尺
run (v) *păo* 跑
runway *păodào* 跑道

S

safe (adj) *ānqúan* 安全
safe (n) *băoxĭan gùi* 保险柜
salad *shālā* 沙拉
　salad dressing *shālā jìang* 沙拉酱
salesman *shòuhùo yúan* 售货员
salt *yán* 盐
same *yī yàng* 一样
sample *yàngpĭn* 样品
sanitary napkin *yùejīng dài* 月经带
satin *dùanzi* 缎子
satisfied *mănyì* 满意

Saturday *Xīngqīliù* 星期六

sausage *xiāngcháng* 香肠

say *shuō* 说

scarf *wéijīn* 围巾

schedule (timetable) *shíjiān biǎo* 时间表

school *xúexiào* 学校

scissors *jiǎndāo* 剪刀

sea *hǎi* 海

seafood *hǎixiān* 海鲜

season (n) *jìjié* 季节

seat (n) *wèizi* 位子

  seat belt *ānquán dài* 安全带

second (in a series) *dì èr* 第一

second (unit of time) *miǎo* 秒

see *kànjiàn* 看见

seem *hǎoxiàng* 好像

sell *mài* 卖

send (deliver, see off) *sòng* 送

send (assign, appoint) *pài* 派

service *fúwù* 服务

  service charge *fúwù fèi* 服务费

settle a bill *jié zhàng* 结帐

seven *qī* 七

seventeen *shíqī* 十七

seventy *qīshí* 七十

several *jǐge* 几个

sew *féng* 缝

shampoo (n) *xǐfà jì* 洗发剂

shave (v) *guā hú* 刮胡

she *tā* 她

sheet (bed) *chuáng dān* 床单

shirt *chènshān* 衬衫

shoe *xiézi* 鞋子

shoelace *xiédài* 鞋带

shop (n) *shāngdiàn* 商店

shop (v) *mǎi dōngxi* 买东西

short (length) *duǎn* 短

short (height) *ǎi* 矮

shorts (briefs) *duǎn kù* 短裤

show to . . . *gěi . . . kàn* 给…看

shower *línyù* 淋浴

shrimp *xiā* 虾

sick *bìngle* 病了

side (location) *pángbiān* 旁边

sightseeing *guānguāng* 观光

sign (poster) *biāojì* 标记

sign (one's name) *qiān zì* 签字

silk *sīchóu* 丝绸

silver *yín* 银

since (until now) *zìcóng* 自从

since (because) *yīnwèi* 因为

sing *chàng* 唱

single *dān* 单

single person *dānshēn* 单身

single room *dānrén fáng* 单人房

sir *xiānsheng* 先生

sister *jiěmèi* 姐妹

  elder sister *jiějie* 姐姐

  younger sister *mèimei* 妹妹

sit *zuò* 坐

six *liù* 六

sixteen *shí liù* 十六

sixty *liù shí* 六十

size (n) *dàxiǎo* 大小

skin (n) *pífū* 皮肤

skirt (n) *qúnzi* 裙子

sleep (v) *shuì* 睡

  to be sleepy *kùn le* 睏了

sleeve *xiuzi* 袖子

slide (photograph) *huàn dēng piàn* 幻灯片

slippers *tuō xié* 拖鞋

slow *màn* 慢

small *xiǎo* 小

smoke (n) *yān* 烟

smoke (v) *chōu yān* 抽烟

snack *xiǎochī* 小吃

snow (n) *xuě* 雪

snow (v) *xià xuě* 下雪

soap *féizào* 肥皂

socks *wàzi* 袜子

soda (pop) *qìshuǐ* 汽水

soda (water) *sūdá shuǐ* 苏打水

sofa *shāfā* 沙发

soft *ruǎn* 软

software *ruǎnjiàn* 软件

soldier *jūnrén* 军人

some *yī xiē* 一些

someone *mǒu rén* 某人

something *shénme* 什么

sometimes *yǒu shíhòu* 有时候

somewhere *shénme dìfāng* 什么地方

son *érzi* 儿子

song *gē* 歌

soon *hěn kuài* 很快

sorry *bàoqiàn* 抱歉

soup *tāng* 汤

south *nánfāng* 南方

souvenir *jìniàn pǐn* 纪念品

soy sauce *jiàngyóu* 酱油

space (place) *dìfāng* 地方

space (outer) *kōngjiān* 空间

spaghetti *Yìdàlì shì miàntiáo* 意大利式面条

speak *shūo* 说

speed *sùdù* 速度

spell (v) *pīn* 拼

spend money *huā qián* 花钱

spice *tiáowèi liào* 调味料

spicy (hot) *là* 辣

spinach *bōcài* 菠菜

spoon *tiáogēng* 调羹

spring (season) *chūnjì* 春季

square (adj) *fāng de* 方的

square (public) *guǎngchǎng* 广场

stadium *yùndòng chǎng* 运动场

stadium *tǐyù chǎng* 体育场

staircase *lòutī* 楼梯

staff member *gōngzuò rényuán* 工作人员

stamp (postage) *yòupiào* 邮票

state (province) *zhōu* 州

state (nation) *gúojiā* 国家

stay (reside) *zhù* 住

steak *niúpái* 牛排

steal *tōu* 偷

stereo system *zǔhé yīnxiǎng xìtǒng* 组合音响系统

steward(ess) *fúwùyúan* 服务员

stock (securities) *gǔpiào* 股票

stockings *chángtǒng wàzi* 长统袜子

stomach (n) *dùzi* 肚子

stone (n) *shítou* 石头

stop (v) *tíng* 停

stop *tíngzhǐ* 停止

store (n) *shāngdiàn* 商店

c = ts; *q* = ch; *x* = sh; *z* = dz; *zh* = j

story (tale) *gùshi* 故事

street *jiēdào* 街道

string (n) *xiàn* 线

strong *qiáng* 强

student *xuésheng* 学生

subtitles *zìmù* 字幕

suburb *jiāowài* 郊外

subway *dìtiě* 地铁

sugar *táng* 糖

suit (clothes) *xīzhuāng* 西装

suitcase *xíngli* 行李

summer *xiàjì* 夏季

sun (n) *tàiyáng* 太阳

Sunday *Xīngqītiān* 星期天

sunglasses *tàiyáng yǎnjìng*
太阳眼镜

supermarket *chāojí shìchǎng*
超级市场

supper *wǎnfàn* 晚饭

surname *xìng* 姓

sweater *máoyī* 毛衣

sweet *tián* 甜

swim *yóuyǒng* 游泳

swimming pool *yóuyǒng chí*
游泳池

syrup *tángjiāng* 糖浆

T

table (n) *zhuōzi* 桌子

tablecloth *zhuō bù* 桌布

tailor (n) *cáifeng* 裁缝

take *ná* 拿

take off (clothing) *tuō* 脱

tampon *yuèjīng yòng*
miánsāi 月经用棉塞

tape (cellophane) *jiāodài*
胶带

tape (for recording) *lùyīndài*
录音带

tape recorder *lùyīn jī*
录音机

taste (flavor) *wèidào* 味道

taste (style) *qùwèi* 趣味

taste (v) *cháng* 尝

taxi *chūzū qìchē* 出租汽车

tea *chá* 茶

teacher *lǎoshī* 老师

team (n) *duì* 队

telecommunications
diànxùn 电讯

telephone *diànhuà* 电话

make a phone call
dǎdiànhuà 打电话

television *diànshì* 电视

tell *gàosu* 告诉

temperature *wēndù* 温度

temple *miào* 庙

temporary *zhànshí* 暂时

ten *shí* 十

tennis *wǎngqiú* 网球

tent *zhàngpeng* 帐篷

Thank you. *Xièxie nǐ.*
谢谢你。

that *nèige* 那个

there *nàli* 那里

there is (are) *yǒu* 有

they *tāmén* 他们

thick *hòu* 厚

thief *xiǎotōu* 小偷

thin (skinny) *shòu* 瘦

thin (not thick) *báo* 薄

thing *dōngxi* 东西

think *xiǎng* 想

third (in a series) *dì sān* 第三

third (fraction) *sān fēn zhī yī*
三分之一

thirsty *kě* 渴

thirteen *shísān* 十三

thirty *sānshí* 三十

this *zhèige* 这个

thousand *qiān* 千

  ten thousand *wàn* 万

three *sān* 三

throat *hòulóng* 喉咙

through (finished) *wán le* 完了

through (passed into) *tōng gùo* 通过

Thursday *Xīngqīsì* 星期四

ticket *piào* 票

  one-way ticket *dānchéng piào* 单程票

  round-trip ticket *láihúi piào* 来回票

ticket window *shōupiào kǒu* 售票口

tie (neck) *lǐngdài* 领带

time (instance) *cì* 次

  once *yī cì* 一次

  twice *liǎng cì* 两次

time (of day) *shíjiān* 时间

  At what time? *Shénme shíhòu?* 什么时候

on time *zhǔnshí* 准时

timetable *shíjiān biǎo* 时间表

tip (n) *xiǎo fèi* 小费

tired *lèi* 累

tissue (facial) *huàzhuāng yòng zhǐ* 化妆用纸

toast (bread) *kǎo miànbāo* 烤面包

toast (with drinks) *zhù jǐu* 祝酒

tobacco *yāncǎo* 烟草

today *jīntiān* 今天

toe *jiǎozhǐ* 脚趾

tofu *dòufu* 豆腐

together *yīqǐ* 一起

toilet *cèsǔo* 厕所

toilet paper *wèishēng zhǐ* 卫生纸

tomato *xīhóngshì* 西红柿

tomorrow *míngtiān* 明天

ton *dùn* 吨

tooth *yáchǐ* 牙齿

toothbrush *yáshuā* 牙刷

toothpaste *yágāo* 牙膏

toothpick *yáqiān* 牙签

touch (v) *mō* 摸

tourist *lǚyóu zhě* 旅游者

toward *xiàng* 向

towel *máojīn* 毛巾

toy *wánjù* 玩具

trade (commerce) *màoyì* 贸易

traffic (vehicular) *jiāotōng* 交通

train (railroad) *hǔochē* 火车

transformer (electrical) *biànyā qì* 变压器

translate *fānyì* 翻译

travel *lǚxíng* 旅行

travel agency *lǚxíngshè* 旅行社

traveler's check *lǚxíng zhīpiào* 旅行支票

tree *shù* 树

trip (travel) *lǚxíng* 旅行

trouble *máfan* 麻烦

truck *kǎchē* 卡车

true *zhēnde* 真的

try (v) *shì* 试

Tuesday *Xīngqìèr* 星期二

tuna fish *jīnqiāng yú* 金枪鱼

turn (v) *zhǔan* 转

c = ts; *q* = ch; *x* = sh; *z* = dz; *zh* = j

twelve *shíèr* 十二
twenty *èrshí* 二十
two (numeral) *èr* 二
two (measure) *liǎng* 两

U

ugly *nánkàn* 难看
umbrella *yǔsǎn* 雨伞
under *zài . . . dǐxià* 在…底下
underpants *nèikù* 内裤
undershirt *nèiyī* 内衣
understand *dǒng* 懂
United Kingdom *Yīngguó*
    英国
university *dàxué* 大学
until *zhídào* 直到
up *shàng* 上
    get up *qǐlái* 起来
    go up *shàng qù* 上去
upstairs *lóushàng* 楼上
urgent *jǐnjí* 紧急
us *wǒmén* 我们
use *yòng* 用
used up *yòng wánle* 用完了
useful *yǒu yòng de* 有用的
useless *wú yòng de* 无用的

V

vacation *jiàqī* 假期
valid *yǒu xiào* 有效
value (n) *jiàzhí* 价值
van *miànbāo chē* 面包车
vase *huāpíng* 花瓶
VCD *shì pín gāomì guāng pán*
    视频高密光盘
vegetable *shūcài* 蔬菜
vegetarian *sùshí zhě* 素食者
very *hěn* 很

vicinity *fùjìn* 附近
videodisc *yǐngdié* 影碟
video game *diànzǐ yóuxì*
    电子游戏
videocassette *lùxiàng dài*
    录像带
    videocassette recorder
        lùxiàng jī 录像机
village *cūnzhuāng* 村庄
vinegar *cù* 醋
visa *qiānzhèng* 签证
visit *fǎngwèn* 访问
volleyball *páiqiú* 排球
volume (sound) *yīnliàng*
    音量
voltage *diànyā* 电压

W

waist *yāo* 腰
wait *děng* 等
waiter; waitress *fúwùyuán*
    服务员
walk (v) *zǒu* 走
    take a walk *sàn bù* 散步
wall *qiáng* 墙
wallet *qiánbāo* 钱包
want *yào* 要
war *zhànzhēng* 战争
warm *wēnnuǎn* 温暖
wash *xǐ* 洗
washing machine *xǐyī jī*
    洗衣机
washroom *xǐshǒu jiān*
    洗手间
watch (wrist) *biǎo* 表
watch (v) *kànkan* 看看
watch out *xiǎoxīn* 小心
water *shuǐ* 水
watermelon *xīguā* 西瓜

way (method) *fāngfǎ* 方法

way (direction) *fāngxiàng*
方向

weak *ruò* 弱

wear (clothing) *chuān* 穿

weather *tiānqì* 天气

Wednesday *Xīngqīsān*
星期三

week *xīngqī* 星期

weekend *zhōumò* 周末

weigh *chēng* 称

weight *zhòngliàng* 重量

welcome (greeting) *huānyíng*
欢迎

well (adv) *hǎo* 好

well done (cooking) *lǎo* 老

West (Occident) *Xīfāng* 西方

Western food *Xīcān* 西餐

wet (adj) *shī* 湿

what *shénme* 什么

when *shénme shíhòu*
什么时候

where (question) *nálǐ* 哪里

which (question) *něige* 哪个

white *bái* 白

who *shéi* 谁

whole *quánbù; zhěnggè*
全部；整个

wholesale *pīfā* 批发

why *wèishénme* 为什么

wife *qīzǐ; tàitai* 妻子；太太

willing *yuànyì* 愿意

win *yíng* 赢

wind (n) *fēng* 风

window *chuāngzi* 窗子

wine *pútáo jiǔ* 葡萄酒

winter *dōngjì* 冬季

wire *diàn xiàn* 电线

wish *xīwàng* 希望

without *méiyǒu* 没有

woman *nǚrén* 女人

won ton *húndùn* 馄饨

wood *mùtou* 木头

wool *yángmáo* 羊毛

word *zì* 字

work *gōngzuò* 工作

work unit *dānwèi* 单位

world *shìjiè* 世界

wrap *bāo* 包

wrapping *bāozhuāng* 包装

write *xiě* 写

wrong *cuò* 错

Y

year *nián* 年

yellow *huáng* 黄

yes *shì de* 是的

yesterday *zuótiān* 昨天

yogurt *suànnǎi* 酸奶

you *nǐ* 你

young *niánqīng* 年轻

You're welcome. *Bú kèqi.*
不客气。

Z

zero *líng* 零

zoo *dòngwùyuán* 动物园

---

c = ts; *q* = ch; *x* = sh; *z* = dz; *zh* = j

CHINESE-ENGLISH DICTIONARY

A

aǐ short (height) 矮
ài love 爱
àn dark 暗
ānjìng quiet 安静
ànmó massage 按摩
ānquán safe; safety 安全
ānquán dài seat belt 安全带
ànzhào according to 按照
Aòdàlìyà Australia 澳大利亚

B

bā eight 八
bàba dad 爸爸
bái white 白
bǎi hundred 百
bǎihùo shāngdiàn department store 百货商店
báilándì brandy 白兰地
bǎiwàn million 百万
bàn half 半
bàng pound (weight) 磅
bāng máng help (assist) 帮忙
bàngōngshì office 办公室
bàngqíu baseball 棒球
bāo wrap 包
bāogǔo package 包裹
bǎohù protect 保护
bāokùo include 包括
bàoqiàn sorry 抱歉
báoxiǎn insurance 保险
bàoyùan complain 抱怨
bàozhǐ newspaper 报纸
bāozhuāng wrapping 包装
bāshí eighty 八十
Bāyùe August 八月
bèi back 背
bēizi cup 杯子
běifāng north 北方
běndì local 本地
bēngdài bandage 绷带
bìanxíe shì dìannǎo laptop computer 便携式电脑
bìanyā qì transformer (electrical) 变压器
bǐao wristwatch 錶
bǐao meter 表
bǐaojì sign (poster) 标记
bíezhēn pin 别针
bǐjì běn notebook 笔记本
bìmiǎn avoid 避免
bīng ice 冰
bǐnggān cookie 饼干
bìngle sick; ill 病了
bīngqílín ice cream 冰淇淋
bīngxīang refrigerator 冰箱
bǐsài contest 比赛
bǐsà bǐng pizza 比萨饼
bìxū necessary 必需
bízi nose 鼻子
bōcài spinach 菠菜
bōlí glass (material) 玻璃
bōlúo pineapple 菠萝

bówùguǎn museum 博物馆

bózi neck 脖子

bùdīng pudding 布丁

bù kěnéng impossible
不可能

bú kèqi you're welcome
不客气

bùliào fabric 布料

bú nèn bù lǎo medium
(cooking) 不嫩不老

bú shì no; not true 不是

bùliào cloth 布料

bùtóng different 不同

C

càidān menu 菜单

cáifeng tailor 裁缝

càihuā cauliflower 菜花

cān meal 餐

cānchē dining car 餐车

cānjīn napkin 餐巾

cánjí rén handicapped person
残疾人

cāntīng dining room 餐厅

cèsuǒ toilet 厕所

chá check; examine 查

chá tea 茶

cháng long 长

cháng taste 尝

chàng sing 唱

chàngpiàn record (disk) 唱片

chángtǒng wàzi stockings
长统袜子

chǎo noisy 吵

cháodài dynasty 朝代

chāojí shìchǎng supermarket
超级市场

chāopiào bill (currency note)
钞票

chātóu electrical plug 插头

chāzi fork 叉子

chēng weight 称

chéngběn production cost
成本

chéngrén adult 成人

chéngshì city 城市

chéngwéi become 成为

chéngwùyuán flight attendant
乘务员

chènshān shirt 衬衫

chī eat 吃

chǐ straightedge ruler 尺

chóngfù repeat 重复

chōu yān smoke 抽烟

chuān wear 穿

chúan boat 船

chúang bed 床

chúang dān bed sheet 床单

chúang diàn mattress 床垫

chuānglián curtain 窗帘

chuāngzi window 窗子

chúanrǎn de contagious
传染的

chúanzhēn fax 传真

chúanzhēn jī fax machine
传真机

chúchòujì deodorant 除臭剂

chúfáng kitchen 厨房

chūkǒu exit; export 出口

chūnàyuán cashier 出纳员

chūnjì spring (season) 春季

chúshī cook; chef 厨师

chūzū qìchē taxi 出租汽车

cì time (instance) 次

cíqì porcelain 瓷器

c = ts; *q* = ch; *x* = sh; *z* = dz; *zh* = j

cōngmíng intelligent 聪明

cù vinegar 醋

cūnzhuāng village 村庄

cuò wrong 错

cuòwù mistake 错误

D

dǎ hit 打

dà big; large 大

dǎ diànhuà telephone 打电话

dài carry 带

dàibiǎo representative 代表

dàibiǎotuán delegation 代表团

dàikuǎn loan 贷款

dàilái bring 带来

dàitì instead of 代替

dàlóu building 大楼

dān single 单

dàn egg 蛋

dāndú alone 单独

dàngāo cake 蛋糕

dāngrán of course 当然

dànhuáng jiàng mayonnaise 蛋黄酱

dànshì but 但是

dānwèi work unit 单位

dānzi list 单子

dǎo island 岛

dàodá arrive 到达

dāopiàn razor 刀片

dǎoyóu guide 导游

dāozi knife 刀子

dǎpò break; smash 打破

dárǎo disturb 打扰

dàshǐguǎn embassy 大使馆

dà suàn garlic 大蒜

dàtīng lobby 大厅

dàxiǎo size 大小

dàxué university 大学

dàyī overcoat 大衣

dǎyìn jī printer 打印机

dàyuē approximately 大约

dédào obtain 得到

dēng lamp 灯

děng wait 等

dēngpào light bulb 灯泡

dī low (height) 低

dì land; ground 地

diàn electricity 电

diànchí battery 电池

dian fàn guō rice cooker 电饭锅

dianhuà telephone 电话

diànnǎo computer 电脑

diànshì television 电视

diàntī elevator 电梯

diàn xiàn wire 电线

diànxùn telecommunications 电讯

diànyā voltage 电压

diànyǐng movie 电影

diànzǐ yóujiàn e-mail 电子邮件

diànzǐ yóuxì electronic game; video game 电子游戏

diào fall 掉

dìdi younger brother 弟弟

dìfāng place; space 地方

dìmiàn floor; ground 地面

dǐpiàn negative (film) 底片

dìqū district 地区

dìtǎn carpet 地毯

dìtiě subway 地铁

dìtú map 地图

dīu lose (misplace) 丢

dìyī first 第一

dìzhǐ address 地址

dǒng understand 懂

Dōngfāng East; Orient 东方

dōngjì winter 冬季

dòngwùyuán zoo 动物图

dōngxi thing 东西

dòufu bean curd; tofu 豆腐

dú read 读

dǔan short (length) 短

dǔan kù shorts; briefs 短裤

duànzi satin 缎子

dùi right (correct) 对

dùi team 队

Dùibuqǐ. Excuse me. (apologizing) 对不起

dùihùan exchange money 兑换

dùihùan lǜ exchange rate 兑换率

dùn ton 吨

dūo many 多

dùzi stomach 肚子

E

è hungry 饿

é goose 鹅

èr two 二

ěrdūo ear 耳朵

ěrhúan earrings 耳环

èrshí twenty 二十

Éryùe February 二月

érzi son 儿子

F

fàng put 放

fāng de square 方的

fāngbìan convenient 方便

fāngfǎ way; method 方法

fángjīan room 房间

fànguǎn restaurant 饭馆

fǎngwèn visit 访问

fāngxìang direction 方向

fángzi house 房子

fānqie jìang ketchup 番茄酱

fānyì interpreter; translate 翻译

fāshāo fever 发烧

fāyán infection 发炎

fāyīn pronunciation 发音

fǎyùan court of law 法院

fēi fly 飞

fēijī airplane 飞机

fēijī chǎng airport 飞机场

fèiyòng fee; charge 费用

féizào soap 肥皂

fēn divide; minute; Chinese cent 分

fēng wind 风

féng sew 缝

fēngjǐng landscape; scenery 风景

fēngmì honey 蜂蜜

fēngsú custom 风俗

fěnhóng sè pink 粉红色

Fó Buddha 佛

fù pay 付

fùjìn vicinity 附近

fùqīn father 父亲

Fūren Mrs. 夫人

fúwù service 服务

fúwù fèi service charge 服务费

fúwùyuán service person 服务员

fùzé responsible for 负责

G

gài cover 盖

gān dry 干

Gānbēi. Cheers. (toast) 干杯。

gǎndào feel 感到

gāngcái just; have just 刚才

gānjìng clean 干净

gānxǐ dry clean 干洗

gāo high 高

gāobǐng diàn bakery 糕饼店

gāo zhōng high school 高中

gāodù height 高度

gàosù tell 告诉

gāozìng happy 高兴

gē cut 割

gē song 歌

gēge elder brother 哥哥

gěi give 给

gěi . . . kàn show to 给…看

gējù opera 歌剧

gèng hǎo better 更好

gēnzhe follow 跟着

gēzi pigeon 鸽子

gōngchǎng factory 工厂

gōngchéng shī engineer 工程师

gōnfēn centimeter 公分

gōnggòng public 公共

gōnggòng qìchē bus 公共汽车

gōngjīn kilogram 公斤

gōnglǐ kilometer 公里

gōnglù highway 公路

gōngsī company (business) 公司

gōngwù cāng business class 公务舱

gōngxǐ congratulations 恭喜

gōngyuán park 公园

gōngzuò work 工作

gōngzuò rényuán staff member 工作人员

gǒu dog 狗

gòu enough 够

guā húzi shave 刮胡子

gūan close; shut 关

Gǔangdōnghuà Cantonese dialect 广东话

gǔanggào advertisement 广告

gǔangpán CD 光盘

guangqu CD-ROM 光驱

gūanguāng sightseeing 观光

gúdǒng antique 古董

gùi expensive 贵

gūidìng rule; regulation 规定

gūizé regulation 规则

gùkè customer 顾客

gúojì international 国际

gùojiā country 国家

gǔojiàng jam 果酱

gùomǐn allergy 过敏

gúowài abroad 国外

gúoyǔ Chinese language 国语

gǔozhī juice 果汁

gūozi pot 锅子

gǔpìao stock (securities) 股票

gùshi story (tale) 故事

gǔtóu bone 骨头

gùyòng hire 雇用

H

hǎi sea 海

hǎigūan Customs 海关

hǎigūan gūanyuán Customs official 海关官员

háishì or (disjunctive) 还是

hǎitān beach 海滩

hǎiwài overseas 海外

hǎixīan seafood 海鲜

hǎiyáng ocean 海洋
hànbǎo bāo hamburger 汉堡包
hángbān airline flight 航班
hángkōng gōngsī airline 航空公司
hángkōng xìn airmail letter 航空信
hángkōng yóujiǎn aerogram 航空邮简
hànyǔ Chinese language 汉语
hǎo good; well 好
hǎokàn handsome 好看
hàomǎ number 号码
hǎoxiàng seem 好像
hē to drink 喝
hé and 和
hé river 河
hēi black 黑
hěn very 很
hěn duō many 很多
hěn kuài soon; fast 很快
héshì lùyīndài cassette 盒式录音带
hétóng contract 合同
hézi box 盒子
hóng red 红
hòu thick 厚
hóulóng throat 喉咙
hòumiàn rear 后面
hú lake 湖
huā flower 花
huà draw; paint; picture 画
huā qián spend money 花钱
huài bad 坏
huáiyùn pregnant 怀孕
huàjù play (drama) 话剧
huàn dēng piàn slide (photograph) 幻灯片

húang yellow 黄
hūanyíng welcome 欢迎
húangyóu butter 黄油
húapíng vase 花瓶
huāshēngmǐ peanuts 花生米
húashì Fahrenheit 华氏
húayǔ Chinese language 华语
huāyuán garden 花园
huàzhuāng pǐn makeup 化妆品
huàzhuāng yòng zhǐ facial tissue 化妆用纸
hūi sè gray 灰色
huídá answer 回答
huìjiàn meet with 会见
huílái come back 回来
huìyì meeting; conference 会议
hūjī pager 呼机
hújiāo pepper 胡椒
hú lúobo carrot 胡萝卜
húndùn wonton 馄饨
huǒ fire 火
húo live; exist 活
huǒchái matches 火柴
huǒchē train 火车
húotuǐ ham 火腿
hùozhě or (conjunctive) 或者
hùshi nurse 护士
hùzhào passport 护照

J

jī chicken 鸡
jí anxious; in a hurry 急
jiā add 加
jiǎ false 假
jiàgé price 价格
jiājù furniture 傢具

c = ts; *q* = ch; *x* = sh; *z* = dz; *zh* = j

jiānádà Canada 加拿大

jiǎndāo scissors 剪刀

jiǎnchá examine 检查

jiāng ginger 姜

jiǎngjià bargain 讲价

jiàngyóu soy sauce 酱油

jiànkāng healthy 健康

jiànyì advice 建议

jiǎo foot (anatomy) 脚

jiao call 叫

jiāojuǎn film (rolls) 胶卷

jiāoshuǐ glue 胶水

jiàotáng church 教堂

jiāotōng traffic 交通

jiāowài suburb 郊外

jiǎozhǐ toe 脚趾

jiǎozi dumpling 饺子

jiàqī vacation 假期

jiǎrú if 假如

jiàshǐ pilot 驾驶

jiātíng family 家庭

jiāyòng diànqì appliance 家用电器

jiāyóu zhàn gas station 加油站

jiàzhí value 价值

jìdé remember 记得

jiè borrow 借

jiēdào street 街道

jiègěi lend 借给

jiéhūn marry 结婚

jiějie elder sister 姐姐

jiěmèi sisters 姐妹

jièmò mustard 芥末

jiémù program 节目

jiérì holiday; festival 节日

jièshào introduce 介绍

jié zhàng settle a bill 结帐

jièzhi ring 戒指

jǐge several 几个

jīhū almost 几乎

jìhuà plan 计划

jīhuì opportunity 机会

jìjié season (time of year) 季节

jīn gold 金

jǐngchá police 警察

jǐngchá jú police station 警察局

jīngcháng often 经常

jīnglǐ manager 经理

jǐngtàilán cloisonné 景泰蓝

jìngzi mirror 镜子

jìnìan pǐn souvenir 纪念品

jǐnjí urgent 紧急

jìnkǒu entrance; import 进口

jīnqiāng yú tuna fish 金枪鱼

jìnrù enter 进入

jīntiān today 今天

jìsùan jī computer 计算机

jìsùan qì calculator 计算器

jiǔ nine 九

jiǔ liquor 酒

jiǔbā bar 酒吧

jiùhù chē ambulance 救护车

jiǔjīng alcohol 酒精

jiǔshí ninety 九十

jì xìn mail a letter 寄信

jízhěn emergency 急诊

júedìng decide 决定

jùjué refuse (v) 拒绝

jùlí distance 距离

jūnrén soldier 军人

júzi orange 桔子

K

kǎchē truck 卡车

kāfēi coffee 咖啡

kāfēi sè brown 咖啡色

kāi open 开

kāi guàn qì can opener
开罐器

kāi huì hold a meeting 开会

kāishǐ begin 开始

kāiwèi xǐaocài appetizer
开胃小菜

kǎlāoūkèi karaoke 卡拉OK

kàn look at 看

kànjiàn see 看见

kǎo bake 烤

kǎo mìanbāo toast (bread)
烤面包

kǎpìan card 卡片

kě thirsty 渴

kè gram 克

kělián poor (pitiful) 可怜

kěnéng maybe 可能

késòu cough 咳嗽

kéyǐ O.K. 可以

kōng empty 空

kōngtíao air conditioning
空调

kǒuhóng lipstick 口红

kòuzi button 扣子

kū cry 哭

kǔ bitter 苦

kùai fast 快

kùai piece 块

kùaijì shī accountant 会计师

kùaizi chopsticks 筷子

kùnnán difficulty 困难

kùzi pants 裤子

L

lā pull 拉

là spicy (hot) 辣

lái come 来

lājī garbage 垃圾

làjīao jìang hot pepper sauce
辣椒酱

lán blue 蓝

lánqíu basketball 蓝球

lánwěi yán appendicitis
阑尾炎

lánzi basket 篮子

lǎo old; well done (cooking)
老

láobǎn boss 老板

lǎoshī teacher 老师

lèi tired 累

lěng cold (adj) 冷

lěngdòng jī freezer 冷冻机

lí pear 梨

lí . . . jìn near to 离…近

lǐan face 脸

líang measure 量

lǐang two (measure) 两

lìang bright 亮

líangkùai cool 凉快

lìanxí practice 练习

lǐfà haircut 理发

lǐfà gǔan barbershop 理发馆

lǐfà shī barber 理发师

líkāi leave; depart 离开

líng zero 零

lǐngdài necktie 领带

língdǐan à la carte 零点

língqían change (coins) 零钱

lǐngshì gǔan consulate
领事馆

língshòu retail 零售

lǐngzi collar 领子

línjū neighbor 邻居

línyù shower 淋浴

c = ts; *q* = ch; *x* = sh; *z* = dz; *zh* = j

lǐpǐn gift 礼品
lìrùn profit 利润
lǐtáng auditorium 礼堂
liú keep 留
liù six 六
liù shí sixty 六十
liú xiě bleed 流血
Lìuyuè June 六月
lǐyóu reason 理由
lìzi example 例子
lóngxiā lobster 龙虾
lóushàng upstairs 楼上
lóutī staircase 楼梯
lóuxià downstairs 楼下
lù road 路
lǜ green 绿
lǚguǎn hotel 旅馆
luòhòu backward 落后
lǜshī lawyer 律师
lùxiàng dài videocassette 录像带
lùxiang jī videocassette recorder 录像机
lǚxíng travel; journey 旅行
lǚxíngshè travel service 旅行社
lǚxíng zhīpiào traveler's check 旅行支票
lùyīndài recording tape; cassette 录音带
lǚyóu shǒucè guidebook 旅游手册
lǚyóu zhě tourist 旅游者

M

mǎ horse 马
máfan trouble 麻烦
mǎi buy 买
mài sell 卖

māma mom 妈妈
màn slow 慢
máng busy 忙
mǎnyì satisfied 满意
māo cat 猫
máojīn towel 毛巾
máoyī sweater 毛衣
màoyì trade 贸易
màozi hat 帽子
mǎshàng immediately 马上
měi every 每
měige each 每个
Měiguó America 美国
Měiguó rén American (person) 美国人
měilì beautiful 美丽
mèimei younger sister 妹妹
měiróng yuàn beauty parlor 美容院
měitiān daily 每天
méiyǒu without 没有
měiyuán dollar (U.S.) 美元
mén door 门
ménlíng doorbell 门铃
mēnrè humid 闷热
mǐ meter 米
miànbāo bread 面包
miànbāo chē van 面包车
miánbèi quilt 棉被
miǎnfèi free; without cost 免费
miánhuā cotton 棉花
miàntiáo noodle 面条
miǎo second (unit of time) 秒
miào temple 庙
mǐfàn rice 米饭
míngtiān tomorrow 明天
míngxìnpiàn postcard 明信片
míngzì name 名字
mō touch 摸

mógū mushroom 蘑菇
mǒu rén someone 某人
mùdì cemetery 基地
mǔqīn mother 母亲
mùtou wood 木头

N

ná hold; take 拿
nǎilào cheese 奶酪
nǎiyóu cream 奶油
nǎli where 哪里
nàli there 那里
nán difficult 难
nán háizi boy 男孩子
nán péngyou boyfriend 男朋友
nán rén man 男人
nánfāng south 南方
nánkàn ugly 难看
něige which 哪个
nèige that 那个
nèikù underpants 内裤
nèiyī undershirt 内衣
nèn rare (cooking) 嫩
néng able; can 能
nǐ you 你
Nǐ hǎo. Hello. 你好。
nián year 年
niánqīng young 年轻
niàobù diaper 尿布
níngméng lemon 柠檬
níunǎi milk 牛奶
níupái steak 牛排
níuròu beef 牛肉
nóngmín farmer 农民
nuǎnqì jī heater 暖气机
nǚ chènshān blouse 女衬衫

nǚ fúwùyuán female service person (waitress, stewardess, etc.) 女服务员
nǚ háizi girl 女孩子
nǚ péngyou girlfriend 女朋友
nuǎnqì heat 暖气
nǚér daughter 女儿
nǚrén woman 女人

P

pà afraid 怕
pài send; appoint 派
páiqiú volleyball 排球
páishúiguǎn drain (n) 排水管
pàng fat 胖
pángbiān side 旁边
pángxiè crab 螃蟹
pánzi dish; plate 盘子
pǎo run 跑
pǎodào runway 跑道
péngyou friend 朋友
piányi cheap 便宜
piào ticket 票
piàoliàng pretty 漂亮
pídài belt 皮带
pīfā wholesale 批发
pífū skin 皮肤
pígé leather 皮革
píjiǔ beer 啤酒
pímáo fur 皮毛
pīn spell (v) 拼
píng flat (adj) 平
píngcháng regular 平常
píngguǒ apple 苹果
píngzi bottle 瓶子
pīnyīn spelling 拼音
pútáo grape 葡萄

pútáo jiǔ   wine   葡萄酒
pǔtōng cāng   economy class
　普通舱
Pǔtōnghùa   Mandarin (dialect)
　普通话

Q

qī   seven   七
qīan   thousand   千
qián   money   钱
qìan   owe   欠
qíanbāo   purse; wallet   钱包
qīanbǐ   pencil   铅笔
qíang   strong   强
qíang   wall   墙
qíanmìan   front; ahead   前面
qīanzhèng   visa   签证
qīaokèlì   chocolate   巧克力
qìchē   automobile   汽车
qìchǔan bìng   asthma   气喘病
qǐlái   get up   起来
qíncài   celery   芹菜
qīng   light (weight)   轻
qǐng   please   请
qīng dǐan   lighter (adj)   轻点
qīngjié jì   detergent   清洁剂
qíong   poor (not rich)   穷
qīpìan   deceive; cheat   欺骗
qīshí   seventy   七十
qìshǔi   soda pop   汽水
qítā   other   其他
qīujì   autumn   秋季
qìyóu   gasoline   汽油
Qīyùe   July   七月
qīzi   wife   妻子
qúanbù   all; entire; whole   全部
qùerèn   confirm   确认
qúnzi   skirt   裙子
qǔxīao   cancel   取消

R

rè   hot   热
rè gǒu   hot dog   热狗
rén   person   人
rènhé   any   任何
rìchéng   itinerary   日程
rìqī   calendar date   日期
róngyì   easy   容易
ròu   meat   肉
rǔan   soft   软
rǔan cípán   floppy disk   软磁盘
rǔanjìan   software   软件
rùchǎng fèiyòng   cover charge
　入场费用
rùo   weak   弱

S

sān   three   三
sān fēn zhī yī   one third
　三分之一
sānshí   thirty   三十
Sānyùe   March   三月
shāfā   sofa   沙发
shālā   salad   沙拉
shālā jìang   salad dressing
　沙拉酱
shān   mountain   山
shàngděng báilándì   cognac
　上等白兰地
shāngdìan   store (shop)   商店
shàngmìan   above   上面
shāngrén   businessman   商人
shàngwǎng   on-line   上网
shànzi   fan   扇子
shǎo   few; less   少
shāoshāng   burn (injury)   烧伤
shéi   who   谁
shēng   liter   升

shēng cài lettuce 生菜

shēng de raw 生的

shēngrì birthday 生日

shénme something; what 什么

shénme dìfāng somewhere 什么地方

shénme shíhòu when 什么时候

shēntǐ body 身体

shèshì Centigrade 摄氏

shèxiàng jī camcorder 摄像机

shī wet 湿

shí ten 十

shì be 是

shì try; test 试

shì de yes 是的

shíbā eighteen 十八

shìchǎng market 市场

shíèr twelve 十二

shíjiān time (of day) 时间

shíjiān biǎo schedule; timetable 时间表

shìjiè world 世界

shíjiǔ nineteen 十九

shíliù sixteen 十六

shípǐn food 食品

shíqī seventeen 十七

shìqing matter; affair 事情

shísān thirteen 十三

shísì fourteen 十四

shítou stone 石头

shīwàng disappointment 失望

shíwǔ fifteen 十五

shíyī eleven 十一

shì zhōngxīn downtown 市中心

shìpín gāomì guāngpán VCD 视频高密光盘

shǒu hand 手

shòu thin 瘦

shǒubei arm 手臂

shōudào receive 收到

shǒudiàntǒng flashlight 手电筒

shòuhuò yuán salesman 售货员

shǒu jī cell phone 手机

shōujù receipt 收据

shǒujuàn handkerchief 手绢

shōurù income 收入

shǒutào glove 手套

shǒuxù fèi processing fee 手续费

shōuyīnjī radio 收音机

shóuzhǐ finger 手指

shǒuzhúo bracelet 手镯

shū book 书

shù tree 树

shuāng pair 双

shuāzi brush 刷子

shūcài vegetable 蔬菜

shūdiàn bookstore 书店

shūfu comfortable 舒服

shuǐ water 水

shuì sleep 睡

shúiguǒ fruit 水果

shuǐlóngtóu faucet 水龙头

shùiyī pajamas 睡衣

shùliàng quantity 数量

shūo say; speak 说

shūzi comb 梳子

sì four 四

sì fēn zhī yī one quarter 四分之一

---

c = ts; *q* = ch; *x* = sh; *z* = dz; *zh* = j

sīchóu silk 丝绸
sījī driver 司机
sīrén private 私人
sìshí forty 四十
sòng send; deliver 送
suàn count 算
suànnǎi yogurt 酸奶
sùdù speed 速度
suǒ lock 锁
sùshí zhě vegetarian 素食者

T

tā he; she; it 他；她；它
tàiyáng sun 太阳
tàiyáng yǎnjìng sunglasses
太阳眼镜
tāmén they 他们
tāng soup 汤
táng sugar 糖
tàng iron (v) 烫
tánggǔo candy 糖果
tángjiāng syrup 糖浆
tǎnzi blanket 毯子
tǎojià bargain (v) 讨价
táoqì pottery 陶器
táozi peach 桃子
tèbié especially; special 特别
tiān day 天
tián sweet 甜
tiānqì weather 天气
tiáogēng spoon 调羹
tiáowèi liào spice 调味料
tǐelù railroad 铁路
tígòng offer (v) 提供
tíkuǎn jī automatic teller
machine (ATM) 提款机
tīng listen 听
tíng stop (v) 停
tīngjiàn hear 听见

tíngzhǐ stop 停止
tǐyù chǎng stadium 体育场
tòng ache; pain 痛
tóngshì colleague 同事
tóngxué classmate 同学
tóngyì agree 同意
tōu steal 偷
tóu head 头
tóuděng cāng first class
头等舱
tóufa hair 头发
tóuyūn dizzy 头晕
tóuzī investment 投资
tǔdòu potato 土豆
tuī push 推
tuǐ leg 腿
tùi kuǎn refund 退款
tuījiàn recommend 推荐
tūo xié slippers 拖鞋
túshūguǎn library 图书馆

W

wàiguó de foreign 外国的
wàimiàn outside 外面
wàitào jacket 外套
wǎn bowl 碗
wǎn late 晚
wǎncān dinner 晚餐
wán le finished; ended 完了
wánchéng finished 完成
wàngjì forget 忘记
wǎngqiú tennis 网球
wǎngzhǐ homepage 网址
wánjù toy 玩具
wánměi perfect 完美
wǎnshàng evening; night
晚上
wáwa baby; doll 娃娃
wàzi socks 袜子

wēibō lú microwave oven 微波炉

wèidao flavor; taste 味道

wéijīn scarf 围巾

wèishénme why 为什么

wéixiǎn dangerous 危险

wèizi seat 位子

wèn ask 问

wēndù temperature 温度

wēnnuǎn warm 温暖

wèntí question; problem 问题

wǒ I; me 我

wǒde my 我的

wòfáng bedroom 卧房

wǒmén us 我们

wǔ five 五

wù fog 雾

wǔcān lunch 午餐

wú yòng de useless 无用的

wūdǐng roof 屋顶

wǔhuì dance 舞会

wùhuì misunderstanding 误会

wǔshí fifty 五十

wǔyè midnight 午夜

Wǔyuè May 五月

X

xǐ wash 洗

xiā shrimp 虾

xià yīgè next 下一个

xiàjì summer 夏季

xiàn string 线

xiǎng think 想

xiàng similar to; resemble 像

xiàng toward 向

xiāngbīnjiǔ Champagne 香槟酒

xiāngcháng sausage 香肠

xiāngfǎn opposite 相反

xiāngjiāo banana 香蕉

xiàngliàn necklace 项链

xiǎngniàn miss (think of, remember) 想念

xiàng qián forward 向前

xiāngshuǐ perfume 香水

xiāngxià countryside 乡下

xiāngxìn believe 相信

xiāngyān cigarette 香烟

xiànkuǎn cash 现款

Xiānsheng Mr.; teacher; gentleman 先生

xiànzài now 现在

xiǎo small; little 小

xiào laugh 笑

xiǎo dìtǎn rug 小地毯

xiǎochī snack 小吃

xiǎofèi tip; gratuity 小费

xiǎohái child 小孩

xiàohuà joke 笑话

xiǎoshí hour 小时

xiǎoshuō novel (n) 小说

xiǎotōu thief 小偷

xiǎoxīn careful 小心

xiàwǔ afternoon 下午

Xīcān Western food 西餐

xiě blood 血

xiě write 写

xiè dùzi diarrhea 潟肚子

xiédài shoelace 鞋带

Xièxie nǐ. Thank you. 谢谢你。

xiěxíng blood type 血型

xiézi shoes 鞋子

xǐfà jì shampoo 洗发剂

Xīfāng West; Occident 西方

xīguā watermelon 西瓜

c = ts; *q* = ch; *x* = sh; *z* = dz; *zh* = j

xīhóngshì tomato 西红柿

xīlánhuā broccoli 西蓝花

xīn new 新

xìn believe; letter; mail 信

xìnfēng envelope 信封

xǐng awaken 醒

xìng surname 姓

xíngli suitcase; baggage; luggage 行李

xīngqī week 星期

Xīngqī'èr Tuesday 星期二

Xīngqīliù Saturday 星期六

Xīngqīsān Wednesday 星期三

Xīngqīsì Thursday 星期四

Xīngqītiān Sunday 星期天

Xīngqīwǔ Friday 星期五

Xīngqīyī Monday 星期一

xīnwén news 新闻

xìnxī information 信息

xīnxiān fresh 新鲜

Xīn Xīlán New Zealand 新西兰

xìnyòng kǎ credit card 信用卡

xīnzàng heart 心脏

xiōngdì brothers 兄弟

xǐshǒu jiān washroom 洗手间

xiū fix 修

xiùhuā embroidery 绣花

xiūlǐ repair 修理

xiūxi take a rest 休息

xiū zhǐjia manicure 修指甲

xiùzi sleeve 袖子

xīwàng wish; hope 希望

xǐyī launder (clothing) 洗衣

xǐyī jī washing machine 洗衣机

xǐzǎo bathe 洗澡

xǐzǎo jiān bathroom 洗澡间

xīzhuāng suit (clothes) 西装

xuǎn choose 选

xuǎnzé choice 选择

xuē boot 靴

xuě snow 雪

xuéshēng student 学生

xuéxí learn 学习

xuéxiào school 学校

xúkězhèng permit; license 许可证

xūnròu bacon 熏肉

xúnwèn chù information desk 询问处

xūyào need 需要

Y

yā duck 鸭

yáchǐ tooth 牙齿

yágāo toothpaste 牙膏

yáqiān toothpick 牙签

yáshuā toothbrush 牙刷

yān smoke 烟

yán salt 盐

yāncǎo tobacco 烟草

yǎng itch 痒

yángcōng onion 洋葱

yángmáo wool 羊毛

yàngpǐn sample 样品

yángròu lamb; mutton 羊肉

yǎnjīng eye 眼睛

yǎnjìng glasses; spectacles 眼镜

yánsè color 颜色

yǎnyuán actor 演员

yāo waist 腰

yào want 要

yào medicine 药

yàofāng prescription 药方

yàofáng pharmacy; drugstore 药房

yāoguǒ cashew 腰果
yāoqǐng invite 邀请
yáokòng qì remote control 遥控器
yàoshi key 钥匙
yáyī dentist 牙医
yě also 也
yěcān picnic 野餐
yī one 一
Yìdàlì shì miàntiáo spaghetti 意大利式面条
yīfu clothing 衣服
yīge a; an; one 一个
yī guì closet 衣柜
yíhàn regret 遗憾
yǐhòu after 以后
yījià clothes hanger 衣架
yǐjīng already 已经
yín silver 银
yíng win 赢
yīngcùn inch 英吋
yǐngdié videodisc 影碟
Yīngguó United Kingdom 英国
Yīngwén English (language) 英文
yínháng bank 银行
yīnliàng volume (sound) 音量
yǐnliào beverage 饮料
Yīngtèwǎng Internet 英特网
yīnwèi because 因为
yǐnxíng yǎnjìng contact lens 隐形眼镜
yīnyuè music 音乐
yīnyuè jiā musician 音乐家
yīnyuè huì concert 音乐会
yìqǐ together 一起
yǐqián before 以前

yīshēng doctor 医生
yìshù jiā artist 艺术家
yìsi meaning 意思
yī xiē some 一些
yī yàng same 一样
yīyuàn hospital 医院
Yīyuè January 一月
yǐzi chair 椅子
yòng use 用
yǒngbù never 永不
yóu oil 油
yǒu have; there is; there are 有
yǒu shíhòu sometimes 有时候
yǒu xiào valid 有效
yǒu yìsi interesting 有意思
yǒu yòng de useful 有用的
yòubiān right (direction) 右边
yóuchāi mailman 邮差
yóufèi postage 邮费
yóujú post office 邮局
yóupiào postage stamp 邮票
yóutǒng mailbox 邮筒
Yóuyì Shāngdiàn Friendship Store 友谊商店
yóuyǒng swim 游泳
yóuyǒng chí swimming pool 游泳池
yóuyǒng yī bathing suit 游泳衣
yú fish 鱼
yǔ rain 雨
yù jade 玉
yuǎn far 远
yuànyì willing 愿意
yuánzhū bǐ ballpoint pen 圆珠笔

---

c = ts; *q* = ch; *x* = sh; *z* = dz; *zh* = j

yùanzi courtyard 院子

yùdìng reservation 预定

yùe month 月

yùedùi orchestra 乐队

yūehùi appointment 约会

yùejīng dài sanitary napkin 月经带

yùejīng yòng míansāi tampon 月经用棉塞

yùetái platform 月台

yùmǐ corn 玉米

yùndòng chǎng stadium 运动场

yùndòng yúan athlete 运动员

yùndǒu iron (clothes) (n) 熨斗

yǔnnùo promise 允诺

yùnqì luck 运气

yùnsòng deliver 运送

yúsǎn umbrella 雨伞

yǔyán language 语言

yǔyī raincoat 雨衣

Z

zài again 再

zài at 在

zài . . . lǐ in 在…里

zài . . . lǐmìan inside 在…里面

zài . . . shàng on top of 在…上

zài . . . zhījīan between 在…之间

zài . . . zhōng among; during 在…中

zài dǐxìa below; under 在底下

zài hòumìan behind 在后面

zài pángbīan beside 在旁边

zài xìamìan below; underneath 在下面

Zàijìan. Good-bye. 再见。

zāng dirty 脏

zǎo early; Good morning. 早

zǎocān breakfast 早餐

zǎopén bathtub 澡盆

zǎoshàng morning 早上

zázhì magazine 杂志

zěnme how 怎么

zhàngfu husband 丈夫

zhánlǎn exhibition 展览

zhànshí temporary 暂时

zhànzhēng war 战争

zhàogù care for 照顾

zhàopìan photograph 照片

zhàoxìang jī camera 照相机

zhèige this 这个

zhékòu discount 折扣

zhèli here 这里

zhēn needle 针

zhēnde true; real; really 真的

zhēnglùn argument 争论

zhēnjiǔ acupuncture 针灸

zhěntou pillow 枕头

zhǐ paper 纸

zhídá de hángbān nonstop flight 直达的航班

zhīdào know; be aware of 知道

zhídào until 直到

zhífēi de hángbān direct flight 直飞的航班

zhìlìang quality 质量

zhīpìao check (an order for money) 支票

zhíyè profession 职业

zhíyǒu only have 只有

zhōng clock 钟

Zhōngguó China 中国

Zhōngguóhùa Chinese (language) 中国话

zhōngjiān middle 中间
zhòngliàng weight 重量
Zhōngwén Chinese (language) 中文
zhōngwǔ noon 中午
zhòngyào important 重要
zhōu state; province 州
zhōumò weekend 周末
zhù reside 住
zhuàn earn 赚
zhuǎnjiē qì adaptor (electrical) 转接器
zhūbǎo jewelry 珠宝
zhǔnbèi prepare 准备
zhǔnbèi hǎole ready 准备好了
zhuō bù tablecloth 桌布
zhuōzi table 桌子
zhǔrén host 主人
zhūròu pork 猪肉
zhúsǔn bamboo shoot 竹笋
zì word; Chinese character 字
zìcóng since; until now 自从
zìdiǎn dictionary 字典

zìmù subtitles 字幕
zǐsè purple 紫色
zìxíng chē bicycle 自行车
zìyóu freedom; liberty 自由
zǒngjī switchboard operator 总机
zǒngjīnglǐ general manager 总经理
zǒngshì always 总是
zǒu walk; go 走
zū rent; hire; charter 租
zuàn diamond 钻石
zǔhé yīnxiǎng xìtǒng stereo system 组合音响系统
zuì drunk; intoxicated 醉
zuì shǎo least 最少
zuǐbā mouth 嘴吧
zuìhòu last; final 最后
zuìjìn recently 最近
zuò make; do 做
zuò sit 坐
zuǒbiān left (direction) 左边
zuótiān yesterday 昨天
zuòzhě author 作者

c = ts; *q* = ch; *x* = sh; *z* = dz; *zh* = j

IMMIGRATION AND CUSTOMS FORMS

The following are the forms you'll have to fill out when either entering or exiting China.

入 境 登 记 卡　**ARRIVAL CARD**
填 写 前 请 认 真 阅 读 背 面 说 明
Please read the points for attention on the back before filling

姓 Family Name	名 Given Name

出 生 日 期 Date of Birth	年 Y	月 M	日 D	性别 Sex

国籍 Nationality	护照 证件号码 Passport or Certificate No.

中国签证号 Chinese Visa No.	签发地 Place of Issue

偕行人数 Accompanying number	航班 (车次) Flight (Train) No.

职业: Occupation　　1.行政管理人员 Legislators & Administrators

2.专业技术人员 Professionals & Technical　　3.办事员 Clerk

4.商业人员 Commerce　　5.服务人员 Service　　6.农民 Farmer

7.工人 Worker　　8.其他 Others　　9.无职业 Jobless

在 华 地 址 Address in China (Hotel)

旅 客 签 名 Signature

官方填写:　　W U Y D Z X F L G C T M　　证件种类
Official Use Only

出 境 登 记 卡 DEPARTURE CARD

填写前请认真阅读背面说明
Please read the points for attention on the back before filling

姓 Family Name	名 Given Name

出 生 日 期 Date of Birth	年 Y	月 M	日 D	性别 Sex

国籍 Nationality	护照 证件号码 Passport or Certificate No.

偕行人数 Accompanying number	目 的 地 (国家) Destination (country)

职业: Occupation   1.行政管理人员 Legislators & Administrators

2.专业技术人员 Professionals & Technical   3.办事员 Clerk

4.商业人员 Commerce   5.服务人员 Service   6.农民 Farmer

7.工人 Worker   8.其他 Others   9.无职业 Jobless

航班 (车次) Flight (Train) No.

旅客签名 Signature

官方填写: W U Y D Z X F L G C T M   证件种类
Official Use Only

入 境 检 疫 申 明 卡
QUARANTINE DECLARATION FORM ON ENTRY

姓名　　　　　　　　性别　　　　　　　　国籍
Name _____ Sex _____ Nationality _____

证件号码　　　　　　到达日期　　　　　　航班号
Passport No. _____ Date of arrival _____ Flight No. _____

来自国家或地区　　　　在华联系地址
From (country/area) _____ Contact Address in China _____

到达前四周内您到过的城市和国家
Please describe the countries and cities (towns)

where you stayed within 4 weeks before arrival : _____

1. 如您以下症状或疾病，请在项目内划"√"
Please mark "√" in the items of following symptom or illness if any now

发热　　　　　　呕吐　　　　　　　　　腹泻　　　　咳嗽
Fever _____ Vomiting _____ Diarrhea _____ Cough _____

精神病　　　　　　艾滋病（包括病毒携带者）　　　麻风病
Mental Psychosis _____ AIDS (Inc. HIV Carrier) _____ Leprosy _____

性传播疾病　　　　开放性肺结核　　　　　其他疾病
STD _____ Active pulmonary tuberculosis _____ Other diseases _____

2. 如携带以下物品，请在项目内划"√"
Please mark "√" in the item of the following articles if you bring any of them

动物　　　　动物产品：如肉，奶制品，动物水产品等　　动物尸体，标本等
Animal _____ Animal products such as meat, milkproducts _____ Animal carcasses and
　　　　　　　_____ Aquatic animal products etc.　　　　　　　　Specimen etc.

植物、种子、种苗和其他繁殖材料　　植物产品：如水果，蔬菜，粮食等　土壤
Plant, seeds, seedling or other　　　Plant products, such as fresh　　Soil
Propagating material　　　　　　　　fruits, grain, vegetable etc. _____

生物制品　　　　　血液或血液制品　　　　废旧衣服
Bioproducts _____ Blood or Blood products _____ Waste clothing _____

我已阅知本申明卡所列事项，并保证以上申报属实。
I declare all the items given are true and correct.

签 名：
Signature of Passenger

WARNING: ANY FALSE STATEMENTS IS LIABLE TO PENALTIES.

EDITION
95

CHINA CUSTOMS

BAGGAGE DECLARATION
FOR ENTERING/DEPARTING PASSENGERS

Name In Full		Sex	M/F
Nationality		From/To	
Passport No.		Purpose	

1. Passengers who, as specified on the reverse of this form, are subject to the declaration formalities shall fill out this form in detail with signature, and submit it to the Customs for verification and endorsement. At the Customs area with "Dual Channel" system, the above passengers shall follow the channel marked "GOODS TO DECLARE."

2. Other passengers do not need to fill out this form and may choose the channel marked "NOTHING TO DECLARE." Any passengers, who are subject to Customs formalities after entry in such cases as taking delivery of commodities with bills, purchasing commodities with foreign currencies, claiming unaccompanied baggage, etc, therefore unable to complete the Customs formalities at one time, shall fill out this form at the Customs offices concerned.

Description	Amount	Type/Model	Customs Note

I HAVE READ THE NOTICE ON THE REVERSE AND HAVE MADE A TRUTHFUL DECLARATION.

SIGNATURE: _____   Y/   M/   D/

FOR CUSTOMS USE ONLY

OFFICER SIGNATURE: _____   Y/   M/   D/

(ORIGINAL: FOR CUSTOMS)

NOTICE: Please read the following before you fill out this form

1. Entering Passengers, under the following circumstances, shall declare:

- Carrying dutiable articles or duty-free articles exclusive of duty-free tobacco & alcoholic drinks under items Ⅱ、Ⅲ of Classification for Entering/Departing Passengers' Baggage within the quantity limitation set by the Customs.
- Non-residents or residents with re-entry visa issued by any foreign country (area) carrying trip necessities exceeding the limitation as set by the Customs: camera, portable taperecorder, mini-movie camera, portable video-recorder, portable word-processor, one piece for each item.
- Carrying more than RMB 6,000 yuan in cash, or gold, silver and ornaments thereof weighing over 66g.
- Non-residents carrying more than US $5,000 (or foreign equivalent) in cash.
- Residents carrying more than US $2,000 (or foreign equivalent) in cash.
- Carrying goods of commercial value, samples or articles other than personal baggage.
- Carrying animals or plants and products thereof under the controll of China Quarantine Law, and other articles subject to Customs formalities.

2. Departing passengers, under the following circumstances, shall declare:

- Carrying the following trip necessities for re-importation: camera, portable taperecorder, mini-movie camera, portable video-recorder, portable word-processor, etc.
- Failing re-exportation of specified articles, or completion of Customs clearance procedures for temporarily imported duty-free articles.
- Carrying foreign currencies, gold, silver and ornaments thereof over the declared quantities or having no export license or certificates therefor.
- Carrying more than RMB 6,000 yuan in cash.
- Carrying cultural relics.
- Carrying goods of commercial value and samples.
- Carrying articles exceeding the limited value and quantity, or other limitations as set by the Customs.
- Having animals or plants and products thereof under the controll of China Quarantine Law, and other articles subject to Customs formalities.

3. Articles prohibited from importation

- Arms, imitation arms, ammunition and explosives of all kinds.
- Counterfeit currencies and counterfeit negotiable securities.
- Printed matter, films, photographs, gramophone records, cinematographic films, loaded recording tapes and video-tapes, compact discs (video and audio), storage media for computers and other articles which are detrimental to the political, economic, cultural and moral interests of China.
- Deadly poison of all kinds.
- Opium, morphia, heroin, marihuana and other addictive drugs and psychotropic substances.
- Animals, plants and products thereof infected with or carrying disease germs, insect pests and other harmful organisms.

- Foodstuff, medicines and other articles coming from epidemic stricken area and harmful to man and livestock or those capable of spreading disease.

4. Articles prohibited from exportation

- All articles enumerated as articles prohibited from importation.
- Manuscripts, printed matter, films, photographs, gramophone records, cinematographic films, loaded recording tapes and video-tapes, compact discs (video and audio), storage media for computers and other articles which involve state secrets.
- Valuable cultural relics and other relics prohibited from exportation.
- Endangered, rare animals and plants, respective specimens, seeds and reproducing materials.

CHINA ON THE INTERNET

The Internet has brought China into the homes and offices of people all over the world. Many Chinese cities have been quick to grasp the power of the World Wide Web to get the word out about investment and trading opportunities as well as tourist destinations and cultural events. And many other organizations have posted interesting and valuable information about China. Here is a smattering of web pages that introduce various aspects of China and things Chinese.

CHINESE GOVERNMENT SOURCES

The **China Internet Information Center** provides official positions of the Chinese government on a variety of domestic and international issues, as well as basic information about China and the Chinese government on-line (*http://www.chinanews.org/*). Other official government sites include those maintained by the **Ministry of Foreign Affairs** (*http://www.fmprc.gov.cn/english/dhtml/*) and the **Ministry of Foreign Trade and Economic Cooperation** (*http://www.moftec.gov.cn/moftec*).

The **Chinese Embassy in Washington** (*http://www.china-embassy.org/*) maintains a web site that provides information about China, its culture, economy, and political structure and the Embassy's own operations, including visa and passport policies and procedures. Other sites are maintained by sister organizations such as **China's Permanent Mission to the United Nations** (*http://www.undp.org/missions/china/*) and its **Consulates-General** in **New York** (*http://www.nyconsulate.prchina.org/*), **Los Angeles** (*http://www.chinaconsulatela.org/*), **San Francisco** (*http://www.chinaconsulatesf.org/*), and **Houston** (*http://www.chinahouston.org*).

Other Chinese embassies in the English-speaking world that are on-line are those in **London** (*http://www.chinese-*

embassy.org.uk/), **Ottawa**
(*http://www.chinaembassycanada.org/*), **Canberra**
(*http://www.chinaembassy.org.au/*), and **Pretoria**
(*http://www.chinese-embassy.co.za/*).

U.S.-CHINA RELATIONS

The **U.S. State Department's Bureau of East Asian and Pacific Affairs** has a page devoted to current issues with China, including links to human rights reports and China-related archival material
(*http://www.state.gov/www/current/debate/china.html*).

The **U.S. Embassy in Beijing** (*http://www.usembassy-china.org.cn/*) provides information on China's agriculture, economy, environment, science, and technology, as well as information on visas and services provided to U.S. citizens visiting China. It also has contact information for the U.S. consulates in Guangzhou, Shanghai, Shenyang, and Chengdu.

The **National Committee on United States-China Relations** (*http://www.ncuscr.org/*) is a nonprofit educational organization that encourages understanding of China and the United States between citizens of both countries. The committee was founded in the belief that vigorous debate of China policy among Americans was essential and that balanced public education could clarify U.S. interests and strengthen American foreign policy.

CANADA-CHINA RELATIONS

Canada's Department of Foreign Affairs and International Trade has a window on China site
(*http://www.canada.org.hk/*) with information about Canada's offices in Beijing, Hong Kong, Shanghai, Guangzhou, and Chongqing, facts about China, and about the bilateral relationship.

MEDIA

Many Western publications that feature extensive China coverage are on the Net. The weekly Hong Kong-based **Far**

Eastern Economic Review (*http://www.feer.com/*) is one of them. The U.S.-China Business' Council's acclaimed **China Business Review** (*http://www.chinabusinessreview.com*) comes out every two months and is known for its in-depth coverage of China's economy and commercial developments. You can catch up on events in Hong Kong through the eyes of its two principal English-language newspapers, the **South China Morning Post** (*http://www.scmp.com/*) and the **Hong Kong Standard** (*http://online.hkstandard.com/today/*). Both include extensive coverage of events in China.

Then there is **ChinaOnline** (*http://www.chinaonline.com/*), a business information service that provides translated news from a wide variety of sources in China, original articles on business topics, and analysis by China experts from around the world.

For the Chinese government's point of view, there's nothing as authoritative as the official **Xinhua News Agency**, the voice of the Communist Party, which maintains an English-language site on the Internet (*http://www.xinhuanet.com/english/index.htm*). The official **People's Daily** is also on the web in English (*http://www.peopledaily.com.cn/english/*). Also available on the Net are the **China Daily** (*http://www.chinadaily.com.cn/*), the **Beijing Review** (*http://dawning.iist.unu.edu/china/bjreview*), and **China Central Television**, or **CCTV** (*http://www.cctv.com.cn/english/index.html*).

DOING BUSINESS IN CHINA

The International Trade Administration of the **U.S. Department of Commerce** has posted useful information for exporters to China on the Net at (*http://www.ita.doc.gov/bems/china.html*). And the **U.S. Census Bureau** provides historical data on the U.S. trade balance with China at (*http://www.census.gov/foreign-trade/balance/c5700.html*).

The United States-China Business Council is the principal organization of U.S. companies engaged in trade and investment in China. The council provides business advisory services and policy advocacy, sponsors conferences and meetings, and issues publications about doing business in China. Its web site (*http://www.uschina.org/*) is an excellent source of information on China's business environment.

The Beijing-based **American Chamber of Commerce of the PRC** (AmCham China) is a central point of contact and exchange for members of the American business community in China; it promotes trade, commerce, and investment between the United States and China. Its web site (*http://www.amcham-china.org.cn/*) features position papers on bilateral issues and other information about the China market.

The **Hong Kong American Chamber of Commerce** has a web site (*http://www.amcham.org.hk/*) that gives information on China in general in addition to material on living and working in Hong Kong. The **Hong Kong Trade Development Council** (*http://www.tdctrade.com*) is also an excellent source on these topics.

See also the web sites of the **Canada-China Business Council** (*http://www.ccbc.com/*) and the **Hong Kong Canada Business Association** (*http://www.hkcba.com/*) for private-sector information on Canada's commercial relations with China.

TRAVEL AND TOURISM

Major tourist destinations in China are described in a web site maintained by **China International Travel Service** (*http://www.cits.net/*).

You can find general information about traveling to China (customs, visas, medical care, crime, and security concerns), as well as any current travel advisories at the U.S. State Department's **China Consular Information Sheet** (*http://travel.state.gov/china.html*). Also visit **Tips for Travelers to the PRC** at (*http://travel.state.gov/tips_china.html*).

There are many web sites devoted to specific cities in China, some official and some not so official. **Beijing** and

Shanghai, for example, are well represented on the Web. Visit the **Beijing Page** (*http://www.flashpaper.com/beijing/*) and **Beijing—The Capital of China** (*http://www.net.edu.cn/beijing/indexsed.html*). And check out **Shanghai on Internet** (*http://www.sh.com/*), **Shanghai-ABC** (*http://www.shanghabc.com/*), or **Shanghai Panorama** (*http://shanghai.muzi.net/*).

Other Chinese localities presented on their own web sites include **Dalian** (*http://www.china-dalian.com/*), **Guangzhou** (*http://www.chinapages.com/guangdong/guangzhou/guangzhou.htm*), **Chongqing** (*http://www.cq.gov.cn/text/english.htm*), and **Chengdu** (*http://www.chinats/chengdu/*). And two sites where you can learn more about **Tianjin** are **Tianjin Municipality** (*http://www.scmp.com/chinamedia/profile.html*) and **Tianjin Window** (*http://sun.ihep.ac.cn/tour/tianjin/*).

You can find out about touring **Taiwan** from any of a number of web pages. Taiwan's official Government Information office has a website: (*http://gio.gov.tw*). General information for visitors to Taiwan, including maps, attractions, and tours, is also provided from the the **Tourism Bureau** at (*http://www.tbroc.gov.tw/*) as well as at several other sites, among them (*http://www.freesun.be/roctourism.html*).

And there is no dearth of **Hong Kong**-related web sites. For basic tourism information, visit the Hong Kong Tourist Association site (*http://www.hkta.org*). General information about Hong Kong can be viewed at (*http://www.glink.net.hk/~hksea/was/s18-hk.html*). And **Hong Kong in Pictures** (*http://www.cuhk.hk/hk/scenery.htm*) provides a lovely cybertour of the region.

ARTS AND CULTURE

China is a central focus for the **Asia Society**, whose programs are described on its web site (*http://www.asiasociety.org/*). The nonprofit organization is America's leading institution dedicated to fostering understanding of Asia, and its programs include art exhibitions and performances, films, lectures, seminars and conferences, publications and materials, and programs for students and teachers.

Washington's **Freer Gallery of Art** and **Arthur M. Sackler Gallery**, both parts of the Smithsonian Institution, have fabulous collections of Asian art that include a large number of priceless Chinese pieces. They also maintain a web page to prove it at (*http://www.si.edu/asia/start.htm*).

Purdue University (*http://pasture.ecn.purdue.edu/~agenhtml/agenmc/china/*) has a site devoted to the art of China, featuring antiquities, painting, crafts, calligraphy, and much more.

The **Shanghai Museum** (*http://www.sh.com/travel/museum/museum.htm*) boasts a huge collection of bronze, ceramics, calligraphy, painting, sculpture, furniture, jade and ivory carvings, oracle bones, seals, coins, minority arts, and bamboo, wood, and lacquer ware. Both it and the **Beijing Art Museum** (*http://china-window.com/beijing/tour/museum/wanshou/index.html*) whose collection includes pieces from the Neolithic Age to the Ming and Qing Dynasties and the twentieth century, feature images of some of their best pieces on-line.

Taipei's **National Palace Museum**, which houses one of the world's finest collections of Chinese art, has a site (*http://www.npm.gov.tw/*) that presents fine pieces from its collection.

Other Chinese museums with their own sites include the **Beijing Museum of Ancient Architecture** (*http://china-window.com/beijing/tour/museum/xiannong/index.html*), an institution devoted to the collection, study, and display of China's ancient architectural relics. Another site (*http://www.warriortours.com/cityguides/xian.htm#xianyang*), provides links to several of the ancient city of Xi'an's museums and cultural relics, including the **Shaanxi Provincial History Museum** and the **Mausoleum of Qinshihuang**, the first Emperor of the Qin Dynasty (221 B.C.–206 B.C.) the site of the famous terra-cotta warriors and horses.

You can get a virtual "taste" of China's **Forbidden City**

(*http://china-window.com/beijing/nbjwe/lvyou/scenic/gg/ index.htm*), the former palace of emperors, a museum in its own right today. Also check out **The Forbidden City** (*http://pasture.ecn.purdue.edu/~agenhtml/agenmc/china/sce nfc.html*), which presents photos from the book *Beijing: Glimpses of History*. Also worth a "virtual visit" is the site of the **Ancient Beijing Observatory** (*http://www.chinatoday.com/culture/abo/abo.htm*), a remnant of the Beijing city wall that displays astronomical instruments made during the Qing Dynasty.

Beijing Opera is the subject of several web sites, including the **Beijing Opera Page** (*http://www.geocities.com/vienna/opera/8692/index0.html*) and **All About Peking Opera** (*http://www.chinapages.com/culture/jje.htm*). There's even a page on the "model operas" that were the only permissible fare during the Cultural Revolution (*http://web.syr.edu/~xwang02/modern.html*). Cantonese Opera has several pages of its own on the Web, among them **Cantonese Opera from Around the World** (*http://members.aol.com/canopera/commun.htm*).

CHINESE CUISINE
The countless varieties of Chinese food are celebrated on a web site (*http://www.chinavista.com/culture/cuisine/ recipes.html*) that is organized by region, from Anhui to Zhejiang. It even includes recipes in case you are moved to try your own hand at some of China's delicacies. Another site (*http://www.bjta.gov.cn/english/meishi_jiayao/default.htm*) gives capsule summaries of regional fare and provides information about several Beijing restaurants.

FURTHER READING
Want to do further reading on China? Of course you can search **Amazon** (*www.amazon.com*) and **Barnes and Noble** (*www.barnesandnoble.com*), which sell everything from soup to nuts. But also check out **China Books and Periodicals** (*http://www.chinabooks.com/*), a specialty shop

that focuses its offerings exclusively on books and other products related to China.

Note: The Internet addresses listed in this section were valid as of the publication date of this book. Web sites may move from time to time, and often even disappear. If a link turns out to be out of date, use a search engine like Yahoo (www.yahoo.com) or Lycos (www.lycos.com) to locate the site's new address.

READY REFERENCE KEY

Here are some phrases and words that you are likely to use often. For a more extensive list of phrases, refer to the appropriate chapter within the book.

SIMPLE WORDS AND PHRASES

Hello. (How are you?)	*Ní hǎo.* 你好。
Do you speak English?	*Nǐ shūo Yīngwén ma?* 你说英文吗？
Do you understand?	*Nǐ tīng de dǒng ma?* 你听得懂吗？
I don't speak Chinese.	*Wǒ bú huì shūo Zhōngguóhùa.* 我不会说中国话。
I don't understand.	*Wǒ bù dǒng.* 我不懂。
Please speak a little more slowly.	*Qǐng shūo màn yīdǐan.* 请说慢一点。
Please repeat.	*Qǐng zài shūo yībìan.* 请再说一遍。

BEING POLITE

please	*qǐng*	请
Thank you very much.	*Fēicháng xìexie.* 非常谢谢。	
Excuse me. (apologizing)	*Dùibuqǐ.*	对不起。

c = ts; *q* = ch; *x* = sh; *z* = dz; *zh* = j

Excuse me. (getting attention)	*Láojià.*	劳驾。
Good morning.	*Zǎo.*	早。
Good night.	*Wǎn ān.*	晚安。

NEEDS AND WANTS

I need ____.	*Wǒ xūyào ____.* 我需要____。
I want ____.	*Wǒ yào ____.* 我要____。
We'd like ____.	*Wǒmén xiǎngyào ____.* 我们想要____。
I'm looking for ____.	*Wó zhǎo ____.* 我找____。
Please give me ____.	*Qǐng géi wǒ ____.* 请给我____。
Please show me ____.	*Qǐng géi wǒ kànkan ____.* 请给我看看____。
Please bring ____.	*Qǐng sònglái ____.* 请送来____。

TIME

What time is it?	*Jídiǎn zhōng?* 几点钟？
What day is today?	*Jīntiān xīngqī jǐ?* 今天星期几？
It's noon.	*Shì zhōngwǔ.* 是中午。

Three in the afternoon.	*Xìawǔ sāndian zhōng.* 下午三点钟。	
A.M.	*shàngwǔ*	上午
P.M.	*xìawǔ*	下午
evening	*wǎnshàng*	晚上
Today is ____.	*Jīntīan shì ____.* 今天是____。	
yesterday	*zúotīan*	昨天
tomorrow	*míngtīan*	明天
tonight	*jīnwǎn*	今晚
last night	*zúowǎn*	昨晚
this week	*zhèige xīngqī*	这个星期
next week	*xìage xīngqī*	下个星期
last week	*shàngge xīngqī*	上个星期
It's early.	*Hái zǎo.*	还早。
It's late.	*Wǎn le.*	晚了。
It's too late.	*Tài wǎn le.*	太晚了。

ADJECTIVES

best	*zùi hǎo*	最好
better	*gèng hǎo*	更好
cheap	*píanyi*	便宜
difficult	*nán*	难
easy	*róngyì*	容易

c = ts; *q* = ch; *x* = sh; *z* = dz; *zh* = j

enough	*gòu le*	够了
expensive	*guì*	贵
fast	*kùai*	快
good	*hǎo*	好
large	*dà*	大
less	*shǎoxīe*	少些
long	*cháng*	长
more	*dūoxīe*	多些
short (length)	*dǔan*	短
slow	*màn*	慢
small	*xǐao*	小
too much	*tài dūo*	太多

DIRECTIONS

I'm lost.	*Wǒ mí lù le.*	我迷路了。
Where is ____?	____ *zài nálì?* ____在哪里？	
Shall I go ____?	*Wǒ yīnggāi xìang* ____ *zǒu ma?* 我应该向____走吗？	
■ to the left	*zúo*	左
■ to the right	*yòu*	右
■ straight ahead	*qían*	前
How far away is ____?	____ *yǒu dūoyǔan?* ____有多远？	
Please show it to me on the map.	*Qǐng zài dìtú shàng zhǐ géi wǒ.* 请在地图上指给我。	

INDEX